CHICAGO

REBECCA HOLLAND

CONTENTS

MAPS

DISCOVER
CHICAGO

Chicago is a thriving, multicultural hub seated on vast Lake Michigan. Fed by the lake, the Chicago River snakes its way through downtown, winding past the soaring architecture of the Loop, slicing across Michigan Avenue's "Magnificent Mile," and cruising along a fusion of skyline sights, impressive museums, and verdant parks and gardens.

In summer, Chicagoans embrace the seasonal warmth by flocking to the lake with sailboats, personal watercraft, and paddleboards. Sunbathers line North Avenue Beach, while the city explodes with street festivals, food fairs, rooftop clubs, and outdoor activities.

Winter holds a certain magic, too. The lake turns icy blue with frozen blocks drifting as far as the eye can see. Crackling frost decorates *Cloud Gate* and drapes the skyline. Chicagoans, bundled in wool jackets and scarves, feel a sense of pride—nothing can stop them from enjoying their city. You'll find them ice-skating at Millennium Park, browsing a bustling Christmas market, packed into comedy clubs and music halls, or sipping a warm cocktail by the fire at a local lounge.

What Chicagoans love most about their city are its colorful neighborhoods, each with its own distinct heritage and character. West Side has the best tacos and the coolest street art. Lincoln Park's boutiques can't be beat. Hyde Park is home to a history and culture so rich it could fill its own book. Each neighborhood is a microcosm of art, culture, and, of course, food, and its residents love it so much it's palpable.

Mostly though, what makes this city special are the people. Chicago is a big city with small-town charm, built by working-class immigrants and filled with folks who say hi to each other on the street. The heart of the Midwest has a lot of heart. Visitors are sure to fall in love.

10 TOP
EXPERIENCES

1 **The Art Institute of Chicago:** One of the country's oldest and largest art museums houses more than 300,000 works and 30 rotating special exhibitions (page 55).

2 **Millennium Park:** World-class architecture, public art, and landscape design come together in this 25-acre park that serves as a hub for Chicago's cultural programs and outdoor activities (page 54).

3 **Willis Tower Skydeck:** At 110 stories, the Willis Tower is the second-tallest building in North America. Enjoy 360-degree skyline views from the beautiful glass-bottom Skydeck (page 56).

4 **Navy Pier:** Its wealth of attractions include the 196-foot-tall Centennial Wheel, one of Chicago's biggest draws (page 60).

>>>

5 **Wrigley Field:** This historic stadium brings in locals and tourists game after game. Whether the Cubs win or lose, it's always a good time (page 67).

>>>

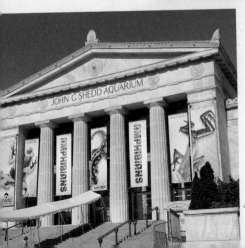

6 **Shedd Aquarium:** The largest indoor aquarium in the world is home to more than 32,000 animals and 1,500 species and features a range of exhibits on everything from local waters to the Amazon (page 58).

<<<

7 **Chicago Architecture River Cruise:** Buildings tell the story of how Chicago grew from a small town to a thriving city. The best way to see them is on this scenic river cruise (page 146).

8 **Lakefront Trail:** These 18 miles pass skyline views, nature sanctuaries, boat harbors, and boardwalks (page 149).

9 **Second City:** The legendary improvisational comedy club where many of *Saturday Night Live*'s stars got their start turns out hilarious revues every night (page 118).

10 **Chicago's Historic Jazz Clubs:** Chicago played a leading role in the evolution of jazz in the early 1900s. Today, jazz clubs are still a vital part of the city's diversity, bringing in acts from around the city and the world (page 125).

EXPLORE
CHICAGO

THE BEST OF CHICAGO

This three-day itinerary covers the best the city has to offer—from must-see sights to neighborhood favorites. Spend the first day downtown, then explore some of the northern neighborhoods on the second day before finishing up with the Museum Campus on the third day. Plan to stay in a hotel in the Loop or Near North for the easiest access to public transportation.

>DAY 1: THE LOOP AND NEAR NORTH

Start your day with a stop at the **Revival Food Hall** for coffee, smoothies, or baked goods from one of the many vendors. The **Chicago Architecture River Cruise** is a picturesque way to begin your morning and get acquainted with the city's history while also taking in the sights. The boat tour ends at Michigan Avenue, where you can walk south to explore **The Art Institute of Chicago**. Spend the rest of the morning taking in the museum highlights (follow the self-guided tour on

Cloud Gate at Millennium Park

TRIBUNE TOWER
This 1925 neo-Gothic structure by architects Raymond Hood and John Mead Howells was the result of a worldwide architecture contest. The 462-foot-tall tower is considered one of the most beautiful in the city (page 61).

WRIGLEY BUILDING
Chicago's most recognizable building was modeled after a cathedral in Seville. Its impressive clock tower has become an icon (page 61).

ROOKERY BUILDING
Frank Lloyd Wright designed the interior lobby of this building, which features a complex ceiling and a beautiful spiral staircase (page 57).

Tribune Tower and the Wrigley Building

ROBIE HOUSE
Built in 1908-1910, this Frank Lloyd Wright-designed house is one of the best examples of his Prairie School architecture (page 71).

MUSEUM OF SCIENCE AND INDUSTRY
Built for the 1893 World's Columbian Exposition, Daniel Burnham's beaux arts-style museum was originally a palace of fine arts. Today, it's one of two remaining examples of the architect's vision for "The White City" (page 69).

CHICAGO CULTURAL CENTER
Built in 1947, the Chicago Cultural Center features a gorgeous interior with an ornate Tiffany dome (the largest in the world) in its main hall (page 129).

---

the museum brochure). Afterward, grab a late lunch at **Seven Lions** just across the street. **Millennium Park** awaits just a few blocks north along Michigan Avenue. Spend the afternoon admiring art installations such as *Cloud Gate*, relaxing on the Great Lawn, or listening to some live music at the Jay Pritzker Pavilion.

Staying at a hotel in the Loop means it's a quick walk back to your room to get ready for a night out. Start with rooftop drinks at **Cindy's Rooftop Bar,** where you'll get amazing views of the skyline and Lake Michigan.

For dinner, head to the hopping River North area where you've made reservations for **Frontera Grill,** chef Rick Bayless's flagship restaurant. After dinner, take a walk along the Riverwalk then go dancing at the **Studio Paris Nightclub** or take in a jazz performance at **Andy's Jazz Club.**

>> **PUBLIC TRANSIT:** To get to the River North area from the Loop, take the Red Line from the Monroe Station north to Grand Station.

BEST VIEWS

WILLIS TOWER SKYDECK
The second-tallest building in North America features glass-bottom ledges for stunning—and stomach-flipping—views over the city (page 56).

360 CHICAGO
The views from the glass TILT platform at 360 Chicago are unlike anything else in the city (page 62).

CENTENNIAL WHEEL
The Navy Pier's Ferris wheel will zoom you 200 feet over the Chicago skyline in comfort (page 61).

CINDY'S ROOFTOP BAR
With floor-to-ceiling windows overlooking Millennium Park, this is the prime spot for dining with a view (page 77).

OAK STREET BEACH
From Chicago's Lakefront Trail, you can gaze over vast Lake Michigan (especially beautiful at sunset) or turn around for iconic skyline views (page 148).

>DAY 2: GOLD COAST, LINCOLN PARK, AND LAKEVIEW

Today, take in Chicago's North Side, starting in the Gold Coast neighborhood. Window-shop your way north along the Magnificent Mile toward **360 Chicago,** arriving when the observation deck opens at 9am for morning views over the city. (Buy a fast pass to avoid spending your morning in line.)

>> **PUBLIC TRANSIT:** From the Loop, take the Red Line to the Chicago Station and walk east along Chicago Avenue until you hit Michigan Avenue.

From 360 Chicago, rent a Divvy bike and ride 2.5 miles along the Lakefront Trail north to **Lincoln Park.** Along the way, you'll pass the historic Lake Shore Drive mansions and the beckoning sands of North Avenue Beach. Just across the street from the park, stop in at **Elaine's Coffee Call** for coffee and a snack.

Enter Lincoln Park, where you can cruise along the park paths, then lock up your wheels before visiting the **Lincoln Park Zoo** and the **Lincoln Park Conservatory.**

>> **PUBLIC TRANSIT:** Buy a 24-hour pass to rent a Divvy bicycle from the station at Mies Van Der Rohe Way and Chestnut Street. There are Divvy docking stations at Broadway and Barry Avenue in

the Lincoln Park Zoo

BEST PEOPLE-WATCHING

Wrigley Field

MAGNIFICENT MILE
Most people come to Michigan Avenue to shop, but it can be just as fun to watch visitors from around the world converge on this bustling street (page 61).

MILLENNIUM PARK
This downtown park is especially popular on summer evenings, when you can watch people pose in front of "The Bean" (the local name for *Cloud Gate*) for photos, catch impromptu music performances at the Pritzker Pavilion, or splash in the cooling waters of *Crown Fountain* (page 54).

WRIGLEY FIELD
Nothing compares to the excitement of a Cubs game at Wrigley Field. Fans deck themselves out in Cubby blue as they chant "Go, Cubs, Go," sing "Take Me Out to the Ballgame," and cheer their hearts out (page 67).

BIG STAR
Grab a seat on the patio at this neighborhood favorite and eat delicious tacos while watching the world go by on busy Damen Avenue (page 102).

LINCOLN PARK
This sprawling park has plenty of sights—including a zoo and two conservatories—plus space to bask in the sun, playgrounds for kids to explore, and tons of Chicagoans enjoying their city (page 149).

Boystown and at Sheffield Avenue and Waveland Avenue near Wrigley Field.

Continue north along the Lakefront Trail, turning west at West Briar Place as you head into Boystown. Stop for brisket and craft brews at **DryHop Brewers,** then browse the shops along North Halsted and North Broadway. From Boystown, it's a one-mile walk or bike ride north to iconic **Wrigley Field.** Snap some photos or take a tour of the stadium. If it's baseball season, try to catch a Cubs game or simply cheer them on at one of nearby bars like **The Cubby Bear.**

At night, stay in Lakeview for dinner at **Chilam Bilam** before catching a comedy show at the

Laugh Factory. Or head back to Old Town for fish tacos at **Buzz Bait** followed by improv at **Second City.**

>> **PUBLIC TRANSIT:** The Addison Station is near Wrigley Field and serviced by the Red Line. To head to Old Town, take CTA bus #22 from Clark Street to the LaSalle Drive stop.

>DAY 3: MUSEUM CAMPUS AND NAVY PIER

Today is all about museums, and you'll want to get an early start as most close by 5pm. Book tickets for the Total Experience Pass online before you head out so that you can skip the lines for entry. Fuel up with coffee from **Cafecito** and grab some Cubano sandwiches to go for the long day ahead. Take either a CTA bus or L train or the Metra Line to the Museum Campus.

>> **PUBLIC TRANSIT:** CTA buses #146 and #130 (summer only) service the Museum Campus. The Metra Electric Line stops at the Museum Campus Station. The Red/Orange/Green L lines stop at the Roosevelt Station, about four blocks west.

Start your day of discovery with **The Field Museum,** whose extensive exhibits and collections of natural history span three floors. Next, cross the campus to the **Shedd Aquarium** where more than 32,000 animals are on exhibit. If you have time, stop in at the **Adler Planetarium** (it closes at 4pm) and gaze among the stars. If you're short on time—or just tired—opt for a picnic on the Planetarium lawn, which has an especially beautiful view of Lake Michigan.

Rent a Divvy bike and ride 2.3 miles north along the Lakefront Trail to **Navy Pier** (or, in summer opt for the water taxi along the lake). Ride the iconic **Centennial Wheel** and explore the pier's many attractions. On summer evenings (Wed. and Sat.), watch fireworks light up the night sky.

>> **PUBLIC TRANSIT:** There are three Divvy bike rental stations on the Museum Campus. The Shoreline Water Taxi (May-Sept.) connects the Museum Campus with Navy Pier. CTA bus #146 can get you to State Street and Illinois, where you can catch bus #29 or #65 to Navy Pier.

Tonight, dig into some deep-dish pizza at **Lou Malnati's** in the River North area.

>> **PUBLIC TRANSIT:** To get to River North, take CTA bus #65 from Navy Pier along West Grand Avenue to the LaSalle stop. To return to the Loop from River North, take the Red Line south from Grand Station.

With More Time

DAY 4

WICKER PARK AND BUCKTOWN
Spend a day in Wicker Park and Bucktown, where you can browse local shops along Damen and Milwaukee Avenues. Start with brunch at **Dove's Luncheonette,** then relax with a stroll to **Wicker Park.** At night, dive into yummy tacos on the patio at **Big Star** and enjoy cocktails at **The Violet Hour.** This neighborhood is best explored on foot and without an agenda.

HYDE PARK
Escape the crowds and see a local side of the city with a day in Hyde Park. Orient yourself with a stroll in **Jackson Park** before visiting the **Museum of Science and Industry.** Browse the wares in **Powell's Books,** then fill up at **Valois** for some local experiences.

CHICAGO WITH KIDS

With interactive museums, a large free zoo, and plenty of kid-friendly restaurants, Chicago is a great choice for a family vacation. These three days are packed with learning experiences, outdoor activity, and sightseeing both adults and kids will love.

>DAY 1

Kick off your Chicago adventure with a day at **Navy Pier.** Breakfast at the hotel or pick up an old-fashioned from **Doughnut Vault.** Spend the morning in the **Chicago Children's Museum,** then grab lunch at **Giordano's** on the pier. Ride on the **Centennial Wheel,** play games on the pier, and wander through Crystal Gardens.

As the sun sets, head to the **Willis Tower Skydeck** or **360 Chicago** for impressive views over the city below. (Kids will get a thrill out of the TILT deck.) Have dinner at **Shake Shack** or **Eleven City Diner** before resting up for a big day of museums tomorrow.

>DAY 2

Chicago's museums are great for kids. **The Field Museum, Adler Planetarium,** and **Museum of Science and Industry** are full of interactive exhibits geared toward all ages. Head to **Shedd Aquarium,** where kids will love learning about underwater life around the world and watching dolphins and otters play. Grab a bite at any of the museum cafeterias or bring a picnic lunch to enjoy on the Museum Campus lawn.

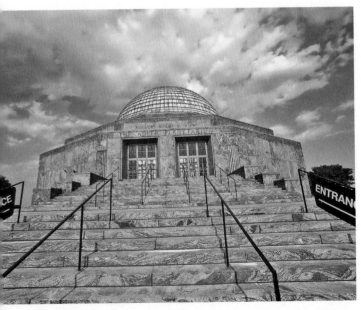

Adler Planetarium

CHICAGO OFF THE CLOCK

CHICAGO ARCHITECTURE RIVER CRUISE
Chicago's best tour offers evening options for business travelers. Catch the twilight cruise at 7:30pm and watch the sun set over the city's famous skyline (page 146).

MILLENNIUM PARK MUSIC SERIES
Millennium Park is the place to be after work during the summer for movies, concerts, and dance performances. Chicagoans come in their work clothes and grab food from food trucks for impromptu picnics (page 24).

WILLIS TOWER SKYDECK
The Willis Tower Skydeck is one of the few Chicago attractions that's open late. Take in sunset or shimmering night views until 8pm (page 56).

CERES CAFÉ
Busy day in the Loop? Stop in at Ceres Cafe, a healthy power lunch institution (page 77).

RPM STEAK
This classic steakhouse is a favorite for after-work meetings, partly because of the innovative cocktail list (page 86).

MONK'S PUB
Visit Monk's Pub during happy hour and you'll find it packed with a relaxed crowd drinking from a huge beer list and snacking on fried food (page 109).

Spend the late afternoon at **Millennium Park,** snapping photos of yourself reflected in the mirror of *Cloud Gate* and splashing around in the *Crown Fountain.* In summer, Millennium Park hosts a **Family Fun Festival** (June-Aug.) with plenty of crafts, music, and activities for kids.

At night, dine on Chicago dogs and Italian beef sandwiches at **Portillo's,** a Chicago tourist hot spot where even locals wait in line.

›DAY 3
Today, visit **Lincoln Park,** where you can walk around the zoo and farm. Grab some coffee and sandwiches to go from **Eva's Cafe,** then make your way into the park. Stop at the monkey house, which is filled with interactive exhibits for kids, like measuring their size and strength against that of a gorilla. At the adjacent farm, children can pet and feed the animals, which is always a hit. The conservatory next door is an easy stop where you and your kids can learn about plants from around the world.

From Lincoln Park, walk across the bridge over Lake Shore Drive to the **Lakefront Trail.** Walk or bike along the path back toward downtown, stopping to spend a couple of hours picnicking on the beach in summer. Sandy **North Avenue Beach** has lifeguards and a concession stand that sells ice cream.

End your Chicago adventure with deep-dish pizza at **Lou Malnati's.**

CHICAGO LIKE A LOCAL

Chicagoans play in the city's parks, tour art exhibits, cheer the Cubs, and eat, eat, eat. Chicago is a foodie city, from the groundbreaking culinary inventions at Alinea to classic, only-in-Chicago staples like beef sandwiches, hot dogs, and, of course, the best pizza anywhere. If there's a Cubs game on, you'll find locals filing into Wrigley Field or watching the game at a Lakeview bar.

Logan Square, in the Bucktown and Wicker Park neighborhoods, and the West Side are popular areas for locals to eat and drink. Wicker Park and Lincoln Park offer great neighborhood boutiques. In summer, Chicagoans flock to the beach, get out on the water, and stroll the Riverwalk at night.

To see Chicago like a local, ride the L train to the city's neighborhoods to explore . . . and avoid the Loop (as do most Chicagoans).

>MORNING

Start your morning in the Bucktown and Wicker Park neighborhoods with an espresso from **Buzz Killer** and a coconut cake doughnut from **Stan's Donuts,** a must-try when in Chicago. **Wicker Park** is packed with local boutiques, art galleries, and specialty food stores. Wander the shops along Damen and Milwaukee Avenues; stop in **Virtu** to admire the unique collection of jewelry and gifts. Once your caffeine wears off, claim a spot on the patio at **Big Star** and order some of their inventive tacos.

Big Star is a favorite taco spot in Wicker Park.

BEST FOR ROMANCE

THE RIVERWALK
Stroll hand in hand along The Riverwalk, stopping for a glass of wine to better admire the historic architecture lining the Chicago River (page 57).

MAUDE'S LIQUOR BAR
Decadent dishes and dim lighting make this a sumptuous place for romance. Sit upstairs for a more private conversation (page 90).

RM CHAMPAGNE SALON
This French champagne bar sits tucked in a secluded alley. With charming lanterns, exposed brick walls, a cozy fireplace, and a wonderfully curated champagne list, it's the perfect spot for a date (page 114).

UNTITLED
Reserve a VIP table at this speakeasy and sip Prohibition-era cocktails while listening to live jazz or watching the Thursday evening burlesque performances (page 113).

THE WALDORF ASTORIA
This classic, elegant hotel in a quiet part of the Gold Coast feels like a retreat. Soak with your sweetie in the large bathtubs, enjoy a cocktail from the bar, and indulge in the luxury spa (page 184).

>AFTERNOON

In the afternoon, head to the Lakeview neighborhood. You'll know whether the Cubs are playing at **Wrigley Field;** just look for sports bars like The Cubby Bear and Sluggers filled with locals. Pop inside for a bit of the excitement or a beer, then walk south along North Broadway. Take time to stop at shops like **Windy City Sweets, Foursided,** and the **Unabridged Bookstore.** Relax with a bite to eat at **Bar Pastoral.**

>EVENING

At night, head to the trendy West Loop for dinner. Make reservations at local favorite **Girl & the Goat** and tuck in to family-style plates off the global menu. After dinner, indulge in inventive cocktails at **The Aviary.** Or, if you're ready for a new 'hood, take the Blue Line north to Logan Square, west Bucktown. Specialty cocktail spots like **Lost Lake, Billy Sunday,** and **Scofflaw** all sit within a few blocks of each other.

PLANNING YOUR TRIP

WHEN TO GO

Summer is high season in Chicago. While it may feel hot and muggy, the city comes alive with festivals, outdoor patios, open-air concerts, water sports, and an overwhelming sense of happiness. Chicagoans love summer and visiting during this season will show you the best of the city. Book hotel and restaurant reservations far in advance and bring sunscreen and a water bottle while outdoors.

Fall is beautiful, especially when the tree-lined streets turn vibrant colors, and **late spring** can also be a pleasant time to visit.

Winters are considered off-season, as they are bitterly cold and long. Visitors should bring warm jackets and shoes, gloves, hats, and scarves to guard against the wind. Snow boots are recommended December-February. However, you'll find better hotel deals and fewer crowds. Sights and museums are open year-round, but if you prefer to avoid the cold, don't visit until at least mid-April.

ENTRY REQUIREMENTS

International travelers will need a **valid passport.** Some international visitors may also need a **visa.** For a list of visa requirements by country, visit the **State**

Millennium Park in winter

DAILY REMINDERS

· **Monday:** The Museum of Contemporary Art, the DuSable Museum of African-American History, and the National Museum of Mexican Art are closed.

· **Tuesday:** The Swedish American Museum is free to all visitors on the second Tuesday of the month.

· **Wednesday:** The Oriental Institute Museum is open until 8pm.

· **Thursday:** The Chicago Children's Museum is free 5pm to 8pm. The Art Institute of Chicago and the Smart Museum of Art are open until 8pm.

· **Saturday:** The Green City Market is held.

· **Sunday:** Jackson Park is closed.

Department website (www.travel.state.gov/visa). Visa requirements can change at any time, and additional restrictions may apply. At time of publication, citizens from Syria, Iran, Yemen, Libya, Somalia, and Sudan required special screenings. If traveling from one of these countries, allow extra time for your visa application and for customs procedures upon arrival.

Canadian citizens do not need a visa to visit the United States, but they must show a passport or passport card. There are no vaccination requirements for visitors to the United States.

TRANSPORTATION

Chicago has two major airports: Chicago O'Hare and Chicago Midway. Most visitors will fly into **Chicago O'Hare International Airport,** which is 17 miles northwest of downtown. **Chicago Midway International Airport** is 10 miles southwest of downtown and serves small and low-cost carriers such as Southwest Airlines, as well as some Delta flights.

Chicago is a hub for Amtrak, which operates its Midwestern and cross-country routes out of **Union Station.**

The Chicago Transit Authority (CTA) offers a public transport system that is comprehensive and inexpensive. **The L** is Chicago's rail system; L trains run through every neighborhood, often stopping every few blocks. **CTA buses** link L stations and neighborhoods for convenient cross-city transport. Tickets for both the L and the CTA buses are sold at CTA station kiosks that accept cash and credit. One ride costs $2.25; transfers are free. Fares can be purchased as single passes, a daily pass, or on a refillable Ventra card.

Taxis are pricey, but readily available. Uber and Lyft are popular alternatives.

Within the downtown Loop, a **car** is not necessary. However, for day trips outside the city or to explore the Pilsen and Andersonville neighborhoods, a car may be needed. Car rentals are available at each airport.

RESERVATIONS

In the summer months and during special events (**St. Patrick's Day** and **Lollapalooza**), lodging can book up quickly; make hotel reservations at least three months in advance. For high-end and fine-dining restaurants, such as **Alinea,** reservations should be made one month in advance for weekends and 1-2 weeks in advance for weeknights. Rooftop seats at **Wrigley Field,** especially for a Cubs game, should be reserved far in advance.

PASSES AND DISCOUNTS

The **Chicago CityPASS** (www.citypass.com/chicago; $99.75 adults, $84.75 children age 3-11) gives you VIP admission to the Shedd Aquarium, Willis Tower Skydeck (fast pass entry), Field Museum, Museum of Science and Industry, 360 Chicago (express entry), Adler Planetarium, and Art Institute of Chicago (fast pass entry). The pass is good for nine consecutive days, starting on the first day of use. If you plan to see most of these sights, the CityPASS can save you 53 percent over general admission costs. Plus, you'll also get to skip many of the lines, saving you time on your trip.

The **Go Chicago Card** (www.smartdestinations.com) has several options. The All-Inclusive Pass offers access to 26 of Chicago's main attractions, including the Shedd Aquarium, Field Museum, Museum of Science and Industry, 360 Chicago, and more. The pass is available in one-, two-, three-, and five-day options ranging from $95 for adults ($69 children age 3-12) up to $195 for adults ($135 children age 3-12).

GUIDED TOURS

The **Chicago Architecture Foundation Tours** (www.architecture. org; $46) are among the most popular and the most worthwhile. During the tour, knowledgeable guides discuss Chicago's history and architecture while sailing along the Chicago River.

Big Bus Chicago (www.bigbustours.com/en/Chicago; $29-59) provides transport via a hop-on, hop-off tour bus. Listen to an audio guide while riding through the city, stopping at some of the most famous spots.

If exploring the city on foot, check out the **Chicago Walking Tours** offered by **Free Tours by Foot** (www.freetoursbyfoot. com/Chicago-tours; by donation). Guided and themed tours explore a variety of Chicago neighborhoods, or you can download one of the free, self-guided walking tours.

For niche interests, **Chicago Elevated** (www.chicagoelevated. com; $23 adults, $10 children) covers the city through a variety of walking tours that explore the Pedway, historic architecture (through binoculars), and disaster sites in the Loop. The **Frank Lloyd Wright Tour** (http://flwright.org/tours; rates vary) explores the architect's life and work through nine specialty tours. **Untouchable Tours** (https:// gangstertour.com; $35) delves deep into the Prohibition era gangster Chicago. **Chicago Food Planet** (www.chicagofoodplanet.com; $50) offers foodie-based tours of Chicago neighborhoods.

CALENDAR OF EVENTS

MARCH

St. Patrick's Day (www.choosechicago.com) is a big deal in Chicago. Home to a large Irish population, the city celebrates with a parade through the downtown Loop and dyes the Chicago River green. Even those who aren't Irish enjoy the yearly festivities, and people come from all over the country to take part.

APRIL-MAY

Chicago Cubs Opening Day at Wrigley Field (1060 W. Addison St.) draws crowds to the neighborhood as they cheer on the Cubbies and kick off a new season with plenty of beer and Chicago dogs. The citywide event even draws baseball fans from neighboring states.

JUNE-AUGUST

Watch free outdoor movies in the Pritzker Pavilion during the **Millennium Park Movie Series** (6:30pm Tues. June-Aug.).

Catch free outdoor concerts during the **Millennium Park Music Series** (6:30pm Mon. and Thurs. June-Aug.).

The free **Grant Park Music Festival** (www.grantparkmusicfestival. com; dates vary June-Aug.) brings classical music to the Pritzker Pavilion.

Chicago Summer Dance (www. cityofchicago.org; dates and locations vary June-Aug.) hosts the largest outdoor dance festival in the United States. Most events take place at Grant Park, with smaller performances at parks around the city.

The **Chicago Blues Festival** (Millennium Park; www.cityofchicago.org; early June) features three days of live music and is the largest free blues festival in the world.

The **Chicago Pride Parade** (Lakeview; http://chicagopride. gopride.com) is held the last Sunday in June. Boystown is enthusiastic with parade-goers and other celebratory events.

Every Fourth of July, the **Fireworks at Navy Pier** (https://navypier.com) hosts a beautiful display. Watch from one of the lakefront beaches for the best views.

The world's largest food festival, the free **Taste of Chicago** (Grant Park; www.cityofchicago. org; early July) is filled with plenty of food and drinks from Chicago's best restaurants.

Lollapalooza (Grant Park; www. lollapalooza.com; early Aug.) is one of the biggest music festivals in the country, with three days of live bands across multiple stages.

The **Chicago Air & Water Show** (North Avenue Beach; www.cityofchicago.org; mid-Aug.) is the largest free air exhibition of its kind. Spread your blanket on one of the lakeshore beaches to enjoy the show.

For one weekend in August, six blocks of North Halsted Street (between Belmont and Addison) fill with hundreds of arts and crafts vendors, plus live music, for the **North Halsted Market Days** (Boystown; www.northalsted.com).

SEPTEMBER

The **Chicago Jazz Festival** (Millennium Park; www.cityofchicago. org; Aug.-Sept.) is a Labor Day weekend tradition featuring free musical performances from local and world-renowned musicians.

OCTOBER

The annual **Halloween Parade of Artists** (Grant Park; www.chicagoculturalmile.

WHAT'S NEW?

- **Sights:** Chicago is constantly transforming, and some big changes are great for visitors. The **Navy Pier** celebrated its 100-year anniversary in 2016 with the christening of the new **Centennial Wheel. Riverwalk** has expanded and now includes floating gardens, fountains, an amphitheater, and even more waterside restaurants. The **606 Trail,** built on the West Side of the city, offers more outdoor activities away from the lakefront.

- **Food:** Restaurants are popping up all the time, constantly elevating the quality of food and drinks in the city. **Cindy's Rooftop Bar, Monteverde,** and many options on the West Side and in Near North have set a high standard. There's never been a better time to eat here.

- **Neighborhoods**: **Pilsen** and **Andersonville,** once known for thriving immigrant communities, now also draw visitors for flourishing food scenes, local boutiques, and museums like the **Swedish American Museum** and the **National Museum of Mexican Art** that showcase the area's immigrant heritage.

org; late Oct.) celebrates the holiday with a parade, musical performances, and more.

NOVEMBER

Sip hot chocolate and watch the lighting of the tree at the **Christmas Tree Lighting Ceremony** (Millennium Park; www.choosechicago.com; mid-Nov.), the unofficial kickoff to the holiday season in Chicago.

At the Lincoln Park Zoo, the pathways and exhibits are lit as part of the festive **Zoo Lights** (www.lpzoo.org; late Nov.-Jan. 1) event, a favorite for families. There's ice carving, holiday snacks, crafts, and photos with Santa.

Taking place on the Saturday before Thanksgiving, one million lights strung across hundreds of trees along Michigan Avenue are lit in the **Magnificent Mile Lights Festival** (www.themagnificentmile.com; mid-Nov.).

DECEMBER

Chicagoans get in the holiday spirit at the **Christkindlmarket** (Daley Plaza; www.christkindlmarket.com; mid-Nov.-late Dec.), a German-style Christmas market in the Loop that runs the month of December. Eat bratwurst, sip mulled wine, and shop for handmade gifts at the outdoor market.

New Year's Eve in Chicago is always a big event with a massive fireworks display over **Navy Pier** (https://navypier.com; Dec. 31-Jan. 1), plus musical performances and other entertainment.

NEIGHBORHOODS

The Loop and Museum Campus

Map 1

In the heart of the city, the Loop is where you'll find the **iconic buildings** that make up **Chicago's skyline,** including the Willis Tower, which for years was the tallest building in the world. **Historic architecture** mixes with newer office buildings in the bustling commercial district, which is separated from the rest of downtown by the **Chi-**

cago River and its many bridges. By day, the Loop is full of businesspeople running to meetings, but at night, it becomes glamorous as the many **theaters** open their doors to adoring crowds.

Farther south, on the beautiful **Museum Campus,** you'll find some of the Chicago's most famed attractions: the Shedd Aquarium, the Field Museum, and the Adler Planetarium.

TOP SIGHTS

- Millennium Park (page 54)
- The Art Institute of Chicago (page 55)
- Willis Tower Skydeck (page 56)
- The Riverwalk (page 57)
- Shedd Aquarium (page 58)

TOP RESTAURANTS

- Cindy's Rooftop Bar (page 77)

TOP NIGHTLIFE

- Buddy Guy's Legends (page 110)

TOP ARTS AND CULTURE

- Oriental Theatre (page 130)
- *The Picasso* (page 132)

TOP SPORTS AND ACTIVITIES

- Grant Park (page 144)
- Chicago Bears (page 146)
- Chicago Architecture River Cruise (page 146)

TOP HOTELS

- Chicago Athletic Association Hotel (page 178)
- Virgin Hotel (page 180)

GETTING THERE AND AROUND

- L Train Stations: State/Lake, Clark/Lake, Washington/Wabash, and Adams/Wabash are served by the Green/Pink/Brown/Orange L lines. La Salle/Van Buren, Quincy, and Washington/Wells are served by the Pink/Brown/Orange L lines.
- Metra Stations: Millennium, Van Buren Street, and La Salle Street Stations
- Major bus hubs: Numerous buses service the Loop. Michigan Avenue at Jackson is a major hub for Millennium Park.

LOOP WALK

TOTAL DISTANCE: 2.5 miles
TOTAL WALKING TIME: 1 hour

This walk through downtown Chicago passes some of the city's most famous sights. You'll admire sculptures by Picasso and Calder, gaze at some of the city's historic architecture, and finish with drinks and a view of the skyline. Start in the late afternoon and finish in time for happy hour at Cindy's Rooftop Bar.

1 Start your exploration of Chicago's Loop by taking the Brown/Pink/Orange L line to the LaSalle/Van Buren Station. Walk one block north on La Salle Street to the Chicago Board of Trade Building, a stunning art deco skyscraper. Power up with a power lunch at the **Ceres Cafe** in the buidling lobby.

2 Walk three blocks east on West Jackson Boulevard and enter the **Willis Tower Skydeck.** Take the high-speed elevator to the 103rd floor observation deck for views across Chicago into four neighboring states.

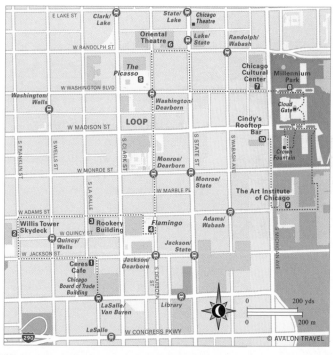

Rookery Building

3 Exit the Willis Tower, walk one block north on South Franklin Street, then turn right onto North Adams Street. Walk three blocks east, then turn right on South LaSalle Street to step inside the **Rookery Building.** The stunning lobby was designed by Frank Lloyd Wright and includes a spiral staircase designed by architect John Root.

4 Continue one block east on West Adams Street to Alexander Calder's bright red, abstract *Flamingo* sculpture. The red color was designed to offset the black and steel dominating Federal Plaza.

5 Turn left onto North Dearborn Street and walk five blocks north toward *The Picasso,* located outside the Richard J. Daley Center. Unveiled in 1967, the 50-foot-tall sculpture was the first major piece of public art in Chicago.

6 Turn right on West Randolph Street and walk one block east, passing the 1926 **Oriental Theatre.** A peek inside the lobby reveals some of its elaborate interior. At North State Street, look left for a photo op of the **Chicago Theatre's** flashing iconic marquee. Built in 1921, the theater still hosts plays and shows (tours are offered daily at noon).

7 Turn right on North State Street and walk one block south, then turn left onto East Washington Street. In two blocks you'll reach the **Chicago Cultural Center.** Step inside to gaze upon one of the most beautiful interiors in the city.

8 Cross Michigan Avenue and enter **Millennium Park.** Snap your photo under *Cloud Gate,* admire the *Crown Fountain,* and wander through the Lurie Garden.

9 From Millennium Park, take the Nichols Bridgeway to cross south over East Monroe Street and enter **The Art Institute of Chicago.** Use the museum brochure to follow a self-guided tour through the impressive collection.

10 Exiting The Art Institute of Chicago, walk two blocks north up Michigan Avenue and stop in at the Chicago Athletic Association Hotel. Head up to **Cindy's Rooftop Bar** for drinks with an amazing view over Millennium Park.

MUSEUM CAMPUS WALK

TOTAL DISTANCE: 1 mile
TOTAL WALKING TIME: 30 minutes

The Museum Campus sits south of the Loop, nestled snugly against the end of Grant Park. It's possible to get there by following the Lakefront Trail south from Grant Park's Buckingham Fountain, which will add one mile to your day. Or opt instead to take the CTA Red/Orange/Green Line to the Roosevelt Station or the Metra Electric Line to the Museum Campus/11th Street Station and save your soles for the worthy sights here. Plan to arrive early (9am) and book tickets online in advance to avoid waiting in long lines.

1 Exit the Museum Campus/11th Street Station walking east across South Columbus Drive. Continue following the tree-lined path east under Lake Shore Drive as you enter the Museum Campus. Looking across the Great Lawn, you'll see The Field Museum to the right and the **Shedd Aquarium** directly ahead. Spend at least an hour admiring some of the more than 32,000 animals at the aquarium and don't leave before catching the Caribbean dive (10:30am).

2 Your next stop is **The Field Museum,** immediately to your left as you exit the aquarium. Arrive in time for the free Museum Highlights Tour (11am), which provides an overview of the museum's extensive natural history collection. Snap your selfie with Sue the T. rex and grab a bite at the on-site café or bistro.

3 After lunch, walk east along Solidarity Drive to the **Adler Planetarium** located on the promontory of Northerly Island. The striking, circular structure offers a variety of shows and exhibits that explore our

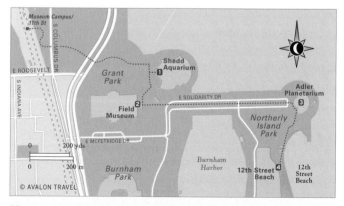

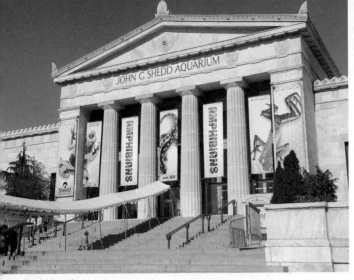

Shedd Aquarium

universe. Catch the afternoon Solar System show then wander the galleries until the planetarium closes at 4pm.

4 Exit the planetarium heading south toward **12th Street Beach,** where you can rest your weary feet on the quiet sand while gazing out over Lake Michigan.

Near North and Navy Pier

Map 2

This trendy neighborhood is the go-to spot in Chicago for drinks and **cocktails.** It's also a prime spot for **views of the city,** with the stunning skyline glittering across the river to the south and Lake Michigan sitting serenely to the east. Browse the **designer stores** along Michigan Avenue's Magnificent Mile, wander inside the art deco Merchandise Mart, and don't miss a ride on the Centennial Wheel at **Navy Pier.**

TOP SIGHTS

- Navy Pier (page 60)
- 360 Chicago (page 62)

TOP RESTAURANTS

- Lou Malnati's (page 80)
- Portillo's (page 81)

TOP NIGHTLIFE

- Green River (page 111)
- Studio Paris Nightclub (page 113)

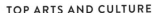

TOP ARTS AND CULTURE

- Museum of Contemporary Art (page 133)

TOP SHOPS

- Magnificent Mile (page 157)
- Knot Standard (page 160)
- Space 519 (page 161)
- Eataly (page 161)

TOP HOTELS

- Four Seasons (page 182)
- The Peninsula Chicago (page 183)
- Freehand Chicago (page 185)

GETTING THERE AND AROUND

- L Train Stations: The Brown/Purple Lines service the Merchandise Mart Station; Blue/Pink/Orange/Green/Purple/Brown Lines service the Clark/Lake Station.
- Major bus hubs: CTA bus #124 runs along Upper Wacker Drive and services Navy Pier.

NEAR NORTH AND NAVY PIER WALK

TOTAL DISTANCE: 2 miles
TOTAL WALKING TIME: 1 hour

On this walk, you'll visit some of Chicago's most famous architectural sights, window-shop the Magnificent Mile, spend some time on the beach, and tour the attractions on Navy Pier. Start in the late morning or late afternoon in order to reach Shake Shack by lunch or dinner.

1 Take the Red Line to the State/Lake Station and walk one block north. Cross State Street heading east to start your stroll on the **Chicago Riverwalk,** where you'll pass historic architecture and view floating gardens. You can also stop for food and drinks.

2 The Chicago River bridges have stairs leading down to the thoroughfare. At Michigan Avenue, take the bridge steps up to the street and look north across the river to see the **Wrigley Building.** The tower is best admired from outside, where you can take in the French Renaissance-style architecture and magnificent clock tower.

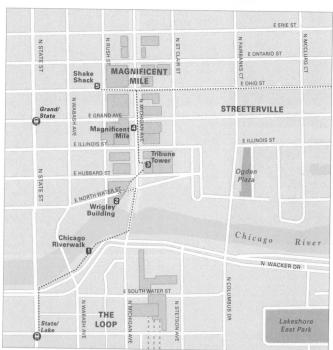

3 Walk north across the DuSable Bridge and cross Michigan Avenue toward the **Tribune Tower.** Admire the giant statue of Abraham Lincoln at the tower's entrance, then look closely at the relief pieces on the lower level—many rocks and materials from famous buildings around the world have been laid into the brick.

4 Continue three blocks north along Michigan Avenue, which offers the chance for window-shopping the famed **Magnificent Mile,** lined with more than 460 luxury, designer, and chain stores.

5 At East Ohio Street, turn east for one block to fuel up with burgers and a custard milk shake at **Shake Shack.** The food is worth the wait.

6 Walk off that burger by heading east along East Ohio Street for 0.5 mile until reaching the pedestrian underpass across Lake Shore Drive. Emerge on the Lakefront Trail at **Ohio Street Beach,** where you can rent lounge chairs and umbrellas in summer.

7 Take the Lakefront Trail east to **Navy Pier,** where your walk ends, but the rest of your day is just beginning. Ride the Centennial Wheel, visit the Chicago Children's Museum, and wander the Crystal Gardens. In summer, fireworks light up the sky (Wed. and Sat. evenings).

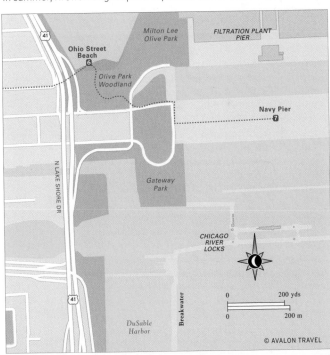

West Side

Map 3

Once a warehouse and factory district, the West Loop and West Side of Chicago has undergone rapid transformation over the past few years. **"Restaurant Row"** along Randolph Street in West Loop features restaurants and **bars** of all kinds along with some of the **best chefs in the city.** A few boutiques and galleries draw creative types to the neighborhood. Chicagoans love that it feels both **sleek and gritty;** visitors love that it feels anything but touristy. The West Side is also home to **Greektown,** so don't forget to stock up on baklava.

TOP RESTAURANTS

- Au Cheval (page 87)
- Momotaro (page 89)

TOP NIGHTLIFE

- The Aviary (page 114)

GETTING THERE AND AROUND

- L Train Stations: Brown/Pink/Orange/Purple Lines service the Quincy/Wells Station; the Blue Line services the Clinton Station.
- Metra Stations: Ogilvie Transportation Center
- Major bus hubs: #7, 28, 126, 151, and 156 bus routes stop along Adams Street.

Lincoln Park, Old Town, and Gold Coast

Map 4

Victorian mansions and **ivy-covered brick homes** characterize Chicago's most affluent neighborhoods. Some of the buildings here survived the Great Chicago Fire; they now sit alongside luxury hotels and **fine-dining restaurants.** The Gold Coast is the area to **see and be seen** in Chicago. A few blocks west in tranquil Old Town, you'll find high-end coffee shops by day countered by a **wild nightlife** scene after dark. Lincoln Park is known as Chicago's "City in a Garden," a fitting name for this neighborhood of brick row houses,

landmark districts, tree-lined streets, and verdant parks. It's also a favorite among families for its **zoo, museums**, and affordable dining. At night, the nearby DePaul University brings a young crowd out to the area's **live music venues** and **sports bars.**

TOP SIGHTS
- Lincoln Park Conservatory (page 64)

TOP RESTAURANTS
- Alinea (page 93)
- Green City Market (page 94)
- Halal Guys (page 96)

TOP NIGHTLIFE
- Second City (page 117)

TOP ARTS AND CULTURE
- Steppenwolf Theatre (page 137)

TOP SPORTS AND ACTIVITIES
- North Avenue Beach (page 148)
- Lakefront Trail (page 149)

GETTING THERE AND AROUND
- L Train Station: The Red Line services the Clark/Division Station.
- Major bus hubs: The #22 and 36 bus lines run along Clark Street.

LINCOLN PARK, OLD TOWN, AND GOLD COAST WALK

TOTAL DISTANCE: 2.7 miles
TOTAL WALKING TIME: 1 hour

This walk explores the history, homes, and gardens of the city's most charming neighborhoods. Start this tour in the morning and enjoy fresh-baked pastries from La Fournette before ending at North Avenue Beach.

1 The Brown Line stops at the Sedgwick Station in Old Town. Walk east along West North Avenue and turn right onto North Wells Street to grab a coffee and a croissant at **La Fournette.**

2 Return to West North Avenue and turn right, continuing to North Clark Street where you'll reach the south corner of **Lincoln Park.**

3 The massive Lincoln Monument greets you a few steps into Lincoln Park. To your left is the **Chicago History Museum,** which is worth a stop for a crash course in Chicago history.

Lincoln Park Conservatory

4 Walk north through the park, following the Nature Boardwalk and stopping to admire the webbed, wooden archway near the bridge over South Pond. Visit the **Lincoln Park Zoo** and farm.

5 After visiting the zoo, stop in the **Lincoln Park Conservatory** for a quick tour through different types of ecosystems.

6 It's just a short walk north across Fullerton Avenue to the **Peggy Notebaert Nature Museum.** The scientific institution houses a 2,700-square-foot greenhouse filled with more than 1,000 butterflies.

7 From Lincoln Park, exit east via West Fullerton Avenue and cross the bridge to walk about one mile south along the Lakefront Trail. Stop at **North Avenue Beach** and stake out a spot in the sand to relax.

Lakeview and Wrigleyville Map 5

Visitors flock to Wrigleyville for **Cubs games** at historic Wrigley Field and beers at Sluggers, but the rest of Lakeview has a lot to offer. The **beaches** are less crowded than those downtown, and there is a cluster of **theater, pubs,** and casual restaurants. While it's not full of must-see sights, it is a great place **browse local shops** and dine outdoors. Within this neighborhood is **Boystown,** an LGBTQ enclave of lively nightclubs with some of the best karaoke in town.

TOP SIGHTS
- Wrigley Field (page 67)

TOP NIGHTLIFE
- The Holiday Club (page 120)
- Trader Todd's (page 122)

TOP SPORTS AND ACTIVITIES
- Chicago Cubs (page 150)

TOP SHOPS
- Nuts on Clark (page 170)

GETTING THERE AND AROUND
- L Train Stations: The Red Line stops at the Belmont, Addison, and Sheridan Stations.
- Major bus hubs: The CTA #22 bus line stops at Clark and Roscoe.

LAKEVIEW AND WRIGLEYVILLE WALK

TOTAL DISTANCE: 1.5 miles
TOTAL WALKING TIME: 30 minutes

This neighborhood is all about sports, food, and entertainment. Plan your walk to start in the early evening so you can take advantage of the neighborhood's late-night offerings. Take in a Cubs game to best experience the spirit of the neighborhood.

1 Take the Red Line to the Belmont Station. The L train conveniently stops right near **Cheesie's Pub & Grub,** where you can order from a wide variety of inventive grilled cheese sandwiches.

2 Walk 0.5 mile north along North Sheffield Avenue to North Clark Street and veer left. Follow Clark Street north to **Sluggers,** a sports bar with its own batting cages that's especially popular during Cubs games.

© AVALON TRAVEL

Wrigleyville

3 Next door, you'll find **The Cubby Bear,** a staple during baseball season. It's worth a stop if the Cubs are playing to see the massive amounts of fans it draws.

4 Leaving The Cubby Bear, you'll be faced with the iconic **Wrigley Field** sign across the street. Catch a game, take a tour, or enjoy the vibe from outside.

5 Walk 0.5 mile east on West Addison Street, then turn right onto North Halsted Street to walk through Boystown, Chicago's vibrant LGBTQ neighborhood. Tons of shops and bars line the four blocks of Halsted Street. Stop at **Roscoe's** for great karaoke in the evening.

6 If your grilled cheese from earlier has worn off, head to the **Chicago Diner** for excellent vegetarian and vegan food or one of their famous milk shakes.

7 Continue walking 0.5 mile south along North Halsted Street and turn right onto Belmont Avenue. Just past Clark Street is **The Annoyance Theater & Bar.** The tiny venue is great for experimental improv.

Wicker Park and Bucktown

Map 6

Northwest of the Loop, the neighborhood once made up of northern European immigrants is now Chicago's **hipster haven.** Baroque-style architecture characterize the area, and it's home to the best **Polish and Ukrainian** food in the city. In 1989, the Around the Coyote festival launched to promote **local artists,** a tradition that continues at the Flat Iron Arts Building and plethora of local **shops and galleries.** More recently, some of Chicago's most **famous chefs** have opened shop in the neighborhood, expanding their downtown reach.

TOP RESTAURANTS
- Mindy's HotChocolate (page 101)
- Big Star (page 102)

TOP NIGHTLIFE
- The Violet Hour (page 123)

TOP SHOPS
- Virtu (page 171)

TOP HOTELS
- The Robey (page 191)

GETTING THERE AND AROUND
- Take the CTA Blue Line to Damen. If needed, transfer from other lines in the Loop.
- There's parking around Wicker Park, some metered, some not. The farther from the park you go, the more likely you are to find free parking.

Hyde Park

Map 7

Hyde Park was a southern suburb of Chicago until the **Columbian Exposition** brought the neighborhood into the city. Today, you'll find green spaces, the Gothic Revival-style University of Chicago, **excellent museums,** and a prime example of Frank Lloyd Wright's **Prairie Style architecture.**

TOP SIGHT

- Museum of Science and Industry (page 69)

GETTING THERE AND AROUND

- Metra Stations: 55th - 56th - 57th Street and 59th Street Stations
- Major bus lines: The #6 Jeffrey Express bus runs from Wacker Drive to Hyde Park. The #1 runs from Union Station to Hyde Park, but takes about an hour.

THE UNIVERSITY OF
CHICAGO

HYDE PARK WALK

TOTAL DISTANCE: 2.5 miles
TOTAL WALKING TIME: 1 hour

This Hyde Park walk is packed with history, culture, and architecture. Plan to start the walk in the late morning, so that you can take advantage of the area's breakfast and lunch options. Take your time, but try to make it to the Museum of Science and Industry before it closes at 4pm.

1 Take the Metra Electric Line to the 59th Street Station. Walk 0.5 mile west along the verdant Midway Plaisance, originally conceived by landscape architect Frederick Law Olmsted and used as a midway for the World's Columbian Exposition. Nearing the **University of Chicago,** admire the institution's beautiful Gothic Revival architecture, which is modeled after Oxford University.

2 Turn north on South Woodlawn Avenue and continue past the stunning Rockefeller Memorial Chapel. Cross East 58th Street to grab coffee and a French pastry at **Plein Air Café.**

Robie House

3 Located next to the café is the **Robie House,** one of Frank Lloyd Wright's most famous works. Simply admire the Prairie School style exterior or opt for one of the guided tours inside.

4 Return to South Woodlawn Avenue and walk south, turning right onto East 58th Street to visit the **Oriental Institute Museum,** the university's archaeology museum specializing in artifacts from the Middle East. Tours of the art deco building are free.

5 Back on South Woodlawn Avenue, walk one block north and turn right on East 57th Street. Stop at **Medici on 57th** for pizza and burgers at this favorite student hangout.

6 Continue four blocks east to **Powell's Books,** a must-stop for any book lover, to browse the extensive collection of used books.

7 The **Museum of Science and Industry** awaits at the end of East 57th Street. Housed in a structure built for the 1893 World's Columbian Exposition, the museum's more than 2,000 exhibits are sure to keep you busy for the rest of the day.

SIGHTS

Chicago is rife with "must-do" experiences. Immerse yourself in history on an architecture boat tour. Test your fear of heights at 360 Chicago. Soak in the best views of the city while riding high in the Navy Pier's Ferris wheel.

Wrigley Building and Tribune Tower

Begin your exploration in the Loop to orient yourself within the city. This downtown area is packed with excellent museums, historic architecture, and iconic sights. The neighborhood's grid layout also means it's very walkable and easy to navigate, with Lake Michigan providing a handy guide to the east. Plan to visit the Willis Tower Skydeck, The Art Institute of Chicago, and Millennium Park for some of the best views, art, and outdoor space in the city. Slightly south of the Loop, the aptly named Museum Campus warrants a full day of museum-going; The Field Museum, the Shedd Aquarium, and the Adler Planetarium all demand (and deserve) your time.

Chicago's northern neighborhoods were shaped in part by the 1871 Great Chicago Fire, which destroyed many of the buildings in this area. The resulting architectural renaissance is today reflected in the Lake Shore mansions and towering skyscrapers in the Near North, Old Town, and Gold Coast neighborhoods. While these neighborhoods differ in many ways, one thing they all have in common is ready access to the beaches lining Lake Michigan. Farther north, you'll experience a more local side of Chicago. Cubs fans will want to pay their respects at Wrigley Field, while artists will be drawn to Wicker Park's vibrant community.

HIGHLIGHTS

✪ **BEST URBAN PARK:** Part sculpture garden, part concert hall, and all of it a place to relax, **Millennium Park** is one of the most popular outdoor spaces in the city (page 54).

✪ **MOST IMPRESSIVE:** Spend the day diving into **The Art Institute of Chicago**'s extensive collection—or simply browse the famous works on a Highlight tour (page 55).

✪ **BEST SKYLINE VIEWS:** The breathtaking views from the **Willis Tower Skydeck** are awe-inspiring, especially at sunset (page 56).

✪ **BEST URBAN WALK:** Lining the Chicago River, **The Riverwalk** provides a scenic taste of Chicago's art, architecture, and dining scene (page 57).

✪ **BEST PLACE TO FEEL SMALL:** With 5,000,000 gallons of water and more than 32,000 animals from the world's reefs, rivers, and oceans, the **Shedd Aquarium** puts humanity into perspective (page 58).

✪ **BEST FOR FAMILIES:** Beachy vibes, a Ferris wheel, and a carnival atmosphere make the **Navy Pier** a hit with families (page 60).

✪ **BEST WAY TO CONQUER YOUR FEAR OF HEIGHTS:** On the 94th floor of the historic John Hancock, the **360 Chicago** experience will tilt you parallel to the ground 1,000 feet below (page 62).

✪ **BEST WAY TO BEAT THE COLD:** Immerse yourself in tropical warmth in the gardens at the **Lincoln Park Conservatory** (page 64).

✪ **BEST CITY PRIDE:** Win or lose, fans go crazy for the Cubs at iconic **Wrigley Field** (page 67).

✪ **MOST WORTH THE TREK:** Situated in Hyde Park, the **Museum of Science and Industry** may be far from downtown, but it's worth the trip for the engineering marvels and interactive exhibits (page 69).

On the South Side of Chicago, Hyde Park was largely formed by the 1893 World's Columbian Exposition. Nowhere is this more evident than at the Museum of Science and Industry in Jackson Park. The domed white building is one of only two structures remaining from that historic fair; however, the museum's enormous offerings in science and technology are excitingly modern.

The Loop and Museum Campus

Map 1

TOP EXPERIENCE

✪ Millennium Park

Built to celebrate the second millennium, this park has become one of Chicago's largest attractions, drawing crowds to its 25 acres of outdoor space in the center of the Loop. Its large collection of public art includes the reflective *Cloud Gate*, an installation commonly referred to as "The Bean." The silver, bean-shaped sculpture offers a magnified reflection of the city skyline and is a popular place for a photo op. South of *Cloud Gate*, the *Crown Fountain* draws kids in summer who play amid the gurgling water spouts from the video sculptures lit with rotating images.

In summer, locals lounge on the Great Lawn and picnic with a good book while the Frank Gehry-designed Jay Pritzker Pavilion hosts free live concerts, comedy routines, and film screenings. In the south corner of the park, the 2.5-acre perennial Lurie Garden is a colorful escape from the busy downtown.

Active travelers can take advantage of free morning workouts on the lawn, and art lovers will appreciate the ever-changing collection of sculptures and exhibitions. In winter, Millennium Park draws skaters to the Maggie Daley Ice Skating Ribbon.

The park has won numerous awards for green design and accessibility and is considered the world's largest rooftop garden (it's on top of a parking garage).

Millennium Park is easily accessible via multiple L trains. The Green/Orange/Brown/Pink/Purple Lines exit at Madison and Wabash or Randolph and Wabash. The Red/Blue Lines exit at Monroe or Washington.

Map 1: 201 E. Randolph St., 312/742-1168, www.cityofchicago.org; 8am-11pm daily; free

reflections in *Cloud Gate* at Millennium Park

✪ The Art Institute of Chicago

The Art Institute of Chicago is the second-largest art museum in the United States and boasts one of the most impressive collections in the world. Nestled within Millennium Park, the museum is comprised of eight buildings and housed in a historic structure built in 1893 for the World's Columbian Exposition. Inside are more than 300,000 works of art and 30 special exhibits. Famous works include Pablo Picasso's *The Old Guitarist*, Georges Seurat's *A Sunday on La Grande Jatte*, Edward Hopper's *Nighthawks*, Grant Wood's *American Gothic*, and Marc Chagall's *America Windows*, as well as pieces by Monet and Renoir among others. The modern wing features a large collection of

NEARBY

- Cocktails with a view await at Cindy's Rooftop Bar (page 77).
- See what's on at the Chicago Cultural Center, or simply admire the stunning interior of this landmark building (page 129).
- In winter, a visit to the Maggie Daley Ice Skating Ribbon can be a fun way to enjoy the snowy city skyline (page 145).

the modern wing of the Art Institute of Chicago, designed by Renzo Piano

pop art with work by Andy Warhol and Charles Ray.

Plan at least a full day to wander through the exhibits or take the **Highlights Tour** which offers in-depth explanations of the most remarkable pieces. Those short on time can grab a museum brochure and follow a self-guided tour to the featured top 10 works.

The museum has three on-site dining options and a sculpture garden. In summer, the **Museum Café** (11am-4pm daily) offers outdoor dining with views of Millennium Park and the sculpture terrace.

The museum is a fast and easy stop from the L train via the Brown/Green/Orange/Pink/Purple Lines (Adams and Wabash) or the Red/Blue Lines at Monroe. The CTA bus line stops at the Van Buren and Millennium Stations along Michigan Avenue. Those driving should reserve space at one of the nearby garages, although valet parking ($28) is also available.

Map 1: 111 S. Michigan Ave., 312/443-3600, www.artic.edu; 10:30am-5pm daily, until 8pm Thurs.; $25 adults, $19 seniors, students, and youth ages 14-17, children under 14 free

NEARBY

- **Seven Lions** is the perfect stop for elevated American food after a morning of exploring The Art Institute of Chicago directly across the way (page 77).

- Catch a performance at the **Chicago Symphony Center**, home of the Chicago Symphony Orchestra (page 130).

- Browse the art galleries and art nouveau murals at the **Fine Arts Building** (page 129).

- Stroll through **Grant Park** and admire the Buckingham Fountain as you gaze across Lake Michigan (page 144).

TOP EXPERIENCE

✪ Willis Tower Skydeck

The best view in Chicago is not for the faint of heart. Atop the former Sears Tower, the second-tallest building in North America is the Willis Tower Skydeck with the highest observation deck in the country. A 70-second elevator ride whisks you up to the 103rd floor of the Willis Tower where the views stretch into four neighboring states. But the most stomach-flipping experience is **The Ledge**: a clear glass box that juts 4.3 feet out from the Skydeck. Standing on The Ledge offers views 1,353 feet down to Wacker Drive and the Chicago River—as well as serious vertigo.

Also on the Skydeck are audiovisual exhibits about the tower's history and a theater film about Chicago landmarks, architecture, and the Great Chicago Fire. While the views are prettiest at sunset, it can also be quite crowded. Plan to arrive 30-45 minutes ahead for sunset views. To beat the crowds, opt for a morning visit instead or purchase a limited **early bird pass** (8am Sat., 8:30am Sun. Mar.-Sept.; 9am Sat., 9:30am Sun. Oct.-Feb., $65) for sunrise views. The **fast pass** ($49) skips the

the views from the Willis Tower Skydeck

theater and exhibits for an express line to the Skydeck elevators.

The Red/Purple/Pink Lines stop nearby at the Quincy/Wells Station. Map 1: 233 S. Wacker, 312/875-9447, www.theskydeck.com; 9am-10pm daily Mar.-Sept., 10am-8pm daily Oct.-Feb.; $23 adults, $15 children under 12

NEARBY

- Admire the Frank Lloyd Wright-designed lobby of the Rookery Building (page 57).
- Perfect the power lunch at Ceres Cafe in the Chicago Trade Building (page 77).
- Alexander Calder's *Flamingo* is one of the most-recognized pieces of Chicago public art (page 132).
- Browse vintage clothing and designer shoes at Floradora (page 157).

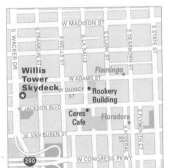

Rookery Building
The Rookery, designed by famous local architecture partners Burnham and Root, was completed in 1888 and has since become one of the most-renowned addresses in Chicago. Frank Lloyd Wright redesigned the lobby in 1905, turning it into a bright, mesmerizing room. The complex, marble-and-gold-patterned ceiling is topped with glass, which adds light to the building (a revolutionary architectural move at the time). The building was added to the National Register of Historic Places in 1970 and designated a Chicago Landmark in 1972. Today it's filled with corporate offices and residences, but visitors can still step inside to take photos of the grand spiral staircase and intricate ceiling in the lobby.
Map 1: 209 S. LaSalle St., 312/553-6100, http://therookerybuilding.com; free

☼ The Riverwalk
Chicago's "second lakefront," the Riverwalk provides a mile-long entertaining stroll past historic architecture, with plenty of opportunities to eat or drink. Highlights include the Vietnam Veterans Memorial Plaza (State and Wabash) and views of the Wrigley Building and Tribune Tower (one block before the Michigan Avenue Bridge). Along the way, sip a glass of wine at City Winery (11 Chicago Riverwalk) and watch the boats go by or grab some gelato at Frost (27 W Riverwalk) to cool down. You can even rent a kayak from Urban Kayaks (435 E Riverwalk) and paddle the Chicago River.
Map 1: Access via Wacker Dr. from N. Lake Shore Bridge to N. Orleans Street Bridge, www.chicagoriverwalk.us; open daily; free

NEARBY

- The patio at **Siena Tavern** is the place to be for brunch (page 84).
- **Andy's Jazz Club** is famed for its jazz performances and one of the best places in the city to hear live music (page 112).
- See the city from the water on the **Chicago Architecture River Cruise** (page 146).

TOP EXPERIENCE

✪ Shedd Aquarium

Built in 1930, the sprawling aquarium holds 5,000,000 gallons of water and is home to 32,000 animals. Permanent exhibits include the 76 habitats in the Waters of the World, the underwater Caribbean Reef, the Amazon Rising rainforest, and dolphins, sea lions, and sea otters in the coastal Abbott Oceanarium. More hands-on experiences include Stingray Touch (May-Oct.), where guests can get their fingers on cownose and yellow-spotted rays, and the sensory overload of the 4-D Experience theater.

The large museum is very popular and admission lines can be long, especially in warmer months. Book tickets online for faster entry and dress for Chicago weather—very hot or very cold—as much of the line forms outdoors. The Total Experience Pass

Shedd Aquarium

($39.95 adults, $30.95 children) provides entry to all exhibits, while the **Shedd Pass** ($30.95 adults, $21.95 children) offers a slightly cheaper option for fewer exhibits. Passes for Illinois residents ($8 adults, $6 children) are more affordable, but with access only to Waters of the World, Caribbean Reef, and Amazon Rising.

The Shedd Aquarium, along with The Field Museum and Adler Planetarium, is part of the Museum Campus. The CTA #130 bus services the Museum Campus (Memorial Day-Labor Day). The closest L station is Roosevelt; Red/Yellow/Green Lines stop here.

Map 1: 1200 Lake Shore Dr., 312/939-2438, www.sheddaquarium.org; 9am-6pm daily June 10-Aug. 20, 9am-5pm Mon.-Fri. and 9am-6pm Sat.-Sun. Aug. 21-June 9; $39.95 adults, $30.95 children

NEARBY

- While on the Museum Campus, time your day to include visits to **The Field Museum** (page 59) and **Adler Planetarium** (page 59).
- Grab a deli sandwich from **Eleven City Diner** to bring with you to the Museum Campus (page 77).
- Relax or enjoy a picnic can at **12th Street Beach** (page 145).

The Field Museum

The Field Museum of Natural History maintains an extensive permanent collection of artifacts and hosts traveling exhibits from around the world. Popular permanent exhibits include **Inside Ancient Egypt**, a re-created Egyptian burial chamber filled with mummies and relics. **Evolving Planet** takes you on a journey of evolution through fossils. And in the **Grainger Hall of Gems,** you can set your eyes on the rare jewels from around the globe. The most beloved member of the museum is 67-million-year-old **Sue**, the most complete and best-preserved *Tyrannosaurus rex* fossil.

Free tours are offered daily at 11am and noon, and there are two restaurants on-site. The CTA #130 bus services the Museum Campus (Memorial Day-Labor Day). The closest L station is Roosevelt; Red/Yellow/Green Lines stop here.

Map 1: 1400 S. Lake Shore Dr., 312/922-9410, www.fieldmuseum.org; 9am-5pm daily; $22 adults, $19 seniors, $15 children

Adler Planetarium

Since 1930, the Adler Planetarium has helped visitors explore the universe through planetarium shows, interactive exhibits, and special events. Located on the tip of the Museum Campus, the striking building was designed by architect Ernest A. Grunsfeld Jr. and features a stunning 12-sided dome that displays each sign of the zodiac. Inside are three theaters, an extensive collection of antique instruments, and the **Doane Observatory**, where you can view planets, stars, and galaxies through the largest telescope in the city. Kids will love crawling through the **Planet Explorers** exhibit or touching pieces of the moon and Mars in **Our Solar System**, while adults can mix cocktails and observatory tours during the **Adler After Dark** events.

The museum has an on-site café and gift shop. Check the calendar for a wide variety of special events, exhibits, and tours. The CTA #130 bus services the Museum Campus (Memorial Day-Labor Day). The closest L station is Roosevelt; Red/Yellow/Green Lines stop here.

Map 1: 1300 S. Lake Shore Dr., 312/922-7827, www.adlerplanetarium.org; 9:30am-4pm Mon.-Fri., 9:30am-4:30pm Sat.-Sun.; $24.95 adults, $19.95 children

Near North and Navy Pier

Map 2

TOP EXPERIENCE

✪ Navy Pier

A makeover in 2016 brought more fun and games to Navy Pier. The half-mile pier is jam-packed with activities for all ages. Spend a day riding the **Centennial Wheel**, exploring three floors of interactive games at the **Chicago Children's Museum** (10am-5pm Mon.-Wed. and Fri.-Sun., 10am-8pm Thurs., $14), watching classic productions at the **Chicago Shakespeare Theater** (www.chicagoshakes.com), touring the indoor **Crystal Gardens** botanical garden, viewing public art, and indulging in plenty of dining options, including Chicago's famous Giordano's deep-dish pizza and an outpost of the Billy Goat Tavern.

In summer, the pier is at its peak with **evening fireworks** (9:30pm Wed., 10:15pm Sat.), boat tours, and special events. In winter, a few turns around the indoor **ice-skating rink** will warm you right up. It's free to stroll the pier, and tickets are available for the individual attractions.

CTA buses #29, #65, #66, and #124 serve Navy Pier daily. The free **Navy Pier Trolley** (10am-10pm Sun.-Tues. and Thurs., 10am-10:30pm Wed., 10am-midnight Fri., 10am-12:30am Sat. June-Sept., weekends only Sept.-May) picks up at locations along Grand Avenue, State Street, Monroe Street, and Columbus Avenue. The seasonal **Shoreline Water Taxi** (312/222-9328, http://shorelinesightseeing.com/water-taxi, May-Nov.) connects Navy Pier with the Museum Campus and Union Station.

the amusement park on Navy Pier

Map 2: 600 E. Grand Ave., 312/595-7437, www.navypier.com; 10am-10pm Sun.-Thurs., 10am-midnight Fri.-Sat. June-Sept.; 10am-8pm Sun.-Thurs., 10am-10pm Fri.-Sat. Sept.-May; general access free, $35 day pass

Centennial Wheel

This is not your average Ferris wheel experience. The Navy Pier's Centennial Wheel lifts you 196 feet above the pier with amazing views of the Chicago skyline. New in 2016 for the Navy Pier's 100th birthday, the wheel features enclosed gondolas: two-sided, blue-and-white cars with a fortified structure and safety glass that can weather 115 mph winds. Inside, guests are treated to TV screens, speakers, plush seats, and 360-degree views. Rides lasts 12 minutes with three rotations. A fast pass ($25) skips holders ahead to the front of the line.

Map 2: 600 E. Grand Ave., 312/595-7437, www.navypier.com; 10am-10pm Sun.-Thurs., 10am-midnight Fri.-Sat. June-Sept.; 10am-8pm Sun.-Thurs., 10am-10pm Fri.-Sat. Sept.-May; $15 adults, $12 children age 3-11, children under 3 free

Tribune Tower

Chicago's 462-foot-tall Tribune Tower looms mightily over Michigan Avenue, its neo-Gothic design making it one of the city's most beautiful and distinctive office buildings. The original Tribune Tower, built in 1868, was a casualty of the Great Chicago Fire. The current building was completed in 1925 and is home to the *Chicago Tribune,* Tribune Media, and WGN Radio. It's a Chicago landmark and part of the Michigan-Wacker Historic District.

The lower level of the building features a series of reliefs incorporating rocks, stones, and other materials donated by *Chicago Tribune* correspondents. Pieces include fragments of the Taj Mahal, the Berlin Wall, the Parthenon, the Great Pyramid of Giza, Notre-Dame, the Great Wall of China, Angkor Wat, and the World Trade Center.

Map 2: 435 N. Michigan Ave.; 8am-6pm daily

Wrigley Building

The Wrigley Building was the first office building erected north of the Chicago River. Architects Graham, Anderson, Probst & White designed two towers of different heights linked by walkways; the 425-foot south tower is topped by a giant clock with multiple clock dials. The glazed terra-cotta exterior glimmers in the sun, takes on a cool tone in winter, and shines at night. The iconic building can be spotted far down Michigan Avenue in either direction, but the best vantage point for unobstructed photos is from along the Riverwalk.

Map 2: 400-410 N. Michigan Ave.; 9am-5pm daily

Magnificent Mile

The Magnificent Mile is luxury shopping at its best. More than 460 stores line this stretch of North Michigan Avenue, from high-end designers like Louis Vuitton and Gucci to popular chains such as the Gap and Crate and Barrel, as well as three shopping centers. Many stores have their flagship location on Michigan Avenue, and their polished storefronts house inventive window displays. This is especially true in December, when holiday window-shopping is an annual event (the window dressers at Macy's go all out). Seasonal decorations line the "Mag Mile" with sparkling lights, and pop-up Christmas markets make for a picturesque and festive walk. Stroll north to south for fabulous views approaching the river.

Map 2: N. Michigan Ave. bet. Chicago River and Oak St., www.themagnificentmile. com; store hours vary

⚙ 360 Chicago

On the 94th floor of the historic John Hancock Center perches the 360 Chicago observation deck with fantastic 360-degree views across the city. For an additional thrill, the TILT experience (timed entry 10:30am-10pm, $7) offers a fun, unique way to gaze down at the city. The clear, glass platform gradually "tilts" visitors outward over the Magnificent Mile; metal bars line the windows and offer a reassuring grip as you parallel the ground 1,000 feet below. (If you're scared of heights, this is not for you.) To skip the lines for the observation deck, make a dinner reservation instead at The Signature Room at the 95th (312/787-9596) and enjoy cocktails and views east over Lake Michigan.

CTA bus #125 stops at the John Hancock Center. The L's Red Line stops at the Chicago Station (N State St. and Chicago Ave.) about four blocks east.

Map 2: 875 N. Michigan Ave., 312/751-3681, www.360chicago.com; 9am-11pm daily, last entry at 10:30pm; $20 adults, $13 youth ages 3-11, children under 3 free

NEARBY

- Take a shopping break with excellent Italian cuisine at Cafe Spiaggia (page 83).

- Grab tickets to a theatrical performance at the Tony Award-winning Lookingglass Theatre (page 134).
- Take a free tour at the Museum of Contemporary Art, with one of the largest modern art collections in the country (page 133).
- More than 460 stores line Michigan Avenue's Magnificent Mile, many of which are housed in the 900 North Michigan Shops complex (page 157).

Newberry Library

This renowned research library houses an extensive collection of rare and historic books, manuscripts, and maps from the past six centuries, all free to the public. Its genealogical research materials date to 1887 and are an excellent source of local history. While you can't remove the research materials, there are plenty of study spaces across the building's three floors. Check the online calendar for exhibitions, lectures, and classes.

Map 2: 60 W. Walton St., 312/943-9090, www.newberry.org; 9am-4pm Tues.-Fri., 9am-noon Sat.; free

West Side

Map 3

SIGHTS

WEST SIDE

Union Station

Chicago's 1925 Union Station bustles with passengers. The beaux arts exterior, designed by architect Daniel Burnham, was completed by Graham, Anderson, Probst & White, who also designed the Wrigley Building. Inside, the Great Hall's high ceilings and Corinthian columns inspire a sense of quiet awe. (Movie buffs might recognize the hall's iconic stairs from a famous scene in the 1987 film *The Untouchables*).

In addition to being an architectural gem, Union Station is a functioning commuter rail station, with Metra and Amtrak service. Other services include a food court, newsstands, and public restrooms. The Chicago History Museum offers 90-minute walking tours (www.chicagohistory.org, $25), where you can learn more about the station's history and architecture.

Map 3: 225 S Canal St., 800/872-7245, www.chicagounionstation.com; open 24 hours

Old St. Patrick's Church

Old St. Patrick's Church was built in 1853 and the Romanesque Revival church is one of the few remaining buildings to predate the 1871 Great Chicago Fire. It was added to the National Register of Historic Places in 1977. The church interior is filled with beautiful pastel illuminations and features a series of stained-glass windows that date to 1912. Tours (8am-11am Mon.-Fri.) are available with advanced

Union Station

notice; mass is held Sunday (7am, 8am, 9:30am, 11:15am, 5pm, and 8pm) and Monday (7am and 12:10pm).

Map 3: 700 W. Adams St., 312/648-1021, www.oldstpats.org; 7am-1pm Mon.-Tues. and Thurs.-Fri., 6:30am-7:30am and noon-12:30pm Wed., 7am-8pm Sun.; free

Haymarket Memorial

Once a bustling economic center in the heart of Chicago, the Haymarket district was thrust into the international spotlight on May 4, 1886. Activists gathered to protest the violent death of workers the previous day, and crowds clustered to listen to speakers address labor issues from a freight wagon outside a factory. When almost 200 police ordered the protest to end, a protester threw a dynamite bomb, killing seven police officers and four civilians. Though the bomber's identity remains unknown, the meeting's speakers and organizers were arrested and tried, and some were sentenced to death. The unfair trials became a symbol for labor and free speech issues around the city.

The *Haymarket Memorial Sculpture* by Mary Brogger depicts the wagon the speakers used as their platform. Today, it stands on the exact location of the original wagon.

Map 3: 175 N. Desplaines St., www. cityofchicago.org; free

Lincoln Park, Old Town, and Gold Coast

Map 4

✪ Lincoln Park Conservatory

Travel through the jungle, the desert, and the Midwest, all in under an hour at the Lincoln Park Conservatory. The conservatory's three acres not only showcase a broad exhibit of exotic plants, but also support the plants used in Chicago's parks. The conservatory's offerings are spread across four display houses, each named for its verdant residents: The Palm House, Fern Room, Orchid House, and Show House.

Located on the conservatory grounds is the Lincoln Conservatory Garden (2391 N Stockton Dr.), a formal public garden and popular wedding spot. Public art fills the garden; look for the Bates fountains, the Shakespeare monument, and the Schiller monument. The gardens are best viewed in the summer, but the conservatory is a welcome place of tropical warmth when visiting in the frigid winter.

CTA buses #151 and #156 stop nearby at Stockton and Fullerton. Parking ($25) is available on-site.

Lincoln Conservatory Garden

LAKE SHORE MANSIONS

The 1200 and 1500 blocks of Lake Shore Drive are home to some of the city's most luxurious homes. These mansions offer a peek at what the area may have looked like in the late 19th century, a prestigious time for Chicago architecture. Famous architects of the era—Benjamin Marshall, Mead & White, Holabird & Roche, and Howard Van Doren Shaw—designed many of these elaborate residences.

For a self-guided tour, start at 1250-1260 North Lake Shore Drive and take in the Romanesque Revival style of 1250 and 1254 North Lake Shore Drive, which are now combined as high-end condos. The Venetian Gothic style is portrayed at 1258 North Lake Shore Drive, while 1260 North Lake Shore Drive was designed with a more Georgian style in mind. Together with 1516, 1524, and 1530 North Lake Shore Drive, these mansions make up the **Seven Houses on Lake Shore Drive District,** which was designated a Chicago landmark in 1989. Residents are used to visitors taking photos from the street, but these are private homes and trespassing is not allowed.

Map 4: 2391 N. Stockton Dr., 312/742-7736, www.chicagoparkdistrict.com; 9am-5pm daily; free

NEARBY

- The Lincoln Park Zoo is home to hundreds of animals housed in a variety of exhibits (page 65).
- Enjoy a bit of Paris near the park at Mon Ami Gabi, a classic French bistro (page 95).
- Sip swanky cocktails while admiring the skyline views from The J. Parker rooftop bar (page 116).
- The kid-friendly Peggy Notebaert Nature Museum is an easy stop in Lincoln Park (page 136).
- Lincoln Park's 1,200 acres have enough sights and activities to fill the day (page 149).

Lincoln Park Zoo

Founded in 1868 and set in the middle of Lincoln Park, this 35-acre zoo is an easy choice for visitors with kids. Start your visit at the Gateway Pavilion for a map and a list of the day's animal antics and shows. Immediately past the Gateway, the Kovler Lion House is home to lions, leopards, and red pandas. African savannah-style outdoor exhibits such as the Regenstein African Journey (north gate) and Camel & Zebra (south gate) feature gazelles, zebras, rhinoceroses, warthogs, and camels. The Center for African Apes, filled with swinging chimpanzees and contemplative gorillas, is a favorite among children for its entertaining primates and interactive games. Other activities include the Lionel Trail Adventure (seasonal, $3) and a vintage carousel, as well as five cafés and an ice-cream stand.

To get here from the Loop, take CTA #36 bus to Dearborn/Clark; exit at the Clark/Wisconsin stop, right outside the zoo's west gate. The L's Brown/Purple Line stops at the nearby Armitage Station. If driving, the parking entrance is at 2400 North Cannon Dr. ($20-35).

THE GREAT CHICAGO FIRE

In 1871, the **Great Chicago Fire** raged from October 8 to 10, destroying 17,000 buildings, killing an estimated 300 souls, and leaving about 100,000 Chicagoans homeless. The fire started in a barn on the lower east side of the Chicago River at 137 DeKoven Street. At the time, most structures (and streets) in Chicago were built of wood—and a severe drought coupled with dry weather helped the fire spread rapidly throughout the city. As the fire jumped the river and sped north, flaming debris lit the city's waterworks structure ablaze and left firefighters without a way to stop the flames. As rain began to fall on October 9, the fire finally began to wane, leaving a four-mile aftermath of destruction in its wake.

Only five buildings in the burned district remain today, including St. Michael in Old Town and the Chicago Water Tower (806 N Michigan Ave.) on the Magnificent Mile. Old St. Patrick's Church also predates the fire.

Map 4: 2001 Clark St., 312/742-2000, www.lpzoo.org; 10am-5pm Mon.-Fri., 10am-6:30pm Sat.-Sun. June-Sept., 10am-5pm daily Sept.-Oct. and Apr.-May, 10am-4:30am daily Nov.-Mar.; free

St. Valentine's Massacre Site

The site of the St. Valentine's Massacre isn't much to look at, but its fascinating history makes up for the simple marker. On February 14, 1929, members of the Al Capone Gang gunned down six members of the Irish American Bugs Moran Gang, along with one unfortunate passerby. Two of the shooters were dressed as police officers, which confused witnesses. The shooting resulted in a bloodstained, bullet-ridden wall, which was sold at auction when the garage it was attached to was torn down. Today, the site is marked by a line of five trees planted in a gated lawn; the middle tree is the exact spot where the massacre occurred.

Map 4: 2122 N. Clark St.; free

St. Michael in Old Town

St. Michael's Roman Church was founded by German immigrants in 1852. Thanks to its redbrick exterior, it was one of only six buildings to survive the 1871 Great Chicago Fire. Today, the church is a haven for the local Puerto Rican community. Visitors can view the beautiful baroque interior with its tall, thin stained-glass windows, a carving depicting *The Last Supper* (purchased from the World's Columbian Exposition), a Kilgen pipe organ, and five painted altars.

Map 4: 1633 N. Cleveland Ave., 312-642-2498, www.st-mikes.org; 9am-5pm daily; free

The Original Playboy Mansion

Built in 1889, this classical redbrick and limestone manor with simple French windows was designed by architect James Gamble Rogers for Dr. George Swift Isham, a surgeon. *Playboy* magnate Hugh Hefner bought the 70-room mansion in 1959, and the "Playboy Mansion" soon became infamous for its owner's hedonistic parties and lifestyle. The original Grotto was housed in the basement and a sign on the front door read *If You Don't Swing, Don't Ring* (in Latin).

When Hefner left Chicago in 1974, the mansion was used as housing for The Art Institute of Chicago students. The building was deeded to The Art Institute in 1989, then sold and turned into luxury condos in 1993. In 2016, the house was for sale for $5.15 million. It remains closed to the public, but is still viewable behind its decorative iron gate.

Map 4: 1340 N. State Pkwy.

Lakeview and Wrigleyville Map 5

TOP EXPERIENCE

✪ Wrigley Field

Wrigley Field, home of the beloved Chicago Cubs, is a historic icon on the North Side of the city. Architect Zachary Taylor Davis designed the park, which opened in 1914. The compact stadium reflects a jewel-box construction, resulting in an intimate venue for fans. It remains the only park to feature an ivy-covered outfield wall. While the Cubs have played here since 1916, the stadium was only named Wrigley Field in 1927 after then-Cubs owner William Wrigley Jr. (of Wrigley Chewing Gum fame). Among the memorable moments Wrigley Field has witnessed are Babe Ruth's "called shot," Gabby Hartnett's famous "Homer in the Gloamin'," Ernie Banks's 500th career home run, and Sammy Sosa's 60th home run.

A 90-minute tour of the park runs April-September ($25). Learn about the history of the stadium while visiting the seating bowl and press box, the clubhouse, and the dugout, and before spending some time on the field.

Map 5: 1060 W. Addison St., 773/404-2827, http://chicago.cubs.mlb.com/chc/ballpark; hours and prices vary

NEARBY

- If you can't score Cubs tickets, join the throngs of fans packed into The Cubby Bear (page 119).
- The Gingerman Tavern offers a respite from the neighborhood's many sports bars (page 119).

Wrigley Field

- On Friday and Saturday nights, dance to 1980s and '90s tunes at **The Holiday Club** (page 120).
- The neon lights of the **Music Box Theatre** evoke the cinema's 1920s origins (page 138).

Graceland Cemetery

The 121-acre Graceland Cemetery is the final resting place for many of Chicago's famous figures such as architect Daniel Burnham; Marshall Field, the Chicago department store magnate; and "Mr. Cub" Ernie Banks. Established in 1860, the lovely Victorian-era cemetery was designed by landscape architect O. C. Simonds. Structural highlights include the beautiful Getty Tomb, the Schoenhofen Pyramid Mausoleum, and the Martin Ryerson Pyramidal Tomb. Sculptor Lorado Taft contributed two works: *The Crusader*, for Victor Lawson's grave, and *Eternal Silence* for the Graves family.

In addition to being a burial site, the cemetery also houses an arboretum and is an active place for public walks. Free, self-guided tours are available with a cemetery road map. The cemetery's main entrance is at Irving Park Road and Clark Street. The L's Red Line stops at the Sheridan Station.

Map 5: 4001 N. Clark St., 773/525-1105, www.gracelandcemetery.org; 9am-5pm daily; free

Wicker Park and Bucktown

Map 6

Logan Square

At the intersection of Logan Boulevard, Kedzie Boulevard, and Milwaukee Avenue, Logan Square is a popular spot to do some people-watching and admire the historic buildings and bungalows that characterize this neighborhood. In the center of the square sits the 70-foot-tall **Illinois Centennial Monument**, built in 1918 and designed by Henry Bacon (Bacon designed the Lincoln Memorial in Washington, DC). The single Doric column was inspired by the Parthenon and is topped with an eagle, which represents the state flag of Illinois. Grab a coffee and a book from the local shops nearby and settle in for an afternoon.

The L's Blue Line stops at the Logan Square Station. CTA bus #76 stops nearby.

Map 6: 3150 W. Logan Blvd.; free

Minnekirken

On the northeast corner of Logan Square sits the Norwegian Lutheran church known as Minnekirken. Built in 1908-1912 by Norwegian immigrants, the picturesque church's vibrant red facade and soaring green steeple design were inspired by a neighborhood in Oslo, Norway. The church remains active in Chicago's Norwegian American community and hosts special events and concerts. Parts of the Sunday services (11am) are in Norwegian.

Map 6: 2614 N. Kedzie Ave., 773/252-7335, www.minnekirken-chicago.org; free

Hyde Park Map 7

⚝ Museum of Science and Industry

Housed inside the former Palace of Fine Arts, built in 1893 for the World's Columbian Exposition, the Museum of Science and Industry is filled with more than 2,000 fascinating interactive exhibits that explore everything from manufacturing and glaciers to robots and engineering marvels. Permanent exhibits include the US-505 Submarine, one of only two German submarines captured during World War II, while rotating exhibits include a giant Lego room. The museum is a favorite with kids and can take a full day to explore. There's a café and cafeteria on-site; parking ($22) is available. Book tickets online to save on admission.

The Metra Electric Line train stops at the 57th Street Station two blocks north.

Map 7: 5700 S Lake Shore Dr., 773/684-1414, www.msichicago.org; 9:30am-4pm Tues.-Fri., 9:30am-5:30pm Sat.-Mon.; $18 adults, $11 children 3-11

NEARBY

- Also part of the 1893 World's Columbian Exposition, Jackson Park's Osaka Garden provides a peaceful stroll through a Japanese-inspired landscape (page 70).
- Burnham Park's Promontory Point offers excellent picnic sites with views of Lake Michigan (page 71).
- Relax at local watering hole The Cove Lounge and check out the Hyde Park mural inside, which features a smiling Barack Obama (page 124).
- Take some time to explore Jackson Park, which was home to the 1893

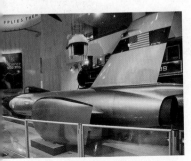

Museum of Science and Industry

THE WHITE CITY

Chicago as we know it today would not exist if not for the **World's Columbian Exposition.** Held in 1893 in Jackson Park and across the Midway Plaisance, this World's Fair covered 600 acres and featured 200 buildings, lagoons, and canals, and the first Ferris wheel. Architects Daniel Burnham, Frederick Law Olmsted, Charles Atwood, and John Root designed the exposition; temporary neoclassical structures were painted a shimmering white and plentiful electricity illuminated the fair, earning it the nickname The White City. Only two of these "temporary" structures survive today: The **Museum of Science and Industry** is housed in the former Palace of Fine Arts and the World's Congress Auxiliary Building is now part of **The Art Institute of Chicago** in Grant Park.

The fair was a huge success and saw 27 million visitors from around the world. It put Chicago on the map in terms of architecture and urban planning. For an excellent read on the subject, pick up *The Devil in the White City* by Erik Larson. Then treat yourself to a walking tour of **Hyde Park** (page 50) and stroll in the steps of history.

World's Columbian Exposition (page 152).

- Browse the vast collection of comics or pop in for a friendly board game at **First Aid Comics** (page 172).

Osaka Garden

Built in Jackson Park for the World's Columbian Exposition in 1893, the Osaka Garden was meant to symbolize the friendship between Chicago and Japan. Originally designed by Frederick Law Olmsted, Calvert Vaux, and Daniel H. Burnham, the garden's small rocks, ponds, and bushes represent the larger landscapes of mountains, lakes, and trees. The strategic placement of the rocks, as well as their geologic age, were considered in the garden design. Strolling the path reveals unique views as you proceed: an ornate Japanese lantern, a walking

Osaka Garden

bridge, and a series of water fountains. The *Sky Landing* sculpture, designed by Yoko Ono, sits just outside the garden's south side. The Osaka Garden is listed on the National Register

the field house at Promontory Point

of Historic Places, and underwent renovations in 2016 to reintroduce native species and reinforce park infrastructure.

Map 7: Jackson Park, 5800 S Lake Shore Dr., www.chicagoparkdistrict.com; free

Promontory Point

At the eastern tip of the Hyde Park neighborhood, Promontory Point juts out of Burnham Park into Lake Michigan. Landscape designer Alfred Caldwell planned the raised meadow to sit in the center of the artificial peninsula and filled the area with used native shrubs, flowers, and trees. In summer, the stone rings along the edge of the lakefront can be used as fire pits, making this the perfect place for a picnic (though the beach is made of rock, not sand). The point is accessible by bike or foot via the Lakefront Trail. From Millennium Park, take the #6 express bus to save time.

Map 7: 5491 S. Shore Dr.; free

Oriental Institute Museum

The University of Chicago's archaeology museum for ancient Near Eastern studies, the Oriental Institute Museum showcases a large collection of artifacts from the Middle East, including pieces from Egypt, Israel, Iran, Nubia, Mesopotamia, and Syro-Anatolia. Notable pieces include treasures from the ancient Persian capital Persepolis, a collection of Luristan bronzes, the Megiddo Ivories, and a giant statue of King Tutankhamun. Founder James Henry Breasted is credited with our current understanding of the Near East's influence on European culture. Visitors can tour the art deco building for free, taking in the eight permanent galleries and rotating special exhibit collection.

Map 7: 1155 E. 58th St., 773/702-9520, www.oi.uchicago.edu; 10am-8pm Wed., 10am-5pm Thurs.-Tues.; $10 donation

Robie House

The Frederick C. Robie House is one of Frank Lloyd Wright's most recognized creations. An icon of the American Prairie School, the house was built in 1908-1910 and exemplifies Wright's trademark low-pitched roofs and strong horizontal lines. It was placed on the National Register of Historic Places in 1966. Guided tours (45-60 min.) offer a rare peek inside the entry hall and living and dining rooms, as well as the master bedroom and children's playroom. Private tours (90 min., $55) offer further access to the servants' wing and third-floor bedrooms.

CTA bus #6 departs stations along State Street and stops at 57th Street, a six-block walk away. The Metra's University Park Line departs Millennium Park to exit at 57th Street. Street parking in the area is limited.

Map 7: 5757 S. Woodlawn Ave., 312/994-4000, http://flwright.org/visit/robiehouse; 10:30am-3pm Thurs.-Mon., $18 adults, $15 students and seniors, children age 3 and under free

Fountain of Time

At the south end of Washington Park, Lorado Taft's impressive *Fountain of Time* statue examines humanity's relationship with time. The 110-foot-long sculpture was constructed in 1920 and displays 100 figures as they explore the universal themes of love, war, and the cycle of life. Taft created the statue (inspired by author Henry Dobson's poem *Paradox of Time*) as a monument to the 100 years of peace between Great Britain and the United States.

Map 7: Washington Park, Cottage Grove Ave. and 59th St.

Smart Museum of Art

The Smart Museum of Art is the fine arts museum of the University of Chicago, featuring a permanent collection of more than 15,000 objects ranging from 20th-century paintings to Frank Lloyd Wright pieces. Named after the founders of *Esquire* magazine (brothers David and Alfred Smart, who originally provided funding), the museum's four galleries house a broad assemblage of modern, Asian, European, and contemporary art. Notable items include furniture from Wright's Robie House, Chinese scroll paintings and Buddhist sculptures, and Goya's *Disasters of War*, as well as the work of Chicago artists. There is also an on-site café.

CTA bus #55 exits at Ellis Avenue, a half-block away. The Metra Electric Line exits at the 57th Street Station, an eight-block walk east.

Map 7: 5550 S. Greenwood Ave., 773/702-0200, https://smartmuseum.uchicago.edu; 10am-5pm Tues.-Sun., 10am-8pm Thurs.; free

Greater Chicago   Map 8

Bahá'í Temple

The Bahá'í House of Worship is the only worship house of its kind in the United States and the oldest surviving Bahá'í House in the world. French Canadian architect Louis Bourgeois designed the magnificent building and nine surrounding gardens with the goal of combining elements of religious architecture from around the world to demonstrate the Bahá'í belief in the unity of religion. The ornamental panels, for example, draw in natural light during the day and illuminate from within in the dark, symbolizing "light and unity" in the temple. The gardens feature a wide variety of color, representing the beauty in diversity,

Bahá'í Temple

Chicago Botanic Gardens

and the reflecting pools are a nod to those found in the East. The temple was opened in May 1953 and has since welcomed thousands of Bahá'ís from around the world through its doors. Visitors are welcome to marvel at the interior or relax for a few hours in the gardens.

Map 8: 1233 Central St., Evanston, 847/733-3400, www.bahai.us; 10am-5pm daily Sept. 16-May 14, 10am-8pm daily May 15-Sept. 15; free

Chicago Botanic Gardens

Set outside the city on six miles of shoreline in Glencoe, the Chicago Botanic Gardens are worth the trip. The 385-acre living plant museum sits across nine islands in the Cook County Forest Preserves and features 27 gardens in four natural habitats. The Bonsai Collection is renowned worldwide, as is the English Walled Garden. The Aquatic Garden, Grunsfield Children's Growing Garden, Circle Garden, Heritage Garden, and Landscape Gardens are popular as well, though each of the others are enchanting in their own way. Architects John O. Simonds and Geoffrey Rausch designed the original garden, though additions have been made since, notably the Japanese Garden by Dr. Koichi Kawana in 1975 and the English Walled Garden by John Brookes in 1991. The mission of the garden has always been to be a living museum and conservation center, and all gardens and educational programs are designed with that in mind. Admission is free, and parking is $25 per car during the week, $30 on weekends. Parking is free for members, a whopping 50,000 people, making it the largest membership of any U.S. public garden.

Map 8: 1000 Lake Cook Rd., Glencoe, 847/835-5440, www.chicagobotanic.org; 8am-7pm daily; free

RESTAURANTS

In Chicago, chefs are celebrated and competition is fierce, which means that there's a never-ending supply of fantastic and innovative cuisine (but without the pretentious vibe that sometimes takes hold of great food cities).

Osmium Coffee Bar in Lakeview

No visit to Chicago is complete without trying a slice of deep-dish pizza at one of the city's competing chains: Lou Malnati's, Uno's, or Gino's East. Tucking in to an Italian beef sandwich or a Chicago hot dog is another must. Fortunately, local favorite Portillo's offers the best of both (although Al's Beef is a close second).

A wealth of farm-to-table restaurants, helmed by fantastic chefs across the city, benefit from the surrounding Midwest farms, where fresh produce, meat, and cheese are easily attainable. Dining at Alinea (if you can get reservations) is a once-in-a-lifetime experience—the Michelin-starred restaurant is considered one of the best in the world. And although you might not expect Chicago to have great Mexican food, chef Rick Bayless's empire—including Frontera Grill and Xoco—will prove otherwise, as will farther-flung (but worth the trip) excursions to spots like Carnitas don Pedro in Pilsen.

Of course, each neighborhood has its own specialties as well. The Loop is great for the coffee and lunch crowd, but most establishments shut down at night and on weekends. In the Near North and West Side, well-known chefs reign over fine-dining establishments, and you'll pay more for the privilege of

HIGHLIGHTS

✪ **BEST BRUNCH WITH A VIEW: Cindy's Rooftop Bar** offers panoramic views over Millennium Park and Lake Michigan accompanied by decadent cocktails and farm-to-table cuisine (page 77).

✪ **BEST CHICAGO-STYLE PIZZA:** When it comes to pizza, you must try deep dish—and most Chicagoans will tell you **Lou Malnati's** does it best (page 80).

✪ **BEST ITALIAN BEEF:** It's worth the wait in line for **Portillo's** addictive Chicago dogs, Italian beef, and famous chocolate cake shake (page 81).

✪ **BEST STEAKHOUSE:** For a date-night splurge, you can't go wrong with the fantastic steak and cocktails at **RPM Steak** (page 86).

✪ **BEST CHEESEBURGER:** Randall Street's "Restaurant Row" is home to **Au Cheval's** decadent and delicious gourmet burgers (page 87).

✪ **BEST SUSHI: Momotaro** is arguably the best sushi restaurant in Chicago. The hefty price tag is worth the expertly prepared fish (page 89).

✪ **BEST OVERALL DINING EXPERIENCE:** With three Michelin stars, **Alinea** is considered one of the best restaurants in the country. Make reservations well in advance to get a seat (page 93).

✪ **BEST PLACE TO EAT LOCAL: Green City Market** is where Chicagoans shop for farm-fresh produce while stocking up on doughnuts and nibbling treats from food trucks (page 94).

✪ **BEST TAKEOUT:** Crowds flock to **Halal Guys** for fast, flavorful gyros and falafel served with a spicy sauce on the side (page 96).

✪ **BEST PLACE TO WARM UP:** James Beard Award-winning pastries, a cozy vibe, and the best hot chocolate in the city make **Mindy's HotChocolate** the perfect refuge from the cold (page 101).

✪ **BEST OUTDOOR PATIO: Big Star** is the place to be in summer. Join the packed patio for happy hour and some of the best tacos in town (page 102).

PRICE KEY

$	Entrées less than $15
$ $	Entrées $15-25
$ $ $	Entrées more than $25

THE DEEP-DISH DIVIDE

Thick and cheesy, delicious and satisfying, pizza both defines and divides Chicago. A few different pizzas fall under the deep-dish umbrella. Stick to one of the five restaurants on this list and you're assured an authentic Chicago deep-dish experience.

Original: Original deep-dish pizza has a flaky crust and is topped with cheese and a chunky tomato sauce. Most places claiming to serve "Chicago-style pizza" serve the original style; this includes **Uno's** (page 80), **Gino's** (page 80), and **Lou Malnati's** (page 80). There's heavy debate over which of the three is the best. They're all good, though many older Chicagoans vie for Uno's, while the younger crowd swears by Lou Malnati's.

Stuffed: Chicago stuffed pizza has a layer of cheese tucked inside the dough (below the sauce). **Giordano's** (page 76) is famous for its stuffed pizza.

Pan: Chicago pan pizza has parmesan cheese ringing the pan and a doughier crust. **Pequod's Pizza** (page 93) is the best for this style.

eating here. The Lakeview and Wicker Park neighborhoods offer more casual and affordable options. And the city's long and rich history of immigration has resulted in pockets of Swedish, Ukrainian, Polish, and Greek communities where delicious ethnic cuisines thrive.

The Loop and Museum Campus

Map 1

PIZZA
Giordano's $$

Chicago has several pizza places that are popular for their deep dish. What sets Giordano's apart is their famous cheese-stuffed crust. The Giordano brothers—Italian immigrants who moved to Chicago in the 1970s—adapted their mother's Easter pie recipe, and the doughy, cheesy, tomato-topped masterpiece quickly became their hallmark. Today, the family-run enterprise has locations all over the city where you can enjoy their stuffed pizza, salads, sandwiches, and pastas.

Map 1: 223 W Jackson Blvd., 312/583-9400, www.giordanos.com; 11am-11pm Sun.-Thurs., 11am-midnight Fri.-Sat.

AMERICAN
Acadia $$$

This upscale South Loop restaurant serves Maine cuisine in a lofty, inviting space awash in grays and creams with furnishings that evoke an elegant seaside retreat. Acadia received two Michelin stars in 2016 for its 5- and 10-course tasting menus with wine pairings. Dine on canapés, hamachi with coconut-infused rice pudding, Wagyu beef with bordelaise, or sweet lobster straight from Maine for an elaborate tasting experience. The service is highly professional, yet friendly, and questions are welcome.

Map 1: 1639 S Wabash Ave., 312/360-9500, www.acadiachicago.com; 5:30pm-9pm Wed.-Thurs., 5pm-11pm Fri.-Sat., 5pm-9pm Sun.

Blackwood BBQ $

The folks at Blackwood BBQ believe good things take time, so they smoke their brisket for up to 15 hours. It's a theory and practice that works. The beef brisket—smoked with hickory and applewood with a ground coffee dry rub—is a highlight. There's also a great brisket and gravy on the breakfast menu. The narrow, simple interior has just enough tables to seat a hungry crowd.

Map 1: 307 W Lake St., 312/621-9663, www.blackwoodbbq.com; 7:30am-3pm Mon.-Fri.

Ceres Cafe $

Ceres Cafe serves burgers and sandwiches for the perfect power lunch. The wood-paneled restaurant sits in the Chicago Trade Building and has been an institution since it opened in the 1980s. The chefs partner with organic farms to bring fresh produce and meat to the menu's turkey, mushroom, quinoa patty, and beef burgers. The happy hour drinks are cheap—and strong. It's what keeps Ceres a favorite.

Map 1: 141 W Jackson Blvd., 312/427-3443, www.cerescafechicago.com; 6am-9pm Mon.-Fri.

✪ Cindy's Rooftop Bar $$$

For cocktails with a view, look no further than Cindy's Rooftop Bar—the giant, panoramic windows overlook Millennium Park, offering some of the best views in the city. Notice the beautiful floors and detailed walls of the historic Chicago Athletic Association Hotel as you head up to the restaurant where the menu features high-end, farm-to-table cuisine—Lake Superior pike, pan-roasted duck breast—served on wooden, communal tables. Brunch (Sat.-Sun. only) is more affordable than dinner and extremely popular. Reservations are highly recommended.

Map 1: 12 Michigan Ave., 312/792-3502, www.cindysrooftop.com; 11am-1am Mon.-Fri., 10am-2am Sat., 10am-midnight Sun.

Eleven City Diner $$

This old-school Jewish delicatessen is a Chicago staple. Matzo ball soup is the perfect cure for a cold Chicago day, and a pastrami or Reuben sandwich is great anytime, as are the giant slices of pie and cake. The decor is classic diner, with leather bar stools, cozy booths, and kitschy signs. Breakfast is served all day.

Map 1: 1112 S Wabash Ave., 312/212-2112, www.elevencitydiner.com; 8am-9:30pm Mon.-Thurs., 8am-10pm Fri., 8:30am-10pm Sat., 8:30am-9pm Sun.

Revival Food Hall $

This large, local dining hall offers a fantastic alternative to the typical Loop chains. More than 15 vendors comprise Revival Food Hall, which sits in the ground floor of the National building, designed by Daniel Burnham in 1907. Get into the spirit at Danke's German food stall, try tacos at Antique Taco Chiquito, or grab a drink at the Revival Cafe-Bar. There's plenty of seating room, so settle in with a hot chocolate from HotChocolate Bakery or grab-and-go a refreshing juice from Harvest Juicery.

Map 1: 125 S Clark St., 773/999-9411, www.revivalfoodhall.com; 7am-7pm Mon.-Fri.

Seven Lions $$

Seven Lions is the perfect stop for elevated American food after a morning of exploring The Art Institute of Chicago directly across the way. The menu's well-executed burgers,

Berghoff

chicken sandwiches, and pasta dishes offer something tasty for everyone. The large space, decorated in wood and leather, is great for large groups. The drink list features American wines, but also has plenty of beer and cocktails.

Map 1: 130 S Michigan Ave., 312/880-0130, www.sevenlionschicago.com; 11am-11pm Mon.-Fri., 10am-11pm Sat.-Sun.

FRENCH
Everest $$$

This high-end restaurant sits on the 40th floor of the Chicago Stock Exchange, an elegant respite with pristine white tablecloths and sweeping views. Chef and owner Jean Joho serves a menu of fine-dining French cuisine with American influence, like Maine lobster, seared New York State foie gras, and dry-aged New York steak. An eight-course tasting menu showcases the full range of Joho's talents; there's a vegetarian option as well. Reservations are highly recommended.

Map 1: 440 S LaSalle St., 40th Fl., 312/663-8920, www.everestrestaurant.com; 5:30pm-9:30pm Tues.-Fri., 5pm-10pm Sat.

GERMAN
Berghoff $$

This Chicago institution has been serving hearty German fare since 1898. The oak paneling and stained-glass windows give the restaurant an old-world feel, as does the live polka entertainment. Berghoff is now fourth-generation owned and still very much steeped in tradition. Corned beef sandwiches, stews, pierogi, Bavarian pretzels, and the like fill the menu, though over the years they've begun to accommodate gluten-free guests and other dietary restrictions as well.

Map 1: 17 W Adams St., 312/427-3170, www.theberghoff.com; 11am-9pm Mon.-Fri., 11:30am-9pm Sat.

LATIN AMERICAN
Cafecito $

This weekday spot offers quick, affordable, and authentic Cuban coffee and sandwiches. The menu offers pressed sandwiches with traditional meat, seafood, and vegetarian options, as well as a few salads and soups and breakfast sandwiches. The Cubano, with its perfectly toasted bread and house-marinated roasted pork shoulder, is considered the best in Chicago. Find a table in the simple, cafeteria-like space or order a Cuban espresso or a Cuban milk shake to go.

Map 1: 26 E Congress Pkwy., 312/922-2233, www.cafecitochicago.com; 7am-9pm Mon.-Fri., 10am-6pm Sat.-Sun.

Latinicity Food Hall and Lounge $$

The flavors of Latin America, Spain, and Portugal come together at Latinicity, a food hall featuring 10 kitchens, a tapas restaurant, a café, a bar, a market, and a lounge. Eat your fill of sandwiches at Tortas & Cocas, or slurp your way through the raw bar at Marisco's. Warm up on a chilly Chicago day with a soup from Sopas or relax at the Cerveceria for a drink in summer. Browse the market for specialty goods from Latin America.

Map 1: Block 37, 3rd Fl., 108 N State St., 312/795-4444, www.latinicity.com; 11am-9pm Mon.-Sat., 11am-3pm Sun.

MIDDLE EASTERN
Naf Naf Grill $

For a quick, cheap lunch between seeing the sights, stop at Naf Naf Grill and feast on falafel, shawarma, and fries. Make your own sandwich or bowl, starting with pita or rice and building meat, falafel, hummus, vegetables, spices, and sauces like tahini and *harissa*. Sit at one of the small tables during the popular weekday lunch hour or take it to go.

Map 1: 309 W Washington St., 312/251-9000, www.nafnafgrill.com; 10:30am-10pm Mon.-Thurs., 10:30am-8pm Fri.

SEAFOOD
Pearl Brasserie $$

Pearl Brasserie is a raw bar serving oysters that are flown in twice daily. In addition to the raw menu options, you'll find lobster rolls, fish-and-chips, salmon teriyaki, large seafood platters, and non-seafood items like burgers and grilled chicken. The restaurant's historic interior gives it an old-world feel, while the marble bar and black booths lend a sleek touch. Or dine outside on the inviting patio on the banks of the Chicago River.

Map 1: 180 N Upper Wacker Dr., 312/629-1030, www.pearlbrasserie.com; 11am-10pm Mon.-Fri.

SPANISH
Mercat a la Planxa $$

This Catalan tapas restaurant inspires the feel of a bustling Barcelona street market. The colorful interior is adorned with fabrics, mosaic tile, sculptures, funky furniture, and large murals. It's the perfect backdrop to sip Spanish wine or seasonal sangria, and to dine on grilled-to-order meats and traditional tapas like bread with tomatoes, Spanish omelets, and serrano ham croquettes.

Map 1: 638 S. Michigan Ave., 312/765-0524; 6:30am-10pm Sun.-Thurs., 7am-11pm Fri.-Sat.

Near North and Navy Pier

Map 2

PIZZA

Gino's East $$

Opened in 1956, Gino's East claims to have invented the Chicago deep dish. Their dense version has a buttery crust and is topped with a sweet, chunky tomato sauce; it takes 45 minutes to bake. While you wait, peruse the colorful graffiti that adorns the walls—and leave your own mark, too. Other locations include River North (500 N. LaSalle St.) and South Loop (521 S. Dearborn St.).

Map 2: 162 E. Superior St., 312/266-3337, www.ginoseast.com; 11am-9pm Sun.-Thurs., 11am-10pm Fri.-Sat.

✪ Lou Malnati's $$

One of Chicago's most iconic restaurants, Lou Malnati's has been using the same family deep-dish recipe since its opening in 1971. The buttery and flaky crust is topped with cheese followed by fresh tomato sauce with chunks of plum tomatoes and sprinkled with more cheese and spices. The result is the best Chicago-style pizza around and worth every filling bite. Other locations are on the Gold Coast (1120 N. State St.), West Side (1235 W. Randolph St.), and in the Loop (805 S. State St.).

Map 2: 439 N. Wells St., 312/828-9800, www.loumalnatis.com; 11am-11pm Mon.-Thurs., 11am-midnight Fri.-Sat.

Uno's $$

Uno's *also* claims to have invented the deep-dish pizza. Whether their claim is true or not, Uno's does serve some delicious Chicago-style deep dish.

The dense, flaky crust is filled with a chunky tomato sauce, plenty of cheese, and large pieces of sausage. The original location has a sports-bar feel and is great for families or groups. Uno's also has a second location (619 N. Wabash Ave.).

Map 2: 29 E Ohio St., 312/321-1000, www. unos.com; 11am-1am Mon.-Fri., 11am-2am Sat., 11am-11pm Sun.

BEEF SANDWICHES AND HOT DOGS

Al's Chicago Beef $

A staple since 1938, Al's Italian beef sandwiches are to Chicago as cheesesteak is to Philadelphia. Their au jus is what gives the beef its flavor and makes this sandwich "Chicago beef." Know that there's a right or wrong way to order: The right way, according to most Chicagoans, is dipped with cheese and hot and sweet peppers. To place your order, ask for "a beef, dipped with hot and sweet." Fries, hot dogs, and burgers are also on the menu if you're feeling less "traditional."

Map 2: 169 W. Ontario St., 312/943-3222, www.alsbeef.com; 10am-midnight Mon.-Thurs., 10am-3am Fri.-Sat., 11am-9pm Sun.

Mr. Beef $

There's strong debate in Chicago about who serves the best Italian beef, but Mr. Beef is always in contention. Juicy and flavorful beef overflows from a roll dipped in au jus and covered with hot peppers; a cult following for their huge portions of just-greasy-enough fries makes this a popular late-night stop. Grab a booth in the no-frills, 1950s diner and dig in.

Map 2: 666 N Orleans St., 312/337-8500; 10am-6pm Mon.-Sat.

✪ Portillo's $

Portillo's is a Chicago institution for hot dogs, Italian beef sandwiches, and sinfully delicious shakes and cheese fries. This flagship River North location is large and chaotic, and that's part of the fun. Ordering lines vary depending on what you want (drinks, hot dogs, sandwiches, etc.); place your order and then wait among the masses as your number is shouted over a speaker. Chicago dogs with all the fixings are the obvious menu choice, but a less obvious star is the chocolate cake shake—the best guilty pleasure in town.

Map 2: 100 W Ontario St., 312/587-8910, www.portillos.com; 10am-11pm Mon.-Thurs., 10am-midnight Fri.-Sat.

AMERICAN
Bandera $$

This dimly lit, intimate restaurant offers out-of-towners a true Chicago experience with views of Michigan Avenue and live jazz every night. The food is simple with a southern twist, like rotisserie chicken, hearty salads, and must-try skillet corn bread.

Map 2: 535 N Michigan Ave., 312/644-3524, www.banderarestaurants. com; 11am-10pm Sun.-Thurs., 11am-11pm Fri.-Sat.

Beatrix $$

Beatrix is a grab-and-go café, a cozy lunch spot, and a unique brunch indulgence. The food is fresh but hearty: Warm pot-roast sandwiches, chili- and chocolate-glazed salmon, and spicy chicken *tinga* are standouts. The fresh-squeezed juices and craft cocktails are also excellent. The cozy restaurant spans two rooms with a mix

Portillo's

of high-top and armchair seating. In summer, the glass wall opens onto the patio.

Map 2: 519 N Clark St., 312/284-1377, www. beatrixchicago.com; 6am-midnight daily

DMK Burger Bar $

Grass-fed burgers, shakes, and fries (with Wisconsin cheese if you're feeling indulgent)—do you need more reasons to visit DMK Burger Bar? Simple high-top tables and exposed brick give it a hipster vibe, as do the craft beers, classic cocktails, and house-made sodas. Other locations include Navy Pier (600 E. Grand Ave.), Lakeview (2954 N. Sheffield Ave.), and Museum Campus (1410 Museum Campus Dr.).

Map 2: 600 E Grand Ave., 312/624-8017, www.dmkburgerbar.com; 11am-8pm Sun.-Thurs., 11am-10pm Fri.-Sat.

River Roast $$

James Beard Award-winning chef Tony Mantuano and executive chef John Hogan serve tavern fare, taking presentation to another level. Whole roasted fish, beef, and chicken are all carved at your table, while other plates are beautifully displayed and meant for sharing. While the food is exceptional, many people come for the spacious patio, which is one of the best outdoor seating areas in the city and overlooks the Chicago River. On weekends, come see local blues musicians noon-3pm at the Blues and Brews Brunch.

Map 2: 315 N LaSalle St., 312/822-0100, www.riverroastchicago.com; 11:30am-10pm Mon.-Thurs., 11:30am-11pm Fri., 11am-11pm Sat., 11am-9pm Sun.

Shake Shack $

When Shake Shack first opened in Chicago in 2014, lines went around the block for their crinkle-cut fries, custard milk shakes (made with local ingredients from Glazed & Infused and Bang Bang Pie), and gourmet Angus beef burgers served on buttered buns with sweet-and-sour ShackSauce. The buzz has since died down, but there are still lines through the door. The interior has plenty of seating, but this is also a nice to-go option. Order ahead using the Shake Shack app.

Map 2: 66 E. Ohio St., 312/667-1701, www. shakeshack.com; 11am-11pm Sun.-Thurs., 11am-midnight Fri.-Sat.

ASIAN
Ramen-San $$

Ramen-san was founded on two principles: Noodles make everything better, and cold beer makes life more fun. The lively restaurant is meant to remind diners of traditional Japanese ramen shops, so it's casual and open late, while still serving food worthy of accolades. Get ramen, of course, and cold beer. There's also a raw bar, dumplings, and craft cocktails.

Map 2: 59 W. Hubbard St., 312/377-9950, www.ramensan.com; 11am-midnight Mon.-Fri., 11am-1am Sat., noon-midnight Sun.

Sunda $$

Sometimes, when restaurants try to do it all, it doesn't work. But at Sunda, where you'll find modern interpretations of traditional Japanese, Chinese, Vietnamese, Cambodian, Indonesian, Thai, and Filipino food, it works very well—so well it's been Michelin-recommended and is consistently packed. The swanky interior and long shared bar tables make it fun for a night out, or cozy up in a booth for date night. Don't forget to check out the large wine and sake menu, too.

Map 2: 110 W. Illinois St., 312/644-0500, www.sundachicago.com; 11:30am-11pm Mon.-Wed., 11:30am-midnight Thurs.-Fri., 10:30am-3pm and 4pm-midnight Sat.-Sun.

FRENCH
Bavette's Bar & Boeuf $$

An American steakhouse with a bit of French flair, Bavette's serves steak cuts, a large salad selection, and hearty non-steak entrées like spiced fried chicken and short rib stroganoff, plus a raw bar. It's on the dark side, and very cozy. Reservations recommended, or you can dine at the bar.
Map 2: 218 W Kinzie St., 312/624-8154, www.bavetteschicago.com; 4:45pm-11:30pm Mon.-Thurs., 4:45pm-12:30am Fri.-Sat., 4:45pm-10:30pm Sun.

Brindille $$$

Visit Paris in Chicago at Brindille, a beautiful, fine-dining French restaurant in the heart of the city. The menu is classic French, from foie gras to squab, though it changes often and is served as a seasonal tasting menu. The fine china, French linens, and extensive wine list covering every region of France add to the Parisian ambience. A perfect spot for special occasions. Make reservations.
Map 2: 534 N Clark St., 312/595-1616, www.brindille-chicago.com; 5pm-11pm Mon.-Sat.

Tru $$$

One of Chicago's finest restaurants, Tru is a AAA five-diamond restaurant and has received four stars from numerous publications and institutions, as well as a James Beard Award for service. Chef Anthony Martin serves modern French cuisine highlighting fresh, local ingredients. The Coral Caviar offering, a selection of fine caviars, is popular, as is the prix fixe menu. Dining at Tru, you'll also take in a large art collection including pieces by Andy Warhol and Gerhard Richter. A dress code is enforced and reservations are highly recommended.
Map 2: 676 N St. Clair St., 312/202-0001, www.trurestaurant.com; 6pm-10pm Tues.-Thurs., 6pm-11pm Fri., 5pm-11pm Sat.

GERMAN
Bohemian House $$

Dine on Bohemian-inspired dishes influenced by Austria, the Czech Republic, and Germany, with fresh and local twists. Think roasted duck or chicken liver with cranberry marmalade, pork schnitzel, roasted beets, and crispy sweetbreads. The interior is beautiful and lighthearted, with cherry wood furniture, exposed brick walls, hanging lanterns, plush blue seating, and details that will bring you back to another era in Europe. Don't forget to check out the drinks menu, which features European beers and bohemian-era cocktails with lots of infusions.
Map 2: 11 W Illinois St., 312/955-0439, www.bohochicago.com; 11:30am-2pm and 5pm-10pm Mon.-Thurs., 11:30am-2pm and 5pm-11pm Fri., 10am-2pm and 5pm-11pm Sat., 10am-2pm and 5pm-10pm Sun.

ITALIAN
Cafe Spiaggia $$$

It's hard to choose the best Italian in a city with so many options, but Cafe Spiaggia often tops the list. This modern, fine-dining restaurant on Michigan Avenue is sleek, with marble tables, gold accents, and impeccable service. The beautifully plated pasta and seafood dishes and extensive, award-winning wine list featuring more than 700 labels make it a perfect place to celebrate a special occasion.

The adjacent café offers a similar but more affordable menu and is a great choice for business lunches or a shopping break.

Map 2: 980 N. Michigan Ave., 312/280-2750, www.spiaggiarestaurant. com; 11:30am-2:30pm and 5:30pm-10pm Mon.-Thurs., 11:30am-2:30pm and 5:30pm-10:30pm Fri.-Sat., 4pm-8pm Sun.

Siena Tavern $$$

Siena Tavern serves modern Italian cuisine and one of Chicago's favorite brunches in a large space with a great outdoor patio. Chef/Partner Fabio Viviani rose to fame as a "fan favorite" on *Top Chef*. His Tuscan aesthetic (with a hint of American influence) flavors the wood-fired pizzas, creamy *burrata*, heaping pastas, and an array of unique vegetable sides and seafood on the menu. Brunch is a mix of sweet and savory dishes, plus pizza and addictive, sweet monkey bread. Reservations are needed for dinner; summer brings more seating so you might luck out walking in.

Map 2: 51 W. Kinzie St., 312/595-1322, www.sienatavern.com; 11:30am-2am Mon.-Fri., 11:30am-3am Sat., 10am-2am Sun.

LATIN AMERICAN
Big & Little's $

At first look, Big & Little's seems like a strange mix: po' boys and tacos alongside Chicago dogs and kimchi fries, plus a huge burger selection. But it's all good, and Big & Little's is consistently named one of the city's best. The atmosphere is extremely casual and friendly. Order at the counter and find a table wherever you can to dig in. It's especially busy around lunchtime.

Map 2: 860 N Orleans St., 312/943-0000, www.bigandlittleschicago.com; 11am-9pm Mon.-Fri., noon-9pm Sat.

Frontera Grill $$

Rick Bayless's flagship restaurant is consistently packed, and serves excellent, authentic Mexican food. Midwestern farms supply most of the ingredients, but the flavors are straight from a kitchen in Mexico, from buttery sweet corn tamales to fiery chiles and Oaxacan carne asada. Colorful Mexican folk art and mariachi music add a playful vibe to this slightly upscale restaurant. Reservations are recommended. If you can't make it during your trip, there's a Frontera Grill in the Chicago O'Hare Airport.

Map 2: 445 N. Clark St., 312/661-1434, www.rickbayless.com/restaurants/ frontera-grill; 11:30am-2:30pm and 5:30pm-10pm Tues., 11:30am-2:30pm and 5pm-10pm Wed.-Thurs., 11:30am-2:30pm and 5pm-11pm Fri., 10:30am-2pm and 5pm-11pm Sat.

Nacional 27 $$$

This high-end Latin restaurant blends the flavors of the 27 countries in Central and South America and the Latino Caribbean Islands for a vibrant menu of tacos, ceviches, empanadas, tapas, steak, and more. Stock up on margaritas and mojitos before your complimentary salsa lesson, which happens every Wednesday at 7:30pm. On weekends the place turns into a dance hall after dinner, with a DJ on Fridays from 11pm to 2am, and salsa, merengue, and bachata on Saturdays from 11pm to 3am.

Map 2: 325 W Huron St., 312/664-2727, www.nacional27chicago.com; 5:30-10pm Wed.-Thurs., 5:30pm-2am Fri., 5pm-3am Sat.

The Purple Pig $$

This lively restaurant off Michigan Avenue is a favorite for tapas and house-cured meats. Crispy pig's ear, roasted bone marrow, and

milk-braised pork shoulder are just a few highlights on the menu, which also features a large wine list. Though it's a tapas restaurant, portions are larger than you might expect. It's always packed, so reserve in advance.
Map 2: 500 N Michigan Ave., 312/464-1744, www.thepurplepigchicago.com; 11:30am-midnight Sun.-Thurs., 11:30am-1am Fri.-Sat.

Xoco

Xoco $

Xoco ("sho-ko") is a quick stop for fresh Mexican street food and snacks, from breakfast sandwiches to empanadas, churros, and tortas. The filling caldo soups are perfect on a cold Chicago day. Xoco boasts Chicago's only bean-to-cup chocolate program; the chocolate is melted and then poured thick and hot as a delicious winter beverage or served iced with mint in the summer. The few booths inside the small, casual eatery are often packed, but the summer patio is spacious and food can be ordered to go. The small **River North location** (449 N. Clark St.) is good for a quick bite or takeout, while the **Wicker Park location** (1471 N. Milwaukee Ave.) has more seating.
Map 2: 449 N Clark St., 312/661-1434, www.rickbayless.com/restaurants/xoco; 8am-9pm Tues.-Thurs., 8am-10pm Fri.-Sat.

MEDITERRANEAN
Bernie's Lunch and Supper $$

Nestled into the corner of Erie and Orleans, Bernie's serves sustainably sourced, seasonal Mediterranean and new American cuisine with family-style seating. Lamb Hashwi, Greek salad, and roasted oysters are just a few popular items. The eclectic restaurant is decorated with a variety of textiles, coffered ceilings, and vibrant turquoise accents. In the summer the rooftop is a nice hub in the center of the city, and on busy nights you can still usually find bar seating.
Map 2: 660 N Orleans St., 312/624-9892, www.bernieslunchandsupper.com; 11am-3pm and 5pm-9pm Tues.-Wed., 11am-3pm and 5pm-10pm Thurs.-Fri., 10am-3pm and 5pm-10pm Sat., 10am-3pm Sun.

Naha $$$

Chef Carrie Nahabedian has won a James Beard Award and several Michelin stars for her seasonal, contemporary menu of Mediterranean and Californian flavors that draw from her Armenian and Greek heritage. You'll find dishes like slow-roasted lamb shank with bean puree, Greek yogurt, and falafel or whole roasted squab with bing cherries, Medjool dates, and foie gras. The vibe is elegant but comfortable, and the food is always beautifully presented.
Map 2: 500 N Clark St., 312/321-6242, www.naha-chicago.com; 5:30pm-9:30pm Mon., 11am-2pm and 5:30pm-9:30pm Tues.-Thurs., 11am-2pm and 5:30pm-10pm Fri., 5:30pm-10pm Sat.

SEAFOOD
GT Fish & Oyster $$$

This buzzy restaurant is one of the hottest spots for seafood in the city. The shareable menu features classics like oysters and lobster rolls, as well as innovative items like cold green-tea soba, bigoli pasta with beer-uni sauce, and caviar service. It's a trendy happy hour or brunch spot too, with clientele dressed to impress. If you don't have a reservation, get a seat at the bar and watch oysters being shucked.

Map 2: 531 N Wells St., 312/929-3501, www.gtoyster.com; 5pm-10pm Mon., 11:30am-2:30pm and 5pm-10pm Tues.-Thurs., 11:30am-2:30pm and 4:30pm-11pm Fri., 10am-2:30pm and 4:30pm-11pm Sat., 10am-2:30pm and 5pm-10pm Sun.

STEAKHOUSE
Chicago Cut $$$

Chicago has no shortage of steak-houses, but Chicago Cut stands out for its sleek interior with floor-to-ceiling windows that overlook the Chicago River. The food is a cut above as well, with steaks dry-aged on-site, excellent *burrata* and kale salads, and a section of Chicago Favorites for those not in the mood for steak. It's open breakfast, lunch, and dinner, but make reservations for the last.

Map 2: 300 N. LaSalle St., 312/329-1800, www.chicagocutsteakhouse.com; 7am-2am Mon.-Fri., 10am-2am Sat.-Sun.

✪ RPM Steak $$$

RPM has all the makings of a great, classic steakhouse—with a contemporary twist. The intimate interior is rich and colorful, with a sunken dining room and modern architectural elements. The menu features classic steak cuts, but includes a wide selection of Wagyu, bison, and local grass-fed beef. It's great for a business lunch or date night—the innovative cocktail list can turn any meal into an occasion. Reservations are recommended, especially for dinner.

Map 2: 66 W. Kinzie St., 312/284-4990, www.rpmrestaurants.com/rpmsteak/chicago; 11am-midnight Mon.-Thurs., 11am-1am Fri., 4pm-1am Sat., 4pm-midnight Sun.

COFFEE AND DESSERT
Doughnut Vault $

This tiny bakery sells a small selection of old-fashioned doughnuts daily until they run out, which is usually around 11am. The line goes quickly and the wait is worth it. There are several famous doughnut shops in Chicago, but many locals agree this is the best for old-fashioned.

Map 2: 401 N Franklin St., www.doughnutvault.com; 8am-3pm Mon.-Fri., 9:30am-3pm Sat.-Sun.

West Side

Map 3

PIZZA

Roots $$

This neighborhood favorite is perfect for watching the game, a casual date night, or satisfying late-night hunger pangs. Slide into one of the large booths to munch on an authentic Quad Cities-style pizza, which comes from a region of Iowa and Illinois and features a nutty crust, spicy tomato sauce, and toppings buried under cheese. Families are welcome; kids will love the organic sweets and house-made sodas. The mozzarella sticks are incredibly filling, but worth every giant bite of cheese.

Map 3: 1924 W Chicago Ave., 773/645-4949, www.rootspizza.com; 11am-midnight Sun.-Thurs., 11am-2am Fri.-Sat.

AMERICAN

✪ Au Cheval $$

The wait at Au Cheval is more than worth it for the renowned cheeseburger, considered the best in Chicago. This indulgence begins with prime beef, then adds cheese, Dijon mustard, pickles, and optional foie gras, egg, or bacon all housed inside a toasted bun and served with fries. Sink into the restaurant's dark leather booths and enjoy. Reservations are not accepted; put your name on the list for a table, then sip a cocktail from one of the Randolph Street bars while you wait.

Map 3: 800 W Randolph St., 312/929-4580, www.auchevalchicago.com; 11am-1am Mon.-Sat., 10am-midnight Sun.

Avec $$$

This wine bar serves a rustic menu that fuses Chicago with the Mediterranean. Local ingredients inspire flavors from Italy, Spain, Portugal, and southern France in small plates like brussels sprouts panzanella with pickled raisins and chorizo chiles or slow-roasted pork shoulder with Tuscan kale and apple. Long wooden tables line one side of the simple restaurant, while the bar offers a window into the kitchen.

Map 3: 615 W Randolph St., 312/377-2002, www.avecrestaurant.com; 11:30am-2pm Mon.-Fri., 3:30pm-1am Mon.-Thurs., 3:30pm-2am Fri.-Sat., 10am-1am Sun.

Blackbird $$$

In Blackbird's simple white interior, James Beard Award-winning chef Paul Kahan showcases the best Midwestern cuisine using farm-fresh ingredients. Start with local vegetables or quail then move on to entrées like pan-roasted striped bass with onion noodle and schmaltz pudding. Finish with the exquisite cheese plate.

Map 3: 619 W Randolph St., 312/715-0708, www.blackbirdrestaurant.com; 11:30am-2pm and 5pm-10:30pm Mon.-Thurs., 11:30am-2pm and 5pm-11:30pm Fri., 5pm-11:30pm Sat., 5pm-10:30pm Sun.

The Dawson $$

This neighborhood spot is great for happy hour, date night, or group gatherings. The menu is packed with elevated comfort food like wood-fired meat, chorizo-stuffed dates, and an addictive mac and cheese with smoked pork shoulder. Craft cocktails recall a bygone era and feature names like Public Enemy #1 and Chicago Typewriter. Reclaimed materials throughout the restaurant interior are

Girl & the Goat

a nod to the industrial 19th century, while the outdoor patio offers views of an energetic street corner perfect for people-watching.

Map 3: 730 W Grand Ave., 312/243-8955, www.the-dawson.com; 4:30pm-11pm Mon.-Thurs., 4:30pm-midnight Fri., 10:30am-midnight Sat., 10:30am-11pm Sun.

Girl & the Goat $$

Stephanie Izard of *Top Chef* fame serves family-style plates at Girl & the Goat. The global menu is varied—from pan-fried shishito peppers to blue-cheese sweet potato pierogi, and, as the name implies, plenty of goat dishes. The drink menu emphasizes local craft beer and wine from small producers. Sit in the lounge or the bar, or opt for a table right against the kitchen for an inside peek into a famous restaurant at work. Reservations are recommended, though the restaurant does save spots for walk-ins.

Map 3: 809 W Randolph St., 312/492-6262, www.girlandthegoat.com; 4:30pm-11pm Sun.-Thurs., 4:30pm-midnight Fri.-Sat.

Homestead $$$

Homestead's tagline is "literal farm-to-table"—the chef is obsessed with buying locally and serving whatever is in season. The menu changes weekly and usually features items like roasted Amish chicken breast, caramelized beets, cauliflower soup, and beignets with seasonal fruit compote. In summer, the cozy interior opens into an 80-seat patio with hanging gardens. The Homestead entrance is through the Roots restaurant, which sits below.

Map 3: 1924 W Chicago Ave., 773/332-2354, www.homesteadontheroof. com; 5pm-9pm Tues.-Thurs., 5pm-9:30pm Fri.-Sat.

Lou Mitchell's $

Lou Mitchell opened this casual breakfast spot for neighborhood residents in 1923. As word of his skillet-fried eggs spread, the place was soon so popular that he needed something to feed people while they waited. That something ended up being doughnut holes, and you'll still enjoy a few while you wait in line today for heaping plates of eggs, pancakes, and breakfast fare served in cozy booths by the friendly staff.

Map 3: 565 W Jackson Blvd., 312/939-3111, www.loumitchellrestaurant.com; 5:30am-4pm Mon.-Fri., 7am-4pm Sat., 7am-3pm Sun.

Publican $$

Oysters, pork, and beer are the stars at Publican. Sustainably harvested seafood along with sustainably raised heirloom pork fill the menu; the porchetta with spaghetti squash, chicory, and hazelnut is a favorite, as is the romesco fish stew. The long communal wood tables and hanging lights recall a European beer hall. Ask a server to guide you through the beer list, which features more than 100 lagers, ales, and ciders.

Map 3: 837 W Fulton Market, 312/733-9555, www.thepublicanrestaurant. com; 3:30pm-10:30pm Mon.-Thurs., 3:30pm-11:30pm Fri., 10am-2pm and 5:30pm-11:30pm Sat., 9am-2pm and 5pm-10pm Sun.

Sepia $$$

Housed in an 1890s print shop, Sepia feels warm and classic. The inviting space is filled with vintage memorabilia and custom art nouveau tile. The rustic elegance extends to the menu where Chef Andrew Zimmerman showcases seasonal ingredients in dishes like roasted rabbit with house bacon, tea-soaked prune and potato puree, and wild mushrooms with Parisian gnocchi, spruce, and soft ripened cheese.

Map 3: 123 N Jefferson St., 312/441-1920, www.sepiachicago.com; 11:30am-2pm and 5:00pm-10pm Mon.-Fri., 5pm-11pm Sat., 5pm-10pm Sun.

Two $$$

Family-run butcher shops were a huge influence in Two's creation. The meat is sourced from small Midwestern farms, while bacon, sausage, cheese, pasta, and other ingredients are made in-house. The refurbished interior features barn doors, water spigots (now faucets), and plenty of Chicago touches. Order a microbrew from the bar, or opt for a sip of the restaurant's barrel-aged vodka.

Map 3: 1132 W Grand Ave., 312/624-8363, www.113two.com; 5pm-10pm Tues.-Thurs., 5pm-11pm Fri.-Sat., 5pm-10pm Sun.

ASIAN
BellyQ $$

This trendy Asian barbecue spot serves a full menu of ceviche, tea-soaked duck breast, and Korean pancakes. Everything is delicious, but for an experience, reserve a grill table where you can settle in for a three-course meal of grilled vegetables, a choice of protein with barbecue sauces, plus dessert. Wash it all down with the sake on tap.

Map 3: 1400 W Randolph St., 312/563-1010, www.bellyqchicago.com; 5pm-10pm Mon.-Thurs., 5pm-11pm Fri.-Sat., 11am-3pm and 5pm-10pm Sun.

☺ Momotaro $$$

The beautiful AvroKO interior makes dining at Momotaro an experience. On the main floor, a room of polished wood and modern Japanese lanterns sets the stage for sushi and *robata* stations. (Their sushi and sashimi program is unrivaled in Chicago.) On the lower level, the Izakaya lounge is decorated with vintage Tokyo signs and feels like a hidden alleyway. Izakaya serves Tokyo street food, sake, and Japanese whiskey. The Izakaya lounge does not take reservations; Momotaro does and reservations are advised.

Map 3: 820 W Lake St., 312/733-4818, www.momotarochicago.com; 5pm-10:30pm Mon.-Thurs., 4:30pm-11pm Fri., 4:30pm-midnight Sat., 4:30pm-10:30pm Sun.

FRENCH
French Market $

This indoor marketplace near Union Station features outlets from more than 30 local restaurants. Choose from Vietnamese soup, Italian sandwiches, Mexican tacos, and, of course, French pastry shops with pretty macarons lining their display and corner bistros serving French onion soup and baguettes. There's also a small grocery for snacks and fruit. Take your goods to go or sit at a table near the back of the market and enjoy the frequent live music.

Map 3: 131 N Clinton St., 312/575-0306, www.frenchmarketchicago.com; 7am-7:30pm Mon.-Fri., 7am-5:30pm Sat.

Maude's Liquor Bar $$

This charming, intimate restaurant serves traditional French dishes and classic cocktails. Oysters, *moules frites,* French onion fondue, and other comforting dishes accompany a large wine, champagne, and beer list. Or opt for something sparkling like a St. Germain Fizz or the intense Smokey Violet Smash and relax in the cozy exposed brick and dark wood interior.

Map 3: 840 W Randolph St., 312/243-9712, www.maudesliquorbar.com; 5pm-10:30pm Sun.-Mon., 5pm-11:30pm Tues.-Thurs., 5pm-12:30am Fri.-Sat.

Chicago's indoor French Market

Artopolis Bakery, Cafe and Agora

GREEK
Artopolis Bakery, Cafe and Agora $

The sweet smell of baking baklava, Grecian cookies, and other treats will draw you into this inviting shop with its open-air kitchen and large wood-burning oven. The café also serves savory items like eggplant moussaka and spanakopita. Dine inside at the small wooden tables or take your order to go.
Map 3: 306 S. Halsted St., 312/559-9000, www.artopolischicago.com; 9am-midnight Mon.-Thurs., 9am-1am Fri.-Sat., 10am-11pm Sun.

Athena Greek Restaurant $$

Athena serve some of the best food in Greektown, with a large menu of salads and authentic Greek dishes like gyros, leg of lamb, pastitsio, and plenty of desserts. Dine on the giant outdoor terrace with a waterfall and retractable roof, or sit inside at stately tables decorated with white linens and blue accents.

Map 3: 212 S. Halsted St., 312/655-0000, www.athenarestaurantchicago.com; 11am-11pm Sun.-Thurs., 11am-midnight Fri.-Sat.

ITALIAN
J. P. Graziano Grocery and Sub Shop $

The oldest Italian market in Chicago has been in the Graziano family for four generations. More importantly, it serves the best Italian subs in the city, stacked with sliced meat and Italian cheeses with house-made *giardiniera*, caper aioli, and other accompaniments served on Italian bread from D'Amato's Bakery. The corner shop still sells imported Italian products like olive oil, cheeses, tomatoes, spices, and wine and has a few tables inside and out (or take your sub to go).

Map 3: 901 W. Randolph St., 312/666-4587, www.jpgraziano.com; 9am-5pm Mon.-Fri., 9am-4pm Sat.

Monteverde Restaurant & Pastificio $$

Simple ingredients and handmade pasta power the food at Monteverde, one of Chicago's best Italian restaurants. Traditional dishes get a slight twist—think tortellini with pumpkin, sage, and apple balsamic. The bustling restaurant with high ceilings feels spacious. From the bar you can watch the *pastificio* station, where chefs hand-roll pasta throughout the day. The wooden barrels hold vinegar from one of Italy's most famous balsamic makers, aging it especially for Monteverde.

Map 3: 1020 W Madison St., 312/888-3041, www.monteverdechicago.com; 5pm-11pm Tues.-Sat., 4pm-9pm Sun.

LATIN AMERICAN

El Taco Veloz $

This casual taqueria serves affordable tacos and enchiladas in a fun setting until late at night. The brightly decorated restaurant is packed with locals who gather on Saturday nights to sing Spanish karaoke. (Even if you don't understand the lyrics, it's fun to watch while sipping pitchers of margaritas or beer.) It may not the best Mexican food in Chicago, but it fits the bill when you're craving something tasty at the end of a night out.

Map 3: 1745 W Chicago Ave., 312/738-0363; 9am-midnight Sun.-Thurs., 9am-3am Fri.-Sat.

Leña Brava $$$

Chef Rick Bayless introduces diners to new regions of Mexico through his cooking, and his colorful and lively Leña Brava is no different. Here the focus is on Baja California Norte, which specializes in live-fire cooking and is home to Mexico's best wine region. Taste your way through the ceviches and raw bar items before moving on to baked cod, pork belly with sweet salsa, and octopus *carnitas*, all cooked in the restaurant's large wood-burning oven.

Map 3: 900 W Randolph St., 312/733-1975, www.rickbayless.com/restaurants/lena-brava; 5:30pm-10pm Tues.-Thurs., 5:30pm-11pm Fri.-Sat., 5:30pm-9pm Sun.

COFFEE AND DESSERT

Atomix $

This simple coffee shop in Ukrainian Village is packed with regulars working on laptops. Primary-colored school tables and mismatched artwork fill the shop, which promotes local artists and events. There's nothing fancy about Atomix, but the unlimited coffee is cheap, and the vegan baked goods and bagel sandwiches are the perfect breakfast or pick-me-up after a long day.

Map 3: 1957 W Chicago Ave., 312/733-2701, www.atomixcafe.com; 6:45am-9pm Mon.-Fri., 8am-9pm Sat.-Sun.

Black Dog Gelato $

Gourmet gelato and sorbet are made fresh daily inside this small, pink shop. While flavors change often, there's always a mix of both the traditional and the unique—chocolate and strawberry sit among goat-cheese cashew caramel or maple cayenne bacon. Black Dog Gelato is cash-only, but there is an ATM inside.

Map 3: 859 N Damen Ave., 773/235-3116, www.blackdogchicago.com; Fri.-Sun. 2pm-10pm

Lincoln Park, Old Town, and Gold Coast

Map 4

RESTAURANTS

LINCOLN PARK, OLD TOWN, AND GOLD COAST

PIZZA
Happy Camper $$

While it's not Chicago-style, Happy Camper serves tasty, reliable pizza in a fun, trendy space. Sit in a tire swing at the bar, perch at a high-top table, or dine in a giant Airstream camper van in the middle of the restaurant. Complement your slice with a craft cocktail or beer from the extensive drink list. In the summer, dine on the expansive, lively patio.

Map 4: 1209 N. Wells St., 312/344-1634, www.happycamperchicago.com; 4pm-midnight Mon.-Wed., 4pm-2am Thurs., 11am-2am Fri., 10:30am-3am Sat., 10:30am-midnight Sun.

Happy Camper

Pequod's Pizza $

While there is some debate about whether Pequod's qualifies as Chicago-style, Chicagoans are in agreement when it comes to the addicting deep-dish, caramelized cheese crusts. The casual atmosphere and late hours are a plus.

Map 4: 2207 N. Clybourn Ave., 773/327-1512, www.pequodspizza.com; 11am-2am Mon.-Sat., 11am-midnight Sun.

HOT DOGS
The Wiener Circle $

Locals and tourists alike file in day after day, hour after hour (especially late at night) at this Chicago icon to undergo the staff's famous verbal harassment as they place their hot dog orders. Talking back is accepted—and expected—and the entertaining and sometimes shocking banter is always good for a laugh. The original location on Clark is still a favorite among Chicagoans and is cash only.

Map 4: 2622 N. Clark St., 773/477-7444, www.wienercircle.net; 10:30am-4am Sun.-Thurs., 10:30am-5pm Fri.-Sat.

AMERICAN
✪ Alinea $$$

Chicago's best restaurant is also one of the best in the world: decorated with three Michelin stars, the AAA Five Diamond Award, a spot on the San Pellegrino World's 50 Best Restaurant List, and a James Beard Award for Outstanding Restaurant. Chef Grant Achatz experiments with playful fine dining, serving dishes like piquant onion and black-pepper cream sandwiches in a purple onion flower and desserts like helium-filled balloons of strawberry taffy. The set menu, while expensive, is worth it not only for the incredible food and creative interpretations but for the experience

93

itself, which often incorporates light and music. Reservations are required weeks or even months in advance.

Map 4: 1723 N. Halsted St., 312/867-0110, www.alinearestaurant.com; 5pm-9:30pm Wed.-Sun.

Boka $$$

This sleek, dimly lit restaurant in Lincoln Park is revered for its Michelin-starred food, beautiful presentation, and intimate atmosphere. Chef Lee Wolen's elevated take on American cuisine includes dishes like shellfish and apple chowder and olive oil-poached walleye. A tasting menu is also available ($120). Reservations are highly recommended.

Map 4: 1729 N. Halsted St., 312/337-6070, www.bokachicago.com; 5pm-10pm Mon.-Thurs., 5pm-11pm Fri.-Sat.

☺ Green City Market $

Chicago's only year-round, sustainable market resides in Lincoln Park, supporting small farms and providing local food to families and restaurants. Fruit, vegetable, and flower stands are plentiful, as are cheese vendors from Wisconsin. There are also plenty of ready-to-eat foods, from pastries to tacos. Lincoln Park hosts the market May-October; November-April, it moves to the Peggy Notebaert Nature Museum (2430 N Cannon Dr., 8am-1pm Wed. and Sat.). A smaller version of the market is available (115 S. Sangamon St., 8am-1pm Sat.) in summer.

Map 4: Lincoln Park, 773/880-1206, www.greencitymarket.org; Lincoln Park, 7am-1pm Wed. and Sat. May-Oct.

Hugo's Frog Bar $$$

This bustling, upscale seafood restaurant is incredibly popular and always packed, though usually with tourists. Locals do stop by in the summer though, when the patio is the place to see and be seen in Chicago. Sit outside and feast on $1 oyster happy hour and a glass of white wine while watching Chicago's best-dressed stroll down Rush Street. If you do stay for dinner, the restaurant specializes in frog's legs, crab cakes, and steak. Reservations are recommended.

Map 4: 1024 N. Rush St., 312/640-0999, www.hugosfrogbar.com; 3pm-2am daily

Summer House Santa Monica $$

Summer House Santa Monica brings sunny, airy California vibes, beachy furniture, and tropical drinks to Lincoln Park. Seasonal dishes emphasize vegetables and seafood, though there are meat options as well. Brunch is especially popular in summer when the atrium lets in additional light. Reservations are recommended.

Map 4: 1954 N. Halsted St., 773/634-4100, www.summerhousesm.com; 11am-10pm Mon.-Thurs., 11am-11pm Fri., 8am-11pm Sat., 8am-10pm Sun.

White Oak Tavern $$

This sleek, airy gastropub is a rustic treasure in the heart of Lincoln Park. The changing menu of regional and expertly prepared cuisine—determined by season and local producers—changes often and is consistently ranked one of the best in the area. The atmosphere is modern yet comfortable, complemented by a knowledgeable staff.

Map 4: 1200 W Webster Ave., 773/248-0200, www.thewhiteoaktavern. com; 11am-3pm and 5pm-9:30pm Tues.-Thurs., 11am-3pm and 5pm-10pm Fri., 9:30am-3pm and 5pm-10pm Sat., 9am-3pm Sun.

FRENCH
Mon Ami Gabi $$

Inside the Belden-Stratford Hotel, Mon Ami Gabi exemplifies the classic French bistro complete with white tablecloths and dark walls. The traditional menu includes exemplary *steak frites* and beef bourguignon, but save room for one of the decadent desserts. A list of more than 80 boutique French wines rounds out the meal.

Map 4: 2300 N. Lincoln Park West, 773/348-8886, www.monamigabi.com; 5pm-9:30pm Mon.-Thurs., 5pm-10:30pm Fri.-Sat., 10am-2pm and 5pm-8:30pm Sun.

GREEK
Athenian Room $

This neighborhood Greek restaurant has been around since the 1970s, and not much has changed since then. The brick columns and arched ceilings will make you feel like you're in Europe as will the friendly Greek family who owns the place. Everything on the menu is good and reasonably priced, but the gyros and fries are especially popular.

Map 4: 807 W. Webster Ave., 773/348-5155; 11am-10pm Mon.-Sat., 11am-9pm Sun.

ITALIAN
Balena $$

Inviting and warmly lit, Balena is a standout Italian restaurant. Choose from a selection of handmade pastas or order pizza from the large brick oven and enjoy a glass from the expansive wine list. For those without reservations, there's a seating section reserved for walk-ins and a large bar where you can order off the menu.

Map 4: 1633 N. Halsted St., 312/867-3888, www.balenachicago.com; 5pm-9pm Mon., 5pm-10pm Tues.-Thurs., 5pm-11pm Fri., 4:30pm-11pm Sat., 10am-8pm Sun.

Sapori Trattoria $$

This cozy Italian spot is bustling with locals, who come for the hearty portions of house-made pasta. The spaghetti *barese* is a local favorite, as is the lasagna di Antonio. The restaurant is bigger than it looks, so you won't have to wait too long for a table, but reservations are a good idea.

Map 4: 2701 N. Halsted St., 773/832-9999, www.saporitrattoria.net; 4:30pm-10pm Mon.-Thurs., 4:30pm-11pm Fri., 4pm-11pm Sat., 3pm-10pm Sun.

LATIN AMERICAN
Buzz Bait $

Beachy vibes greet you at this taqueria serving a small but delicious menu that focuses on fish tacos. The ahi and crispy shrimp are favorites as are the bowls that mix seafood, protein, and veggies together in a filling, beautiful pile. Counter service makes the experience fast and casual, perfect before a night out or for a quick lunch on the weekends.

Map 4: 1529 N. Wells St., 312/664-2899, www.buzzbaitchicago.com; 4pm-9pm Mon.-Thurs., 11am-10pm Fri.-Sat., 11am-9pm Sun.

Velvet Taco $

Velvet Taco's handmade tortillas are stuffed with homemade fillings like fried paneer, falafel, and ahi along with the more traditional steak, pork, and chicken. Order at the counter, then find a table in this casual restaurant. Don't forget the margaritas, which are made with sorbet.

Map 4: 1110 N. State St., 312/763-2654, www.velvettaco.com, 11am-midnight Mon.-Wed., 11am-3am Thurs., 11am-4am Fri., 9am-4am Sat., 9am-midnight Sun.

MIDDLE EASTERN
✪ Halal Guys $

New York's famous Halal Guys opened this Chicago branch in 2016, bringing a small but flavorful menu to the city. Order a bowl or sandwich of gyro, chicken, or falafel with red sauce—and when they tell you it's spicy, believe them. The counter service shop is tiny, so grab a bite to go.

Map 4: 49 W. Division St., 312/877-5575, www.thehalalguys.com; 11am-11pm Sun.-Thurs., 11am-4am Fri.-Sat.

Halal Guys

STEAKHOUSE
Gibson's Bar & Steakhouse $$$

Gibson's bills itself as *"the* steakhouse" in Chicago, and it's definitely up there when it comes to food and ambience. It's also a favorite among celebrity visitors, as the photo-adorned walls will attest. Steak is the obvious, and best, menu choice. Make reservations in advance and plan to dress up.

Map 4: 1028 N. Rush St., 312/266-8999, www.thegibsonsteakhouse.com; 11am-2am daily

COFFEE AND DESSERT
Elaine's Coffee Call $

Though it's part of the Hotel Lincoln, a separate entrance and warm decor make this feel like anything but a hotel coffee shop. Sit and relax at one of the tables or grab a cup of La Colombe coffee and a pastry to go on your way to nearby Lincoln Park.

Map 4: 1816 N. Clark St., 312/254-4665, www.bokagrp.com/elaines.php; 6:30am-5pm daily

Eva's Cafe $

This cozy café with brick walls and a blazing fireplace is a favorite for huddling away from Chicago winters with a good book or a pile of work. The friendly staff makes great specialty coffee drinks, and a small food menu offers sandwiches, breakfast items, and soup. Located just steps from the Sedgwick Brown Line, it's the perfect spot to rejuvenate after a day of sightseeing.

Map 4: 1447 N. Sedgwick St., 312/280-8900, www.evasoldtown.com; 7am-8pm Mon.-Fri., 8am-8pm Fri.-Sat.

Floriole $

Floriole began as a pastry stand at the Green City Market. Today, this storefront location is one of Chicago's most popular bakeries for bread, sandwiches, and sweets. Stop inside the bright and surprisingly spacious shop for a breakfast sweet or a wonderfully fluffy quiche.

Map 4: 1220 W. Webster Ave., 773/883-1313, www.floriole.com, 7am-5:30pm Tues.-Thurs., 8am-5:30pm Sat.-Mon.

French onion soup at La Fournette

La Fournette $

This small, authentic French café in Old Town is the perfect spot to grab a coffee and a croissant, or to hide out from chilly weather with a bowl of French onion soup (the best in the city).

Map 4: 1547 N. Wells St., 312/624-9430, www.lafournette.com; 7am-6:30pm Mon.-Sat., 7am-5:30pm Sun.

Lakeview and Wrigleyville Map 5

AMERICAN

Bar Pastoral $

The original Pastoral location is part cheese shop, part deli, part wine shop, and always a good idea. While you could stop in for a cheese and charcuterie basket to take home, it's better to come hungry and indulge in one of the innovative sandwiches, like goat cheese with almond butter, celery, and avocado. You could also pick up a Pastoral Picnic selection and head to the lakefront or park. Another dining location is in Andersonville (5212 N. Clark St.).

Map 5: 2947 N Broadway St., 773/472-4781, www.pastoralartisan.com; 5pm-10pm Mon.-Wed., 5pm-11pm Thurs., 5pm-midnight Fri., 11am-midnight Sat., 11am-10pm Sun.

Cheesie's Pub & Grub $

Grilled cheese is great, but Cheesie's makes it even better with 11 variations on this classic. The Mac doubles down on the cheddar with macaroni and cheese plus cheese slices on Texas Toast, while The Caprese pretends to be a healthy option with mozzarella, tomato, basil, and pesto. Order your food at the counter and get a number, then head to the bar where you'll find plenty of local and domestic beer. Cheesie's is very much a sports bar, and there are enough TVs lining the walls that you can find whatever game you're hoping to catch.

Map 5: 958 W Belmont Ave., 773/388-1574, www.cheesieschicago.com; 11am-3am Sun.-Thurs., 11am-5am Fri.-Sat.

DryHop Brewers $

This kitchen and brewery serves seasonal, elevated bar food and craft beer that is only available in Lakeview. The brisket and short rib burger with aged cheddar, pickled onions, arugula, and a chile-tomato jam is consistently rated one of the best in the city. The beer selection skews hoppy (no surprise) and can be taken home in growlers.

Map 5: 3155 N. Broadway St., 773/857-3155, www.dryhopchicago.com; 11am-midnight Sun.-Thurs., 11am-2am Fri.-Sat.

DryHop Brewers

Golden Apple Grill & Breakfast House $

Fans of *This American Life* may recall the radio show's excellent piece about this 24-hour diner. It's a comfortable and affordable place for a late-night bite (sandwiches, soups, salads, pasta, etc.) or the popular all-day breakfast. Service is casual and friendly—and if they ask if you want a slice of pie, say yes.

Map 5: 2971 N. Lincoln Ave., 773/528-1413, www.goldenapplediner.com; 24 hours daily

Southport Grocery and Café $

This small grocery stocks locally made goods like sauces, baking mixes, and homemade bitters. It also serves breakfast and sandwiches all day— the stuffed French toast is worth the line that forms on weekends. Get there early or visit during the week to snag a seat.

Map 5: 3553 N. Southport Ave., 773/665-0100, www.southportgrocery.com; 7am-4pm Mon.-Fri., 8am-4pm Sat.-Sun.

ASIAN
Crisp $

Crisp's Korean chicken wings have a cult following in Chicago for their spicy Seoul Sassy sauce, big portions, and cheap prices. For the full experience, skip dining in the tiny restaurant and order your wings to go (or for delivery).

Map 5: 2940 N. Broadway St., 773/697-7610, www.crisponline.com; 11:30am-9pm daily

LATIN AMERICAN
Chilam Balam $$

Farm-to-table Mexican small plates in an intimate setting—that's Chilam Balam, though you wouldn't guess it from the exterior. (The tiny awning is easy to miss while walking down Broadway.) Pork shoulder tacos get an upgrade with tomato guajillo and quesadillas are served with grape guacamole, among other unique twists on the menu. The cash-only restaurant is BYOB—but bring in a bottle of wine and they might make sangria for you.

Map 5: 3023 N. Broadway St., 773/296-6901, www.chilambalamchicago. com; 5pm-10pm Tues.-Thurs., 5pm-11pm Fri.-Sat.

SWEDISH
Ann Sathers $

Ann Sathers is a Swedish restaurant that feels like an American diner. They claim to have the best cinnamon rolls in town—and so far, no one has proved them wrong. Share one of their huge rolls over breakfast, which is the most popular time to come. For dinner, try the Swedish platter. The restaurant is BYOB, and there are additional locations in Boystown (3415 N. Broadway) and Edgewater (1147 W. Granville).

Map 5: 909 W. Belmont Ave., 773/348-2378, www.annsather.com; 7am-3pm Mon.-Fri., 7am-4pm Sat.-Sun.

VEGETARIAN
Chicago Diner $

The tiny Chicago Diner has been "meat free since '83." Menu items are vegan takes on classic diner food—Thai chili wings with seitan, tofu quesadillas, and truffle-mushroom lentil loaf. Gluten-free options are available, and they even have vegan milk shakes! Seating is limited and reservations are not accepted, but the Halsted crowd does breakfast late. If you make it in before 11am, you'll have a better chance at getting seated right away. A second location is in Logan Square (2333 N. Milwaukee Ave., 773/252-3211).

Map 5: 3411 N. Halsted St., 773/935-6696, www.veggiediner.com; 11am-10pm daily

COFFEE AND DESSERT
Bittersweet Pastry Shop & Café $

This European-style café and pastry shop just off the Belmont Red Line serves a small and reasonably priced breakfast and lunch menu. French toast, French onion soup, and the quiche of the day are local favorites. Pick up a box of macarons or other pretty pastries to bring home.

Map 5: 1114 W. Belmont Ave., 773/929-1100, www.bittersweetpastry. com; 7am-7pm Tues.-Fri., 8am-7pm Sat., 8am-6pm Sun.

Jeni's Splendid Ice Creams

Jeni's Splendid Ice Creams $

It's impossible to walk into Jeni's and not order a scoop of ice cream, so sweet is the smell of their unique flavors. Order sweet corn in the summer, Thai curry pumpkin in the fall, or pistachio and honey anytime. All ice cream is made from scratch with natural ingredients and known for its supercreamy texture. There's a second location near the Damen stop in Wicker Park (1505 N Milwaukee Ave., 872/802-4668).

Map 5: 3404 N. Southport Ave., 773/348-7139, www.jenis.com; noon-11pm daily

Osmium Coffee Bar $

For good, local coffee with a twist, go to Osmium. This coffee bar just off the Belmont CTA stop serves Dark Matter coffee in Agave Lattes or Mayan Mochas, or iced on draft. It's a great spot to get some work done; the mix of obscure, upbeat music and other patrons on their laptops are motivating factors.

Map 5: 1117 W Belmont Ave., 773/360-7553, www.darkmattercoffee.com; 6am-9pm daily

Wicker Park and Bucktown

Map 6

PIZZA
Piece Brewery and Pizza $$

Piece Brewery and Pizza serves New Haven-style pizza. The style is different than traditional Chicago deep dish—thin and crispy and served on a sheet pan (the white pizza is a local favorite). The large sports bar/restaurant is always buzzing with TVs playing an array of games and live bands some nights. The on-site brewery makes decent, small batch, handcrafted beer.

Map 6: 1927 W. North Ave., 773/772-4422, www.piecechicago.com; 11am-10:30pm Mon.-Wed., 11am-11pm Thurs., 11am-12:30am Fri.-Sat., 11am-10pm Sun.

AMERICAN
Cellar Door Provisions $$

Small and simple is the theme at Cellar Door Provisions, which limits seating to 20 to inspire a community feel. The food is sourced from local farms and includes a menu of pastries, quiche, and tartines, with a few salads and soups. Dinner features a changing prix fixe menu of American dishes ($38-48), including appetizers, 2-3 courses, and dessert. Reservations are accepted for dinner; breakfast and lunch are walk-in only.

Map 6: 3025 W. Diversey Ave., 773/697-8337, www.cellardoorprovisions.com; 8am-3pm Sun. and Wed.-Thurs., 8am-3pm and 5:30pm-9pm Fri.-Sat.

Longman and Eagle $$

Craft cocktails, a massive whiskey selection, and locally sourced, seasonal food with an old Chicago vibe characterize this small corner restaurant in Logan Square. Sit on the patio outside or in the cozy, wooden bar for a rare bourbon or expertly mixed cocktail. Entrées include fried chicken with duck-fat biscuits and pork jowl with brussels sprouts. Reservations are not accepted, so be prepared to wait in line on weekends.

Map 6: 2657 N. Kedzie Ave., 773/276-7110, www.longmanandeagle.com; 9am-3pm and 5pm-1am daily

Lula Cafe $$

Lula Cafe has been serving farm-to-table cuisine to Logan Square locals since 1999. The casual restaurant rewards with locally sourced salads and sandwiches and brunch dishes like baked egg with avocado and lemon brioche French toast. Dinner is elevated to dishes like beet dumplings with black trumpet mushrooms and scallop crudo. Reservations are accepted for dinner, but prepare to wait in line for brunch.

Map 6: 2537 N. Kedzie Ave., 773/489-9554, www.lulacafe.com; 9am-10pm Sun.-Mon. and Wed.-Thurs., 9am-11pm Fri.-Sat.

☺ Mindy's HotChocolate $$

Mindy's HotChocolate serves fantastic, locally sourced food (like crispy chicken with polenta and risotto with truffle sauce and foraged mushrooms), but dessert is the star of the show. Owner Mindy Segal has won a James Beard Award for Outstanding Pastry Chef, so save room for homemade cookies, cheesecake, and chess pie. To truly indulge, pair your dessert with rich hot chocolate served with house-made marshmallows. The cozy, contemporary restaurant is full of dark wood furnishings—the perfect place to hide out during a Chicago snowstorm.

Map 6: 1747 N. Damen Ave., 773/489-1747, www.hotchocolatechicago. com; 5:30pm-10pm Tues.-Thurs., 5:30pm-midnight Fri.-Sat., 5:30pm-10pm Sun.

ASIAN
Fat Rice $$

This small Logan Square restaurant serves Macanese food, the ultimate fusion of flavors from Southeast Asia, India, China, and Portugal. The menu changes often, but includes piri piri chicken or Malay vegetable curry with ginger-lime pickled cauliflower or Sichuan peanuts as sides. Dine at communal tables or on bar stools and watch the chefs through the open kitchen as they prepare *arroz gordo*, or fat rice (get it?) with prawns, clams, chicken, eggs, peppers, and sausages piled on top of crispy jasmine rice in a clay pot.

Map 6: 2957 W. Diversey Ave., 773/661-9170, www.eatfatrice.com; 5:30pm-10pm Tues., 11am-2pm and 5:30pm-10pm Wed.-Sat., 11am-3pm Sun.

Yusho $$

Chef Matthias Merger, former executive chef at Charlie Trotter's, opened Yusho after falling in love with the bustle of Tokyo's fish markets. At Yusho, fresh seafood is prepared over a *binchotan*, or Japanese grill, which gives the food a crispy layer while sealing the flavors inside. The idea may be foreign, but the food is not; meat, vegetables, and spices are locally sourced and served as small plates. The restaurant interior is simple and comfortable, with a row of booths and a long bar offering a menu of craft cocktails, beers, and Japanese whiskeys and spirits. You can even order customized meal pairings.

Map 6: 2853 N. Kedzie Ave., 773/904-8558, www.yusho-chicago.com; 5pm-10pm Mon. and Wed.-Thurs., 5pm-11pm Fri.-Sat., noon-9pm Sun.

GREEK
Taxim $$

Enter the beautiful dining room at Taxim, with its Byzantine-style artwork, high ceilings, and marble floors, and prepare yourself for a meal of delicious, regionally inspired Greek dishes. Graze through a selection of small plates, or opt for an entrée of grilled quail, lamb chop, or fish, among others. The octopus and housemade yogurt with fava beans and lamb confit are favorites. A large salad and vegetable selection make this a good option for vegetarians. The wine list is Greek, and the staff is well-versed in the selections.

Map 6: 1558 N. Milwaukee Ave., 773/252-1558, www.taximchicago.com; 5:30pm-10pm Mon.-Thurs., 5:30pm-11pm Fri.-Sat., 5pm-9:30pm Sun.

ITALIAN
Osteria Langhe $$$

Osteria Langhe specializes in cuisine from the Piemonte region in northern Italy. Inside the small and intimate restaurant order comfort food like *plin* (hand-pinched ravioli with parmesan, butter, and thyme) or prosciutto-wrapped rabbit with wild mushrooms. The wine list is regional, and your server and sommelier are happy to describe Piemonte's often-overlooked wines.

Map 6: 2824 W. Armitage Ave., 773/661-1582, www.osterialanghe.com; 5:30pm-10pm Mon.-Thurs., 5:30pm-11pm Fri.-Sat., 5:30pm-9pm Sun.

LATIN AMERICAN
✪ Big Star $

There's contention over who serves the best tacos in Chicago, but Big Star is always in the running. The tacos (the pork shoulder and fish are fantastic) are more Texan than Mexican, with a bourbon and beer drink list that elicits a honky-tonk feel. Come summer, the spacious patio is the busiest in the neighborhood. Grab an umbrella-shaded seat outside or pull up to the large center bar where you can admire the neon art and vintage beer signs. If you're in a rush, there's a to-go stand next door.

Map 6: 1531 N. Damen Ave., 773/235-4039, www.bigstarchicago.com; 11:30am-2am Mon.-Fri., 9am-3am Sat.-Sun.

Dove's Luncheonette $$

Southern meets Mexican at this diner serving hearty food, local coffee, and a tequila and mescal-heavy cocktail list. Bar stools line the small restaurant, which features a jukebox and '60s and '70s memorabilia. For brunch, dine on pancakes, eggs over grits with Texas toast, and posole with guajillo chile. At lunch or dinner, feast on chicken-fried chicken, Cajun flounder, tacos, and chili. If coming for weekend brunch, grab a coffee and prepare to wait in line; Dove's does not take reservations.

Map 6: 1545 N. Damen Ave., 773/645-4060, www.doveschicago.com; 9am-9pm Sun.-Thurs., 8am-10pm Fri.-Sat., 8am-9pm Sun.

MIDDLE EASTERN
Sultan's Market $

This small grocery store serves falafel, shawarma, and other Middle Eastern options with a large salad bar. The lentil soup and falafel sandwiches are especially delicious. If there's no room at one of the few tables inside, grab your meal to go and sit in the nearby park. Cash only.

Map 6: 2057 W. North Ave., 773/235-3072, www.chicagofalafel.com; 10am-10pm Mon.-Sat., 10am-9pm Sun.

COFFEE AND DESSERT
Buzz Killer Espresso $

For great coffee without a pretentious, hipster vibe, come to Buzz Killer Espresso. The sleek white walls and simple tables make this a popular spot for people to relax. While the coffee drinks and pastries may be a tad bit pricier, Buzz Killer serves its own roasted beans and espresso blends.

Map 6: 1644 N. Damen Ave., 773/366-8377, www.buzzcoffeeroasters.com; 7am-7pm Mon.-Fri., 8am-7pm Sat.-Sun.

Ipsento Coffee $

This hip café is serious about coffee. The owners source their beans from world-class coffee farms that highlight each region. Ipsento's owners want you to care about coffee too, so they offer classes, which you can register for online. Sip coffee from the bar or purchase beans to go. For coffee with a side of booze, look for a small drink menu at the bar.

Map 6: 2035 N. Western Ave., 773/904-8177, www.ipsento.com; 6am-6pm Mon.-Fri., 7am-6pm Sat.-Sun.

Stan's Donuts $

Stan's Donuts, a Los Angeles staple since the 1960s, came to Chicago through a partnership with Labriola, a local baking company. Stan's California-style doughnuts are baked with Chicago bread and served in flavors like old-fashioned, glazed, Nutella banana pocket, coconut cake, and more. They also serve gelato, bagels, and coffee from Stumptown Coffee Roasters.

Map 6: 1560 N. Damen Ave., 773/360-7386, www.stansdonutschicago.com; 6:30am-9pm Sun.-Wed., 6:30am-10pm Thurs., 6:30am-10:30pm Fri.-Sat.

Hyde Park   Map 7

AMERICAN
Medici on 57th $$

Medici on 57th is a hangout for University of Chicago students, who gather for pizza, burgers, shakes, and baked goods. Medici also does a decent brunch and serves hearty salads. The casual interior of brick walls and wooden tables is covered in scribbles from students and visitors. Scrawl your own political prose or poetic lines in a booth before heading out. Grab some beer on the way in—the restaurant is BYOB.

Map 7: 1327 E. 57th St., 773/667-7394, www.medici57.com; 7am-11pm Sun.-Thurs., 7am-midnight Fri.-Sat.

Valois $

Comfort food and friendly counter service make Valois a neighborhood favorite for many Hyde Park residents including Barack Obama, who apparently can't get enough of the perfectly crunchy hash browns. Valois serves a huge variety of breakfast dishes, burgers, and hot sandwiches with simple cafeteria-style seating. With good food, great prices, and a presidential endorsement, Valois doesn't need to be fancy to draw a crowd.

Map 7: 1518 E. 53rd St., 773/667-0647, www.valoisrestaurant.com; 5:30am-10pm daily

FRENCH
Plein Air Cafe $$

This sunlit, modern café across from the Robie House is the perfect spot to grab coffee on a cold day or a light lunch while exploring Hyde Park. High-quality coffee is served alongside French menu items like tartines, quiche, and soup. Seating can fill, but turnover is usually pretty quick.

Map 7: 5751 S. Woodlawn Ave., 773/966-7531, www.pleinaircafe.co; 7am-8pm Mon.-Fri., 8am-6pm Sat.-Sun.

ITALIAN
A10 $$

Named after the highway that runs between Italy and France, A10 serves Italian and French cuisine with an American twist. Rigatoni with Bolognese is served alongside beet salad and hand-cut fries in a warmly lit space amid brick walls and tiled tables. Craft cocktails, beer, and wine provide libations for all. For Sunday brunch, try a house-made pastry with a savory main dish.

Map 7: 1462 E. 53rd St., 773/288-1010, www.a10hydepark.com; 5pm-10pm Tues.-Thurs., 5pm-11pm Fri.-Sat., 5pm-9pm Sun.

COFFEE AND DESSERT
Cafe 53 $

This cozy café serves espresso drinks, Arabic coffee, homemade chai, and a huge selection of teas. The menu is halal, with plenty of vegetarian and vegan options. The roast beef sandwich, *kufta* sandwich, *fattoush* salad, and hummus plate are popular, as is the gelato bar. The small interior is filled with Chicago artwork and busy students; in warmer months, the crowds overflow into the cute, leafy patio.

Map 7: 1869 E. 53rd St., 773/493-1000; www.cafe-53.com; 8am-9pm daily

Greater Chicago   Map 8

BARBECUE
Smoque BBQ $

Barbecue may not be what comes to mind when you think of Chicago, but Smoque could change your mind. The five guys behind this operation are passionate about their barbecue and work to bring the natural flavors of the meat, the savory smoke, the spicy rub, and the sweet sauce all together in one perfect dish. All rubs and sauces are made in-house as are the sides, which include corn bread, mac and cheese, and beans. The 14-hour smoked brisket and pulled pork smoked over apple and oak are particularly delicious. The vibe is very casual and BYOB. You might have to wait in line, but it's worth it.

Map 8: Irving Park, 3800 N. Pulaski Rd., 773/545-7427, www.smoquebbq.com; 11am-9pm Sun.-Thurs., 11am-10pm Fri.-Sat.

ITALIAN
Spacca Napoli $

At family-run Spacca Napoli, the pizza is heavy on tomatoes and mozzarella, soft in the middle, and charred on the edges. That's because Spacca Napoli bakes its pizzas in an oven made in Naples. They source everything from Italian vendors, from flour to tomatoes, cheese, and even salt. You're getting the real deal, so order as you would in Naples: buffalo mozzarella, daily fried appetizers, and a simple margherita pizza. Sitting near the giant brick oven will give you the full experience, but the patio is nice for alfresco dining in warm months. Reservations are recommended, especially on weekends.

Map 8: Ravenswood, 1769 W. Sunnyside Ave., 773/878-2420, www.spaccanapolipizzeria.com; 11:30am-9pm Tues.-Thurs., 11:30am-10pm Fri.-Sat., noon-9pm Sun.

Spacca Napoli

MEXICAN
Carnitas Don Pedro $

Part butcher shop, part no-frills restaurant, Carnitas Don Pedro serves some of the best meat and tacos in Chicago. Opt for a mix of *carnitas,* which will include rib sections, dark meat, white meat, and more; it's ordered by weight. Take it to go or eat at the plastic tables, where it will be served with fresh tortillas, cilantro, onion, an array of salsas, lime, and peppers.

Map 8: Pilsen, 1113 W. 18th St., 312/829-4757; 6am-6pm Mon.-Thurs., 5am-6pm Fri.-Sat., 5am-3pm Sun.

SEAFOOD
Calumet Fisheries $

Smokehouses used to be big in Illinois, but now there are only a few left and Calumet Fisheries is one of them. The restaurant smokes its seafood on-site with oak logs, after marinating the fish in a special brine overnight. The result is smoky, mouthwatering fish that is truly unique to most other seafood places in the country. The owners of Calumet Fisheries pride themselves on tradition rather than newer smoking methods, though that means despite immense popularity they haven't updated to an actual restaurant either.

Calumet Fisheries is basically a shack, so take your fish to go.

Map 8: South Chicago, 3259 E. 95th St., 773/933-9855, www.calumetfisheries.com; 10am-9:45pm Sun.-Wed., 9am-9:30pm Thurs., 9am-9:45pm Fri.-Sat.

SOUTHERN
Big Jones $$

Heirloom southern cooking from Chef Paul Fehribach focuses on traditional southern cooking, with a regional bent toward Virginia. Inside the small and rustic restaurant, sturdy wooden tables are filled with diners tucking into popovers, creamy grits, or omelets stuffed with crawfish and andouille. Slow-cooked sausages, chicken fried in lard and clarified butter, flavorful greens, and honey-glazed corn bread pair with the vast bourbon and whiskey cocktail selection. Brunch is incredibly popular, but you can make a reservation!

Map 8: Andersonville, 5347 N. Clark St., 773/275-5725, www.bigjoneschicago.com; 11am-9pm Mon.-Thurs., 11am-10pm Fri., 9am-10pm Sat., 9am-9pm Sun.

SWEDISH
Svea $

This little Swedish diner is one of the few Swedish restaurants left in Chicago. The blue countertops and kitschy paintings provide a cozy setting for heaps of Swedish comfort food. Breakfast is best; order the Viking Breakfast, a local favorite that consists of two eggs, two Swedish pancakes with lingonberry, a large sausage, toast, and potatoes. It's as filling as it sounds. Later in the day, dine on Swedish meatballs, salmon, and lutefisk.

Map 8: Andersonville, 5236 N. Clark St., 773/275-7738; 7am-2pm Mon.-Fri., 7am-3pm Sat.-Sun.

southern fried chicken at Big Jones

COFFEE AND DESSERT
Middle East Bakery $

This small bakery/restaurant is a bit out of the way, but if you're craving Middle Eastern food, it's the best in the city. Lentil soup, perfectly fluffy falafel sandwiches, Syrian-style shawarma with pickled vegetables and garlicky tahini, plus baklava all compete for the best dishes. The simple restaurant, with wooden tables and minimal decorations, is good for a quick lunch. In the bakery are Middle Eastern pastries, to-go hummus, salads, and fresh bread. A grocery section sells spices, figs, dates, and olives.

Map 8: Andersonville, 1512 W. Foster Ave., 733/561-2224, www. middleeastbakeryandgrocery.com; 9:30am-8pm Mon.-Sat., 11am-5pm Sun.

NIGHTLIFE

Once a hub for jazz music, Chicago's Prohibition-era speakeasies left behind a legacy of boundary-pushing cocktails. The many talented mixologists, bar-

Three Dots and a Dash

tenders, and craft brewers mean that Chicagoans will never be without a cool drink. Live music and dance clubs are options every night of the week, whether it's grooving to underground DJs or listening to classic jazz. Oh, and those speakeasies? They're still some of the hottest spots in town.

In summer, Chicagoans bask in the warm weather, taking advantage of the city's numerous outdoor patios and rooftop bars. At night, they sweat it out at River North dance clubs like Studio Paris or cool down with innovative cocktails at Green River or The Violet Hour. Of course, if the Cubs are in town, everyone will be at one of the many Lakeview sports bars, which can get crazy on game days.

Hugely influential in the evolution of jazz and blues, Chicago is still home to historic jazz clubs such as the Green Mill, Kingston Mines, and Buddy Guy's Legends. Today, those stages are graced by veteran musicians and new acts alike. More music acts pop up at any number of venues throughout the city. Big-name bands like Broken Social Scene play beneath the chandeliers at the enormous Aragon Ballroom, while local, under-the-radar bands rock the cramped stage at the tiny Hideout.

The city is also a hub for improv comedy clubs. Famous performers like Stephen Colbert and Tina Fey got their start at Second City and the iO Theater.

HIGHLIGHTS

✪ **BEST BLUES CLUB:** Visit **Buddy Guy's Legends** for a night of music and dancing in the place where many blues legends got their start (page 110).

✪ **BEST OUTDOOR DRINKS:** With a picturesque terrace overlooking the Chicago skyline and creative cocktails that evoke the city's past, the outdoor patio at **Green River** is the place to be in summer (page 111).

✪ **HOTTEST DANCE CLUB:** Famous DJs and local celebrities like Chance the Rapper have been known to pop in at **Studio Paris Nightclub** (page 113).

✪ **MOST UNIQUE:** **The Aviary**'s bartender/chefs craft each delicious drink like a science experiment that transforms before your eyes (page 114).

✪ **BEST COMEDY CLUB:** **Second City** has been churning out comedy icons for decades. Grab a seat and get ready for a night of laughter (page 117).

✪ **BEST SPORTS BAR:** Batting cages and arcade games mean there's always a game on at **Sluggers**, even when the Cubs aren't playing next door at Wrigley Field (page 119).

✪ **BEST THROWBACK DANCE CLUB:** Travel back to the '80s and '90s at **The Holiday Club,** where you can dance to the music and videos of decades past (page 120).

✪ **BEST KARAOKE:** **Trader Todd's** exceptionally strong tiki drinks make karaoke that much easier and more enjoyable (page 122).

✪ **BEST COCKTAILS:** It's worth the wait for the expertly mixed drinks at **The Violet Hour.** The speakeasy is one of the city's best cocktail bars (page 123).

✪ **BEST JAZZ CLUB:** **The Green Mill** has barely changed since Al Capone frequented its dimly lit booths (page 126).

COCKTAIL BARS
Vol. 39

Settle into Vol. 39, the upscale bar and lounge in the Kimpton Gray Hotel, and sip a classic cocktail or glass of rare wine. The dark, intimate lounge is lined with massive bookshelves of law books and filled with plush leather couches. Aside from expertly made drinks, there's tableside silver champagne and caviar service, along with other small plates like artisanal cheeses, poached shrimp, and oysters.
Map 1: 39 S. LaSalle St., 312/750-9012, www.vol39.com; 3pm-midnight Mon.-Fri., 3pm-11pm Sat.

CRAFT BEER
First Draft

Inside this historic Printer's Row building are more than 20 craft beers on tap, each served in specialty glassware meant to elevate the taste. The warm brick and wood interior offers a welcome place to chat up the knowledgeable staff who can offer suggestions (and samples) to find the perfect beer for you.
Map 1: 649 S. Clark St., 312/461-1062, www.firstdraftchicago.com; 11am-2am daily

Monk's Pub

A local favorite, this German-style pub is stocked with old books, wooden barrels, and vintage taps. Try one of the more than 100 bottles of beer plus around 16 on tap at any given time, and dig into pub food like cheese curds, burgers, and Reubens. Monk's is extremely relaxed, always gives off a cozy vibe, and is usually bustling in the afternoon with a happy hour crowd.
Map 1: 205 W. Lake St., 312/357-6665, www.monkspubchicago.com; 9am-midnight Mon.-Fri., 11am-5pm Sat.

SPORTS BARS
The Bar Below

This basement bar in the Loop became popular during Prohibition, and so it remains today, thanks to its affordable drinks and cozy atmosphere. The underground space features a fireplace, wooden tables, a tin ceiling, and the menu of classic Prohibition-era cocktails includes the Chicago Old-Fashioned and the Classic Hot Toddy. Bar food and plenty of TVs make it a favorite during sports events, although it also has a popular happy hour.
Map 1: 127 S. State St., 312/372-2987, www.thebarbelowchicago.com; 11am-2am Mon.-Fri., 11am-3am Sat., 10am-10pm Sun.

Kasey's Tavern

The second-oldest tavern in Chicago still draws a crowd for its classic look and easygoing vibe. The small neighborhood bar serves beer and mixed drinks, with a patio in warmer months that adds space. Vintage wood and dim lighting give Kasey's a pub feel, with the jukebox a finishing touch. It's especially popular during happy hour and with locals on weekends.
Map 1: 701 S. Dearborn St., 312/427-7992, www.kaseystavern.com; 11am-2am daily

LIVE MUSIC

✪ Buddy Guy's Legends

Buddy Guy's Legends is a legend itself, drawing world-renowned jazz and blues acts for nightly shows. Since its opening in 1989, the club has hosted Otis Rush, The Rolling Stones, Eric Clapton, Willie Dixon, Stevie Ray Vaughan, and David Bowie, just to name a few of the many famous performers. Buddy Guy himself performs from time to time; his Grammys are on display, along with a pair of Muhammad Ali's gloves, one of Eric Clapton's guitars, and a scarf from Jimi Hendrix. Photos and records adorn the walls, many of which were autographed by their artists.

The full-bar serves affordable drinks at tables near the stage and there's a menu of New Orleans-style Cajun food, like po' boys and gumbo. This is one of the best live music spots in the city, with plenty of space for dancing. Buy tickets online for big shows, or show up at the door.

Map 1: 700 S. Wabash Ave., 312/427-1190, www.buddyguy.com; Mon.-Tues. 5pm-2am, Wed.-Fri. 11am-2am, Sat.-Sun. noon-2am

Buddy Guy's Legends

Chicago winters are brutal. In January, the average temperature is 21°F, but close to Lake Michigan, strong, biting winds bring a windchill effect that can dip temps below zero. Chicagoans don't let the cold get to them; they warm themselves at bars with fireplaces, enjoy leisurely dinners in cozy restaurants, and dance in River North nightclubs until they sweat. Of course, they also pile on the winter gear.

So, how can *you* survive Chicago in winter? First, layer up: Wool socks, down jackets, waterproof boots, and bulky scarves are key. Ladies can trade high heels for stylish boots, buy a pair of fleece-lined leggings, and shop for a wool scarf. Bring a heavy winter coat, and then leave it at coat check.

For a cozy place to sip a cocktail and wait out a snowfall, try **The Violet Hour** (page 123), **Scofflaw** (page 123), or **RM Champagne Salon** (page 114). Each features a fireplace or offers warm winter beverages to ward off the cold.

Near North and Navy Pier

Map 2

BEERCADE

Headquarters Beercade

Sip craft cocktails and local beer while playing your favorite vintage arcade games like pinball and Pac-Man at Headquarters, a local favorite for happy hour and weekend day drinking. The best part? All games are free to play! The kitchen is open late and serves burgers, big salads, wings, and other bar food. Come in, relax, and go back to your childhood (but with alcohol) at one of the first beercades in the country.

Map 2: 213 W. Institute Pl., 312-291-8735, www.hqbeercade.com; 5pm-2am Mon.-Thurs., 3pm-2am Fri., 11am-3am Sat., 11am-2am Sun.

COCKTAIL BARS

✪ Green River

The outdoor terrace at Green River is one of the best in the city and reason enough to visit. But the food and drinks inspired by the Irish Americans who make Chicago the city it is today are the reason to stay. Cocktails hint at flavors like rye and molasses, while salt cod fritters and saffron spaghetti highlight the bar menu. If the patio is closed, the marble booths and long bar in the modern interior make almost as pretty a setting.

Map 2: 259 E. Erie St., 312-337-0101, www.greenriverchi.com; 11:30am-10pm Mon.-Wed., 11:30am-11pm Thurs.-Fri., 11am-3pm and 5pm-11pm Sat., 11am-3pm Sun.

Pops for Champagne

The champagne list at Pops is unrivaled and—with around 250 selections—heralded as the best in the country. Pair a glass of bubbly with a selection of small plates or opt instead for a delicious champagne cocktail. At night, the sleek bar turns clubby.

Map 2: 601 N. State St., 312-266-7677, www.popsforchampagne.com; 3pm-2am Mon.-Fri., 1pm-2am Sat.

Three Dots and a Dash

This tiki bar from Chicago cocktail king Paul McGee is raucous, with a fun mix of island tunes and pop songs, and serves festive well-made drinks. The fun menu describes tiki staples like the mai tai and includes the inspiration behind each cocktail. Large drinks like the Treasure Chest and the Diver Down serve up to eight people and are a hit with groups and bachelorette parties. A small appetizer menu extends the tropical theme with offerings like coconut shrimp and crab Rangoon. Make a reservation or prepare to wait in line. Map 2: 435 N. Clark St., 312/610-4220, www.threedotschicago.com; 5pm-2am Mon.-Fri., 5pm-3am Sat.

SPORTS BARS
Green Door Tavern

This historic tavern opened just after the Great Chicago Fire, and has been a local favorite ever since for its vintage feel, great burgers and pub food, and strong beer selection. Just after the bar was built the city passed an ordinance banning wooden commercial buildings, so it's one of the only remaining wooden bars or restaurants around. Upstairs is fun for happy hour

or dinner, but if you're feeling swanky, head down to the small door across from the bathrooms. Here you'll find a dimly lit speakeasy, though you might have to wait in line.

Map 2: 678 N. Orleans St., 312/664-5496, www.greendoorchicago.com; 11:30am-2am Mon.-Fri., 10am-3am Sat., 10am-midnight Sun.

LIVE MUSIC
Andy's Jazz Club

This well-established club opened in 1951 and still hosts Chicago's famed jazz artists on a nightly basis. The intimate setting offers a chance to watch some of the top jazz performers in the world; Franz Jackson, Joey DeFrancesco, Eddie Johnson, and Marcus Roberts have all played here. While Andy's colored lighting, vintage signs, and wooden beams evoke an older era, most performers are younger musicians who seek to promote jazz. There is an admission fee

Andy's Jazz Club

and a two-hour seating limit. Guests under 21 can attend 5pm and 7pm shows, but later shows are 21 and over. The club's casual restaurant serves steak, chicken, pasta, and salads.

Map 2: 11 E. Hubbard St., 312/642-6805, www.andysjazzclub.com; hours vary; $10-15

Untitled

This large speakeasy bar and restaurant changes with each room. Drink Prohibition-era cocktails within the dark wood and intimate candlelight of the Whiskey Library. Dine on Michelin-recommended charcuterie boards, salads, steak, and seafood in the Champagne Room. Then move Backstage to listen to live jazz and blues nightly. Request a VIP table and order bottle service—brought out on steamer trunks.

Map 2: 111 W. Kinzie St., 312/880-1511, www.untitledsupperclub.com; 4:30pm-1am Tues.-Wed., 4:30pm-2am Thurs.-Fri., 4:30pm-3am Sat.

DANCE CLUBS

Sound Bar

This upscale nightclub never feels pretentious and is always a safe bet for a fun night. Local and visiting DJs pack the 4,000-foot dance floor, and the huge space is filled with flat-screen monitors, laser lights, and floor-to-ceiling video projection. With nine bars, ordering a drink is never an issue, and there are several lounges for a quieter retreat. Reserve a table online for faster entry and dress to impress.

Map 2: 226 W. Ontario St., 312/787-4480, www.sound-bar.com; 10pm-4am Thurs.-Fri., 10pm-5am Sat.

Spy Bar

This grungy basement club blasts electronic music from resident and visiting DJs. The large dance floor is the draw. If you love techno and want to get your dance on without any pressure—or dressing up much—Spy Bar is your spot. There's a seating area and basic cocktails when you need a break.

Map 2: 646 N. Franklin St., 312/337-2191, www.spybarchicago.com; 10pm-4am Tues.-Fri., 10pm-5am Sat.

✪ Studio Paris Nightclub

Dance alongside local and international celebrities at one of the hottest spots in the city. Big-name DJs like Calvin Harris and Tiesto spin here, while nightly performances bring incredible audio and sound experiences. Neon lights, large windows, and a glass ceiling give the one-room club a spacious feel. For a big night out, opt for bottle service at one of the large couches; you'll feel like you're in an exclusive lounge on the other side of the world. Expect to wait in line— but not before 11pm, when it will be dead inside.

Map 2: 59 W. Hubbard St., 312/377-9944, www.studioparisnightclub.com; 9pm-2am Wed.-Fri., 9pm-3am Sat.

The Underground

Multiple rooms and pulsing sounds make The Underground a favorite with late-night dance crowds. Head to the lounge, full of leather couches and dark brick walls, for a more relaxed night, or stay in the club's larger room to enjoy the flashing, colored lights and gyrating dancers on stage. Order champagne, wine, or cocktails, or opt for bottle service—a popular choice. This is the place to go after other venues have closed; be prepared to wait in line.

Map 2: 56 W. Illinois St., 312/644-7600, www.theundergroundchicago.com; 10pm-4am Wed.-Fri. and Sun, 10pm-5am Sat.

COCKTAIL BARS

✪ The Aviary

The Aviary isn't a cocktail bar—it's an experience. Watch as bartenders (called chefs) mix drinks in a lab, layering alcohols and experimenting in liquid density, building elaborate ships in a bottle, and inventing cocktails that change color as you sip. Book your experience online and choose from a table for two to a full tasting menu of seven cocktails. Walk-in seating is available, but there may be a line.

Map 3: 955 W. Fulton Market, 312/226-0868, www.theaviary.tocktix. com; 5pm-midnight Sun.-Wed., 5pm-2am Thurs.-Fri., 5pm-3am Sat.

CH Distillery

CH Distillery focuses on vodka. If that sounds bland, it's only because you haven't tried it yet—ice cold with rye bread and cornichons on the side. The distillery also makes gin, rum, and a variety of infused spirits that can be sampled in the modern tasting room. Try the Baron Takes Tea (Earl Grey-infused gin with lemon, simple syrup, egg white, and soda) and order a few plates to nibble on while you sip.

Map 3: 564 W. Randolph St., 312/707-8780, www.chdistillery.com; 4pm-10pm Tues.-Thurs., 4pm-11pm Fri., 5pm-11pm Sat.

G&O

This former gas station-turned-lounge is laid-back and intimate, with delicious cocktails made using in-house liquor infusions and a local craft beer list with something for everyone. The small bar becomes spacious in summer, when the garage doors slide open onto the patio. A bar menu includes burgers and short ribs, but it's best to focus on the drinks and cool atmosphere.

Map 3: 459 N. Ogden Ave., 312/888-3367, www.grandandogden.com; 4pm-midnight Mon.-Wed., 4pm-2am Thurs., 4pm-3am Fri.-Sat., 10am-midnight Sun.

RM Champagne Salon

Whisk yourself away to France at this classy champagne bar decorated with exposed brick, hanging lanterns, and cherry wood accents. French bistro fare complements the wide variety of sparkling wines, champagne, and cocktails. The bar is tucked away in an alley, adding to its charm.

Map 3: 116 N. Green St., 312/243-1199, www.rmchampagnesalon.com; 5pm-midnight Mon.-Thurs., 5pm-2am Fri.-Sat., 5pm-11pm Sun.

CRAFT BEER

The Aberdeen Tap

This friendly bar makes everyone feel at home, whether they're from the neighborhood or visiting for the weekend. Inside, the mahogany accents and dark lighting add a cozy vibe in which to enjoy the large and rotating list of up to 65 beers from around the world. Bar food with a twist includes mac-and-cheese squares and tasty open-faced sandwiches with duck confit.

Map 3: 440 N. Aberdeen St., 312/929-3845, www.theaberdeentap.com; 11am-2am daily

Five Star Bar

If you like rock and roll, bourbon, and beer, you'll love Five Star Bar. The rock theme is prominent throughout—from vintage tattoo posters to a rock-and-roll playlist to weekend DJs. Nurse one of more than 30 bourbons at the large L-shaped bar or nestled into a plush booth. If you get hungry, order tempura chicken fingers or a sandwich. In warm months, the windows slide open and seating spills onto the sidewalk.

Map 3: 1424 W. Chicago Ave., 312/850-2555, www.fivestarbar.com; 4pm-2am daily

Haymarket Brewery

This old-school brewpub serves a rotating selection of drafts within view of its fermentation room. Bartenders and servers can walk you through the beer list; while Haymarket doesn't offer flights, the small sizes mean you can try a few. It's a popular place to grab a drink and wait for your turn at Au Cheval across the street. Or make a meal of the shareable appetizers (sausage plates and wings), hearty burgers, and sandwiches.

Map 3: 737 W. Randolph St., 312/638-0700, www.haymarketbrewing.com; 11am-2am daily

SPORTS BARS
Lone Wolf Tavern

This neighborhood tavern serves craft beers, classic cocktails, and a limited menu of gourmet hot dogs and fries in a simple brick and wood setting with giant leather booths. Try the popular Rosemary Sling or choose from the hand-selected bourbon list, which is always a hit. The beer selection is an interesting mix that is heavy on local brews. Lone Wolf Tavern isn't fancy, but for a good bar full of locals and a

great beer or a perfectly mixed drink, it's the place to go.

Map 3: 806 W. Randolph St., 312/600-9391, www.lonewolftavern.com; 4pm-2am Mon.-Fri., noon-3am Sat., noon-2am Sun.

Richard's Bar

Richard's Bar has been a dive bar since the Rat Pack days. Memorabilia from that era decorates the walls, right alongside a retro jukebox and a pay phone. Richard's is one of the cheapest bars in Chicago, stocked with everything from PBR to top-shelf liquor. It's not nice or especially clean, but it's unpretentious and a lot of fun. The downside: Some patrons here disregard Chicago's smoking ban.

Map 3: 491 N. Milwaukee Ave., 312/733-2251, Mon.-Fri. 7am-2am, Sat. 9am-2am, Sun. noon-2am

WINE BARS
City Winery

This winery is best in summer, when patrons spill out onto the Riverwalk with wineglasses in hand to take over the bar tables and sit on the steps by the water. Order at the counter and sip away while watching water taxis cruise by. Inside, you'll find live music and Mediterranean food. The building has great acoustics, so if you're seeing a specific show, you won't be disappointed. But if you're just hoping to relax with a glass of wine, outdoors is where this place shines.

Map 3: 1200 W. Randolph St., 312/773-9463, www.citywinery.com/chicago; 11am-9pm daily

Lincoln Park, Old Town, and Gold Coast

Map 4

BARS
Marge's Still

It's fitting that the oldest pub in Chicago is in Old Town, and Marge's Still maintains the same relaxed neighborhood feel it's always had. The antique aesthetic and quiet atmosphere offer a welcome change from other neighborhood bars, while the comfortable, family-friendly vibe includes a large menu of American food.
Map 4: 1758 N. Sedgwick St., 312/664-9775, www.margeschicago. com; 4:30pm-2am Mon.-Fri., 11:30am-2am Sat.-Sun.

COCKTAIL BARS
Barrelhouse Flat

Barrelhouse Flat gives off the vibe of an old-fashioned bar, with lots of warm wood interior, a fireplace, chandeliers, and a pool table. Come for the classic cocktails and stay for the better-than-average bar food.
Map 4: 2624 N. Lincoln Ave., 773/857-0421, www.barrelhouseflat.com; 6pm-2am Sun.-Wed., 6pm-4am Thurs.-Fri., 6pm-5am Sat.

The J. Parker

The J. Parker is the swanky rooftop bar of the Hotel Lincoln. Lounge on outdoor couches and sip classic cocktails while enjoying some of the best views of the Chicago skyline and the lake. At night, DJs and dancing liven things up.
Map 4: 1816 N. Clark St., 312/254-4747, www.thejparkerchicago.com; 5pm-2am Mon.-Thurs., 3pm-2am Fri., 11:30am-2am Sat.-Sun.

Luxbar

This bar and restaurant was inspired by the American Bar in Vienna, an architectural beauty of stone, brass, deep wood, and natural light. The simple and elegant menu is full of fresh, seasonal foods and specialty cocktails. Brunch is a favorite among those in the area, as is the outdoor patio.
Map 4: 18 E Bellevue Pl., 312/642-3400, www.luxbar.com; 11am-2am Mon.-Fri., 8am-3am Sat., 8am-midnight Sun.

Sparrow

This 1930s-style rum-heavy cocktail bar is reminiscent of grand hotel bars of another era. Imagine you're in Havana while sipping a Cuban-inspired cocktail like La Floridita or Hotel Nacional. Housed in an art deco building, this intimate bar is popular among locals, but is undiscovered by tourists.

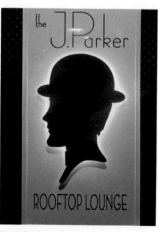

The J. Parker

Map 4: 12 W Elm St., 312/725-0732, www.sparrowchicago.com; 4pm-2am Sun.-Fri., 4pm-3am Sat.

CRAFT BEER
Local Option

The exterior may look punk, but the interior does not. Ignore the design and come for the beer, which includes a large tap selection of mostly local brews as well as a few of their own. The bar menu features decent Cajun food.

Map 4: 1102 W. Webster Ave., 773/348-2008, www.localoptionbier.com; noon-2am Sun.-Fri., noon-3am Sat.

SPORTS BARS
Dublin's

This casual Irish pub is open late and gets more crowded as the surrounding bars close. Locals will tell you to come for the cheap drinks, the fried bar food, the spacious patio, and the friendly bartenders. Come ready to talk to everyone around you and stay for some good people-watching around 4am.

Map 4: 1050 N. State St., 312/266-6340; 11am-4am Sun.-Fri., 11am-5am Sat.

Old Town Ale House

This cash-only bar is one of Chicago's favorite dive spots, mainly for its proximity to Second City and the cast's inclination to hang out here after shows. The interior resembles a pub from decades past and is decorated with random paintings. It's packed on weekends, and loud, but that's what makes it so fun.

Map 4: 219 W. North Ave., 312/944-7020, www.theoldtownalehouse.com; 3pm-4am Mon.-Fri., noon-5am Sat., noon-4am Sun.

Old Town Social

Old Town Social is primarily a bar, but one that happens to serve great bar food. In addition to craft beer and cocktails, the gourmet pub fare includes a fried chicken sandwich and a charcuterie board. There are 23 TVs throughout the bar, showing all the big games of the day.

Map 4: 455 W. North Ave., 312/266-2277, www.oldtownsocial.com; 5pm-2am Mon.-Fri., 11am-3am Sat., 11am-2am Sun.

COMEDY CLUBS
iO Theater

iO is next to Second City when it comes to great improv comedy in Chicago, and also famous alumni. The theater has four stages: two for cabaret and two for a mix of weekly mainstays, sketch shows, and improv. There's always a show going on, so check the schedule online and look at all the stages. The bar is big (as is the beer garden, open in the summer), and a good spot to drink before a show or to hang out after and mingle with performers. iO isn't known for food, but the bar menu, with empanadas, dips, and other snacks, isn't bad.

Map 4: 1501 N. Kingsbury St., 312/929-2401, www.ioimprov.com; 11am-2am Sun.-Fri., 11am-3am Sat.

TOP EXPERIENCE

✪ Second City

This famous theater and improv school began in Chicago. *Saturday Night Live* legends Chris Farley and Tina Fey and comedy kings Steve Carell and Stephen Colbert have all graced its stage. Shows are still hosted nightly on the main stage and in the UP Comedy Club; the sketch shows are particularly popular. Book tickets online in advance and catch the next great comedians before they're famous.

SECOND CITY

Since it opened in 1959, Second City has been the place for improv in Chicago. Founder Viola Spolin taught innovative techniques that were later used as foundations for improvisational comedy. She started the theater as a place to showcase material created through these methods. From its founding, skits had a satirical bent and focused on current events, something that is still true today. The slew of *Saturday Night Live* stars and famous alumni include Bill Murray, Chris Farley, Steve Carell, Stephen Colbert, Mike Myers, Tina Fey, Rachel Dratch, and Amy Sedaris. Catch a show at Second City in Old Town, a few blocks from the original location, and you just might see the next big star.

Map 4: 1616 N. Wells St., 312/337-3992, www.secondcity.com; showtimes vary

Map 4: 940 W. Weed St., 312/337-3486, www.joesbar.com; hours vary

LIVE MUSIC

The Hideout

What began as a working-class bar in the 1930s is today a small music venue with a big history and a reputation for being *the* place to see a show—any show. The tiny old house is decorated with twinkle lights; fans fill the rows of folding chairs in front of the stage to watch performers like The White Stripes, Billy Corgan, Jeff Tweedy, as well as an eclectic variety of blues, punk, open mike, and works in progress. The wooden bar is well stocked, and bands often engage with the crowd. Get there early to stake out a spot.

Map 4: 1354 W. Wabansia Ave., 773/227-4433, www.hideoutchicago.com

Joe's On Weed St.

The huge stage and large dance floor make this bar and music venue a cool place to see a show. Simple Remedy, Sunfallen, and Blackened (Chicago's Metallica cover band) play here often. A mix of country acts and cover bands also take the stage, and there are occasional parties. Take the L train to get here, as valet parking is expensive and street parking is limited.

Kingston Mines

With two stages and music almost every night, this has been one of the city's most popular blues clubs since 1968. Koko Taylor, Magic Slim, and Carl Weathersby have all performed here, while famous musicians like Ronnie Hicks and Mike Wheeler still play regularly. It's always busy, but the spacious place includes plenty of tables with room to dance or hang by the bar.

Map 4: 2548 N. Halsted St., 773/477-4646, www.kingstonmines.com; 7:30pm-4am Mon.-Thurs., 7pm-4am Fri., 7pm-5am Sat., 6pm-4am Sun.; $12-15 cover

Lincoln Hall

Lincoln Hall books well-known and up-and-coming bands almost every night of the week on the main floor and balcony stage. Dave Matthews and Modest Mouse played here when they were first starting out; Parachute and Bastille have played more recently. Multiple bars mean you don't have to wait long for a drink, and food is also served. Tickets are inexpensive, but often sell out—buy them online.

Map 4: 2424 N. Lincoln Ave., 773/525-2501, www.lh-st.com; hours vary

Lakeview and Wrigleyville Map 5

SPORTS BARS

The Cubby Bear

Situated across from Wrigley Field, The Cubby Bear is packed with Cubs fans before, during, and after every home game. Fortunately, the huge place can fit most everyone, and the staff is adept at pouring quickly. Drinks are expensive, but you're paying for proximity to Cubs fandom. Try to visit during baseball season for an experience you won't have anywhere else in Chicago.

Map 5: 1059 W. Addison St., 773/327-1662, www.cubbybear.com; 11am-2am Wed.-Fri. and Sun, 11am-3am Sat.

The Gingerman Tavern

This tavern, though right next to Wrigley Field, is more old-school dive bar than crazy sports bar. With a conversational staff, an eclectic crowd, and a diverse jukebox, you can while away hours sipping craft beer and playing pool or board games. On weekends, be prepared for an impromptu dance party. Cash only.

Map 5: 3740 N. Clark St., 773/549-2050; 3pm-2am Mon.-Fri., noon-3am Sat., noon-2am-Sun.

Guthrie's Tavern

Step into Guthrie's Tavern and you'll be transported into a small-town neighborhood dive bar, complete with red-and-white-checkered tables and bookshelves stocked with board games. The bar serves beer, mixed drinks, and a very limited food menu. Hungry patrons can order delivery from one of the many nearby restaurants; menus are on hand.

Map 5: 1300 W. Addison St., 773/477-2900, www.guthriestavern.com; 5pm-2am Mon.-Fri., 2pm-3am Sat., 2pm-1am Sun.

✪ Sluggers

Sluggers is the ultimate sports bar with dozens of TVs, batting cages, a beer garden, arcade games, and dueling pianos all steps from Wrigley Field. It's incredibly popular and often crowded, but if you want to be in the midst of Cubs fan action, this is the place.

Map 5: 3540 N. Clark St., 773/248-0055, www.sluggersbar.com; 3pm-2am Mon.-Thurs., 11am-2am Fri. and Sun., 11am-3am Sat.

Southport Lanes

This vintage bowling alley has a large craft beer selection and a fascinating history. Originally built by Schlitz Brewery to house beer, the building later became a speakeasy and then a brothel during Prohibition. Today, the place has an old-timey feel with four bowling lanes, billiards, and pool, as well as some of Southport's best bar food.

Map 5: 3325 N. Southport Ave., 773/472-6600, www.southportlanes.com; 4pm-2am Mon.-Thurs., noon-2am Fri., noon-3am Sat., 11:30am-1am Sun.

LIVE MUSIC

Martyr's

This small live music venue is a popular spot to take in international acts and jam bands. Local rock groups and cover bands like Tributosaurus play regularly, drawing a crowd in their 40s and 50s. The space is intimate and the drink service fast, though the food menu leaves something to be desired.

Eat beforehand so you can stay and dance at Martyr's all night.

Map 5: 3855 N Lincoln Ave, 773/404-9494, www.martyrslive.com; hours vary

Schubas Tavern

Schubas Tavern sits in a historic, neo-Gothic building that was once part of Schlitz Brewery (now a Chicago Historic Landmark). Orange brick and terra-cotta patterns grace the exterior facade, while inside you'll find a beautiful mahogany bar and tin roof. The tavern serves affordable beer and has nightly music acts ranging from indie to mariachi.

Map 5: 3159 N. Southport, 773/525-2508, www.lh-st.com; hours vary

The Vic Theatre

The Vic is often home to Lollapalooza after-parties and shows. This five-story former vaudeville house still retains luxurious details like an Italian marble staircase and a lobby with sculptures and paintings throughout. Bands such as Feist and Old Crow Medicine Show have played here, as do plenty of local talent. The balcony seats offer great views. Check the calendar website for details; tickets are available at www.ticketfly.com.

Map 5: 3145 N. Sheffield Ave., 773/472-0449, www.victheatre.com; hours vary

DANCE CLUBS
Berlin

Berlin is Lakeview's most clubby bar, drawing crowds of all kinds for late-night dancing to a wide range of music—electronic, pop, '80s, and everything in between. Ignore the strip-mall exterior and head inside the dark, cave-like club, lit only by a few purple lights. The crowd picks up after midnight, and the bar is cash only.

Map 5: 954 W. Belmont Ave., 773/348-4975, www.berlinchicago.com; 10pm-4am Sun.-Tues., 5pm-4am Wed.-Fri., 5pm-5am Sat.

✪ The Holiday Club

The Holiday Club has a split personality: The casual bar in front serves food and cheap beer, while the dance club parties in back. Come on Friday for '80s night or on Saturday for '90s tunes, and dance the night away to music videos of decades past. The unpretentious vibe means there's no need to dress up to have fun.

Map 5: Uptown, 4000 N. Sheridan Rd., 773/348-9600, www.holidayclubchicago.com; 6pm-2am Sun.-Fri., 6pm-3am Sat.

Smart Bar

The Smart Bar is all about techno dance music and brings in famous DJs from around the world to spin each night until the early morning hours. The online calendar lists free events and specials, such as $1 Dollar Disco Sundays. Tickets are required and must be booked online.

Map 5: 3730 N. Clark St., 773/549-0203, www.smartbarchicago.com; 10pm-4am Sun. and Thurs.-Fri, 10pm-5am Sat.; $10 tickets

GAY AND LESBIAN
D.S. Tequila Company

In the heart of Boystown, D.S. Tequila Company specializes in Tex Mex cuisine and margaritas. The mood is fun and a bit raucous, especially when a DJ sets up later in the evening. Patrons must be age 21 and over.

Map 5: 3352 N. Halsted St., 773/697-9127, www.dstequila.com; 11am-midnight Sun.-Wed., 11am-2am Thurs.-Fri., 11am-3am Sat.

Boystown, an area in east Lakeview, just south of Wrigleyville, is home to one of the largest lesbian, gay, bisexual, and transgender communities in the country. In 1998, Mayor Richard M. Daley commissioned bronze statues that marked Boystown as the first officially designated gay neighborhood in the United States. (The move drew both criticism and acclaim from different groups across the country.) In 2014, Boystown was voted the "World's Most Incomparable Gay Neighborhood" by readers of *Out Traveler*. **Halsted Street** and **Broadway** are the main crossroads: More than 30 gay and lesbian bars, nightclubs, and restaurants line these blocks north to south.

There's always a party in Boystown, whether it's dancing at **Roscoe's** or **Sidetrack** or shopping at one of the eclectic (and delightfully inappropriate) boutiques. The **Chicago Pride Parade** and **Northhalsted Market Days** are both held here in the summer and draw more than one million visitors. Can't make it in the summer? The neighborhood goes all out for Halloween, too.

Kit Kat Lounge

The Kit Kat Lounge offers a little bit of Hollywood glamour in Lakeview. The cocktail list features 200 martinis and specialty drinks, plus entrées named after classic starlets such as Elizabeth Taylor (fish-and-chips) and Lauren Bacall (ravioli). The nightly drag shows by the Kit Kat Divas are a real highlight.

Map 5: 3700 N. Halsted St., 773/525-1111, www.kitkatchicago.com; 5:30pm-2am daily

Roscoe's

Roscoe's is the place to go in Boystown if you're looking for dancing *and* karaoke. The extremely popular LGBTQ club plays dance music nightly and gets packed quickly on weekends, with crowds spilling onto the patio in summer months. Order a $15 Long Island pitcher and let go of your inhibitions.

Map 5: 3356 N. Halsted St., 773/281-3355, www.roscoes.com; 5pm-2am Mon.-Fri., 2pm-3am Sat., 2pm-2am Sun.

Sidetrack

This popular gay and lesbian bar is spacious, with multiple levels for dancing or chatting with friends. The patio fills quickly in the summer when the neighborhood flocks to Sidetrack for its alcoholic slushies.

Map 5: 3349 N. Halsted St., 773/477-9189, www.sidetrackchicago.com; 3pm-2am Mon.-Fri., 1pm-3am Sat., 1pm-2am Sun.

COMEDY CLUBS

The Annoyance Theater & Bar

Chicago is improv city. While The Annoyance may be the smallest of its improv theaters, it's no surprise that you'll still walk away laughing. The Annoyance performers aren't afraid to experiment at this small venue and the owner often lets students (classes are available) perform. The types of shows vary; check the schedule ahead of time. The bar serves basic, but reasonably priced drinks. Guests age 14 and older are welcome.

Map 5: 851 W. Belmont Ave., 773/697-9693, www.theannoyance.com; hours vary

Laugh Factory

Since opening in 1979, the Chicago Laugh Factory has hosted big names like Jerry Seinfeld, Robin Williams, and Chris Rock and constantly tests new talent through open mike nights. Stand-up, improv, and recurring shows fill almost every night of the week; check the online calendar to see what's on. A two-drink minimum is enforced during most shows.

Map 5: 3175 N. Broadway St.,
773/327-3175, www.laughfactory.com;
hours vary

the Laugh Factory

Public House Theatre

If you like drinking and you like comedy, you'll like the Public House Theatre, home to the long-running *Bye Bye Liver: The Chicago Drinking Play*. Through a series of sketches, the show makes fun of all those times you've done something idiotic while drinking—all while getting you drunk through hilarious social games. The no-frills venue serves cheap beer and mixed drinks, making it easy to participate. Of the two theaters in the venue, the smaller stage features up-and-coming sketch groups and one-off scripted shows; it's a great place to see new comedy in the city. Attendees must be age 21 and older.

Map 5: 3914 N. Clark St., 312/265-1240,
www.publichousechicago.com;
7pm-midnight Tues.-Sun.

KARAOKE
❂ Trader Todd's

This dive bar is famous for its karaoke, held in the front and back bars every night of the week. A menu of tiki drinks offers liquid courage, and the bar food shares this tropical twist with items like mango chutney wings and conch fritters.

Map 5: 3216 N Sheffield Ave.,
773/348-3250, www.tradertodd.com;
4pm-2am Mon.-Fri., 9am-2am Sat.,
9am-midnight Sun.

Wicker Park and Bucktown

Map 6

COCKTAIL BARS
Billy Sunday

Don't let the polished wood and high-backed stools at Billy Sunday fool you: This bar isn't a hangout for whiskey drinkers. Instead, expect craft cocktails made with rose bitters, fruit, and house-made tonics. Mulled white wine, saffron, ginger, carob, cognac, and baking spices come together in one cocktail, while another fuses sparkling white wine, rum, cognac, raspberry, and pineapple with hand-cut ice. Bar snacks like fried pig ears and duck confit soak up the sweetness.

Map 6: 3143 W. Logan Blvd., 773/661-2485,
www.billy-sunday.com; 5pm-2am Mon.-Fri.,
3pm-3am Sat., 3pm-2am Sun.

Heavy Feather

From the owners of Scofflaw and Lost Lake comes Heavy Feather, a kitschy-yet-classy 1970s fern bar serving excellent sweet drinks. Settle into a rolling armchair in the dimly lit room and admire the peacock-print wallpaper and throwback atmosphere while sipping an amaretto sour, made with bourbon and egg white or the plum gin fizz with gin liqueur, cynar, lemon, and egg white. Enter through Lost Lake and head upstairs.

Map 6: 2357 N. Milwaukee Ave., 773/799-8504, www.heavyfeatherchicago. com; 7pm-1:30am Mon.-Sat., 7pm-midnight Sun.

Lost Lake

This tropical tiki bar is fun, exotic, and elegant all at once. Inside, the banana-leaf wallpaper and tiki decor will instantly transport you to a glamorous, tropical escape. Sip award-winning cocktails made with aged Jamaican and Trinidadian rum, tequila, tamarind shrub, coconut, and other tropical ingredients.

Map 6: 3154 W. Diversey Ave., 773/293-6048, www.lostlaketiki.com; 4pm-2am daily

Mezcaleria Las Flores

At Mezcaleria Las Flores, you'll get an education with your cocktail. The bartenders can walk you through their extensive mescal selection and explain what makes each one different. Sip one alone, or in a signature cocktail like the Bridges Not Walls, made with *banhez* mescal, ancho chile, strawberry, Thai basil, lime, and salt. The bar is small, but the bright blue walls and hanging plants make it feel spacious and welcoming.

Map 6: 3149 W. Logan Blvd., 773/278-2215, www.mezcalerialasflores.com; 5pm-2am daily

Scofflaw

This dimly lit, rustic bar focuses on gin cocktails. Settle into plush, baroque armchairs amid the exposed brick walls and sip thoughtfully made seasonal cocktails served in funky glassware. While gin is the star, craft beers and other spirits make an appearance as well. Scofflaw also serves affordable small plates; the *guapichosa* is a local favorite.

Map 6: 3201 W. Armitage Ave., 773/252-9700, www.scofflawchicago. com; 5pm-2am Mon.-Fri., 11am-3am Sat., 11am-2am Sun.

✪ The Violet Hour

This James Beard Award-winning cocktail bar serves pre-Prohibition drinks in a swanky setting behind an unmarked door right across the street from the popular Big Star. Find the entryway (a large black door that blends in with the wall) and inside are revealed small white tables, high-backed leather chairs, and dimly lit crystal chandeliers. The elegant interior is matched by expertly mixed cocktails that play off classics like an old-fashioned and the Sazerac, as well as the bar's own creations. Reservations are not accepted and there's often a wait; visit on a weeknight to ensure a quicker entry.

Map 6: 1520 N Damen Ave., 773/252-1500, www.theviolethour.com; 6pm-2am daily

CRAFT BEER
Map Room

This casual corner bar is filled with map paraphernalia—from wallpaper to framed posters to country flags that hang from the ceiling. In addition to more than 200 craft and imported beers from around the world, Map Room serves coffee in the morning and wine and cider at night. You'll often find folks playing cards or reading from the great selection of travel books on hand.

Map 6: 1949 N Hoyne Ave., 773/252-7636, www.maproom.com; 6:30am-2am Mon.-Fri., 7:30am-3am Sat., 11am-2am Sun.

Revolution Brewing

Settle in at the mahogany bar in this German-style beer hall for samplers, pints, and growlers of rotating craft beers. The brewery, one of the largest in Illinois, also offers tours. Bar food includes pizzas, burgers, and salad, but the beer is where they shine.

Map 6: 2323 N Milwaukee Ave., 773/227-2739, www.revbrew.com; 11am-1am Mon.-Fri., 10am-1am Sat., 10am-11pm Sun.

DANCE CLUBS
Evil Olive

Evil Olive hosts late-night dance parties featuring EDM music and local DJs when the edgy club is aglow with colored lights and stenciled walls and packed with young hipsters. If you get tired of dancing, lounge in one of the U-shaped booths, play a game of pool, or goof around in the photo booth. The club is especially popular on Monday, when it hosts Porn and Chicken night, when chicken is served while porn is broadcast on giant screens.

Map 6: 1551 W. Division St., 773/396-4904; 11pm-4am Tues. and Thurs.-Sat.

Hyde Park

Map 7

BARS
The Cove Lounge

The Cove Lounge is Hyde Park's local bar with cheap beer, basic drinks, music on the jukebox, and regulars playing darts. It's nothing fancy, but it's the place to be if you want to feel like a Chicagoan. Inside, check out the giant wall mural of Hyde Park, which features a smiling Barack Obama who is beloved in the area.

Map 7: 1750 E. 55th St., 773/684-1012, www.thecovelounge.com; 11am-2am daily

Woodlawn Tap

This cash-only dive bar is a popular student hangout spot, which means it's always a good time. Chicago sports play on TVs in the relaxed interior while students have intellectual conversations (at least for the first few beers) over the decent bar food (burgers, fries, and fried food).

Map 7: 1172 E. 55th St., 773/643-5516; 10:30am-2am Mon.-Fri., 11am-3am Sat., 11am-2am Sun.

LIVE MUSIC
The Promontory

Come for the food, stay for the music. The Promontory serves hearth-roasted cheese, meat, and fish, as well as large salads and meze in a warm and inviting space of wooden beams and twinkling lights. The second-floor live music venue hosts all kinds of acts, from smooth jazz to DJ dance parties. Both sections host a full bar with craft cocktails, wine, and affordable beers.

Map 7: 5311 S. Lake Park Ave., 312/801-2100, www.promontorychicago. com; 11am-11pm Mon.-Thurs., 11am-1am Fri., 9am-1am Sat., 9am-11pm Sun.

CHICAGO'S HISTORIC JAZZ CLUBS

Chicago played a leading role in the popularization and evolution of jazz. In the early 1900s, the Great Migration drew African Americans from the southern states to the Midwest. Those who came to Chicago settled mostly on the South Side and brought with them a need for music, expression, and entertainment. Jazz performers from New Orleans and the Mississippi Delta—Louis Armstrong, Warren Dodds, Earl Hine, and Jimmy Noone—were some of the big names cutting records for Chicago labels, which gave the city a reputation for authentic jazz recordings.

Listening to live jazz music is a favorite pastime among Chicagoans and a must for music lovers. Two of the most famous and historical spots are The Green Mill and Andy's Jazz Club.

Buddy Guy's Legends

Greater Chicago   Map 8

COCKTAIL BARS
Marty's Martini Bar

For a strong, classic drink, head to Marty's Martini Bar. The small yet swanky lounge features black-and-white tile floors and gold accents that give the place a French vibe. The bartenders are famous here for pouring heavy; order a classic martini, one of the bar's own creations, or opt for a "junior" option (a slightly lighter pour). The place is packed with neighborhood regulars for predinner drinks, then becomes a gay bar late at night.
Map 8: 1511 W. Balmoral Ave., 773/561-6425, www.martysmartinibar.com; 5pm-2am Mon.-Thurs., 4pm-2am Fri., 4pm-3am Sat., 2pm-2am Sun.

SPORTS BARS
Schaller's Pump

Open since 1881, Schaller's Pump is a favorite among White Sox fans and politicians—it's located near the Sox stadium and across the street from the Democratic headquarters. Conversations may get heated and the crowd can get rowdy, but the cheap beer and whiskey and satisfying pub food make this a good spot to watch the game.
Map 8: 3714 S. Halsted St., 773/376-6332; 11am-2am Mon.-Fri., 4pm-3am Sat., 4pm-2am Sun.

LIVE MUSIC
Aragon Ballroom

Built in the 1920s, this Uptown music venue exudes a Moorish style, with a lofty feel to the arched walls and high ceilings. Today, the Aragon Ballroom hosts big acts of all kinds—from indie bands to techno DJs and Top 40 pop stars. It's a cool venue to see a show thanks to its spacious dance floor, ornate balconies, and a ceiling painted to resemble the night sky. Book tickets online.

✪ The Green Mill

The Green Mill is a Chicago icon. Believed to be the oldest continually running jazz club in the United States, the lounge has been home to jazz greats through the decades, including Von Freeman, Kurt Elling, Wilbur Campbell, Eric Alexander, and Orbert Davis. The club still hosts live music nightly. Settle into a booth and admire the walls covered in nostalgic decor—look for Al Capone's favorite booth, rumored to be just off the west end of the bar. The bar is cash only; outside food is permitted.

Map 8: Uptown, 4802 N. Broadway, 773/878-5552, www.greenmilljazz.com; noon-4am Mon.-Fri., noon-5am Sat., 11am-4am Sun.; $4-15 cover

The Riviera Theatre

The Riviera's neon sign and redbrick exterior still look as it did when it was built in 1917. Inside, the former movie theater has been transformed into a concert hall. While the historic element adds charm, it also means the theater is a bit outdated, with basement bathrooms and weak acoustics. Still, The Riviera books solid acts—indie musicians like Conor Oberst, The Cranberries, and Ben Harper have all played here. Stand in front of the stage to watch a show, or head for the balcony seating.

Map 8: 4746 N. Racine Ave., 774/275-6800, www.rivieratheatre.com; hours vary

ARTS AND CULTURE

It would take years to explore all the art and culture Chicago has to offer—from modern art museums to local galleries, public art installations, and a rotating schedule of varied and innovative theater performances. Check out the city's offerings by neighborhood, or simply pick a few highlights to see during your stay.

The Museum of Contemporary Art contains one of the largest modern art collections in the country. Of course, the exhibits don't end there; public art adorns the downtown city streets and parks. Make your way to Daley Plaza to admire *The Picasso* sculpture, then explore the business district to find Calder's *Flamingo*. Millennium Park's *Cloud Gate* and *Crown Fountain* offer a fun, interactive experience for art aficionados of all ages.

The history-making Steppenwolf Theatre still offers innovative productions with ensemble casts, while the PrivateBank Theatre is where to go for musicals like *Hamilton*. Even if you don't have time for a show, it's worth stepping inside the Chicago Cultural Center or the Lyric Opera to admire their

Chicago Theatre

beautiful interiors and to stop for a photo op outside the Chicago Theatre's historic, flashing marquee.

Stroll-worthy stops around the city include browsing the River North's contemporary art galleries, learning about the history of Chicago's Polish, Ukrainian, Swedish, and Mexican immigrants at museums dedicated to their heritage, or simply taking in the latest flick at a historic movie house like the Music Box Theatre.

HIGHLIGHTS

✪ **PRETTIEST PLACE TO SEE A SHOW:** The ornate design and colorful interior of the historic **Oriental Theatre** offers a stunning setting for any production (page 130).

✪ **MOST ACCESSIBLE PUBLIC ART:** Walk through the Loop to gaze at *The Picasso,* one of the artist's largest sculptures (page 132).

✪ **QUICKEST WAY TO FEEL CULTURED:** Challenging, controversial, and exciting, the collection of the **Museum of Contemporary Art** offers a crash course in culture (page 133).

✪ **BEST THEATER:** The **Steppenwolf Theatre** is one of only two Chicago theaters to win a regional Tony for its incredible productions in an intimate setting (page 137).

✪ **BEST LESSON IN THE BLUES:** The stories and history that have passed through **Willie Dixon's Blues Heaven** make it a fun and educational stop in the South Loop (page 140).

Oriental Theatre

The Loop and Museum Campus

Map 1

CULTURAL CENTERS

Chicago Cultural Center

This landmark building is one of the prettiest in the city. Built in 1897, it housed Chicago's first public library before becoming the Cultural Center in 1991. Today, visitors flock to admire the imported marble and Favrile glass mosaics, the beautiful stone staircases, and the Tiffany stained-glass dome (the largest in the world). The center is home to many free exhibits, performances, lectures, and film screenings. **Map 1:** 78 E. Washington St., 312/744-3316, www.cityofchicago.org; 9am-7pm Mon.-Thurs., 9am-6pm Fri.-Sat., 10am-6pm Sun.

Fine Arts Building

Built in 1884, this redbrick building houses some serious history. Inside, you'll find art nouveau murals from the 1900s as well as 10 floors of art, dance, and music studios such as the FAB Second Floor Art Gallery and the PianoForte shop (first floor). While there are no public performances or classes, art lovers will enjoy visiting the open spaces and seeing the artists in action. **Map 1:** 410 S. Michigan Ave., 312/566-9800, www.fineartsbuildingstudios.com; 7am-10pm Mon.-Fri., 7am-9pm Sat., 9am-5pm Sun.

the Tiffany dome in the Chicago Cultural Center

PERFORMING ARTS

✪ Oriental Theatre

Opened in 1926, the Oriental Theatre showed motion pictures and staged vaudeville acts amid its ornate, over-the-top east Asian decor. Today, the beautiful theater hosts pre- and post-Broadway shows (it was home to *Wicked*, the theater's most successful show), concerts, and other events. Check the schedule online to see what's on. Even if you don't see a performance, peek inside the lobby to admire the elaborate architecture and design.

Map 1: 24 W. Randolph St., 312/977-1700, www.oriental.theaterchicago.net; box office hours vary

Chicago Symphony Center

The Chicago Symphony Center is home to the Chicago Symphony Orchestra, which is consistently named one of the world's leading orchestras. The grand building features marble staircases, a classic balcony, and ornate ballrooms. The acoustics are predictably amazing, and the curved structure of the balconies means there's never a bad seat. Classical musicians also perform here throughout the year, including Yo-Yo Ma and Kirill Gerstein. Tickets can be purchased online or at the box office.

Map 1: 220 S. Michigan Ave., 312/294-3000, www.cso.org; box office opens one hour before showtime

Chicago Theatre

The Chicago Theatre is one of the most-photographed buildings in the city for its flashing marquee built in 1921. Part of the Balaban and Katz movie theaters when it first opened, today it hosts post-Broadway plays, musicals, concerts, and comedy shows.

A one-hour behind-the-scenes tour (noon daily, $15 adults, $10 children 12 and under) will take you onstage where you'll learn about the baroque interior and can view a backstage wall autographed by dozens of movie stars.

Map 1: 175 N. State St., 312/462-6300, www.thechicagotheatre.com; box office noon-6pm Mon.-Fri. and one hour before showtime

Goodman Theatre

Opened in 1925, the Goodman Theatre presents contemporary and classic productions that highlight diversity. Notable performances include adaptations of Leonard Bernstein's *Candide*, the Philip Glass opera *Galileo Galilei*, and an annual production of *A Christmas Carol*. The company won a regional Tony Award in 1992, as well as numerous Joseph Jefferson Awards. There's not a bad seat in the small theater. Tickets are available online or at the box office.

Map 1: 170 N. Dearborn St., 312/443-3800, www.goodmantheatre.org; box office open noon-5pm daily

Joffrey Ballet

The Joffrey Ballet established permanent residency in Chicago in 1995. Twyla Tharp, Alvin Ailey, George Balanchine, and many beloved choreographers have worked with the company to perform classic and modern ballets like *The Nutcracker*. The group performs at the Auditorium Theatre in Roosevelt University (Sept.-May). Tickets can be bought online, by phone, or at the Joffrey Tower or Auditorium Theatre box offices. Drop-in ballet classes are offered at Joffrey Tower, where the company rehearses. Class schedules are available online.

Goodman Theatre

Map 1: Joffrey Tower, 10 E. Randolph St., 312/386-8905, www.joffrey.org; Auditorium Theatre, 50 E Congress Pkwy.; box offices open noon-6pm Mon.-Fri.

Lyric Opera

The Lyric Opera of Chicago is one of the most respected opera houses in the country for its devotion to classical opera while bringing in new works and making efforts to promote the arts in the community. The opera performs in Civic Opera House, a limestone skyscraper with a colonnaded portico and large bronze doors. Inside, stenciled ceilings and sparkling chandeliers produce a stunning effect. The curtain depicts a scene from *Aida*, and there are comedy-tragedy masks at the entrances meant to replicate the Paris Opera House. Each season hosts a mix of classic, well-known operas and a few lesser-known shows. Tickets are available online or at the box office. One hour before each show you can join in a free pre-opera talk, where you'll learn about the performance and the theater.

Map 1: 20 N. Upper Wacker Dr., 312/332-2244, www.lyricopera.org; box office hours noon-6pm Mon.-Fri., hours vary Sat.-Sun.

PrivateBank Theatre

The PrivateBank Theatre (originally the Majestic Theatre) opened in 1906 as a venue for vaudeville acts. Today, the Chicago Historic Landmark is home to Broadway productions of *Rent, South Pacific, A Chorus Line, Book of Mormon,* and *Hamilton.* The interior has a grand, opulent feel with gold lights, ornate details, and red seats; however, outdated features include hard seats, a tiny elevator, and obstructed views. Review the seating layout online before booking.

Map 1: 18 W. Monroe St., 312/977-1700, www.broadwayinchicago.com/theatre/the-privatebank-theatre; box office hours vary

ART IN CHICAGO

Flamingo, by Alexander Calder

Public art is plentiful throughout Chicago. The city encourages the placement of sculptures, murals, fountains, and decorative public pieces in order to enhance city buildings and residential spaces. Public art graces many parks, bridges, and exterior walls. More than 500 works of art are found in municipal facilities, like libraries, CTA stations, and police stations.

A few highlights include: *Cloud Gate* and the *Crown Fountain* in Millennium Park; the Buckingham Fountain in Grant Park; the lions outside The Art Institute; and *The Picasso*, the *Flamingo*, and the *Monument With Standing Beast* in the Loop. Statues of generals and presidents line **Lincoln Park,** murals decorate the underpasses at **Oak Street Beach,** and historic Chicago moments are captured in monuments like the **Haymarket Memorial** on the West Side.

Free Tours by Foot (www.freetoursbyfoot.com) offers free walking tours of public artwork in the Loop.

PUBLIC ART

✪ *The Picasso*

When *The Picasso* was unveiled in Daley Plaza in 1967, it was the first major piece of public art in the city. Commissioned by the architects of the Richard J. Daley Center, the abstract, 50-foot-tall steel sculpture was modeled by Picasso, who made a gift of it to the city. Today, people stop to admire the statue on their way to work, visitors line up for photos, and kids climb up and slide down its base.

Map 1: 50 W. Washington St.

Flamingo

One of the most-recognized public art pieces in Chicago, the *Flamingo* is a 53-foot sculpture created in 1974 by artist Alexander Calder and painted the famous "Calder Red." Calder, who pioneered the stable abstract structure art form, was commissioned to create a work to offset the surrounding rectangular buildings. The arching shape combines the natural and the animal and was integrated into the plaza so that viewers could walk through it.

Map 1: 50 W. Adams St.

Near North and Navy Pier

Map 2

ARTS AND CULTURE

NEAR NORTH AND NAVY PIER

MUSEUMS

✪ Museum of Contemporary Art

The Museum of Contemporary Art houses one of the largest modern art collections in the country. The bright, modern building was designed by German architect Josef Paul Kleihues. Inside, permanent collections and rotating exhibits include the works of such well-known iconoclasts as Larry Clark and Chuck Close, as well as theatrical and dance productions. Free tours highlight artists' methods, materials, and ideas.

Map 2: 220 E. Chicago Ave., 312/280-2660, www.mcachicago.org; 10am-9pm Tues. and Fri., 10am-5pm Wed.-Thurs. and Sat.-Sun.; $15 adults, $8 students

Chicago Children's Museum

The enormous Chicago Children's Museum at Navy Pier is filled with exhibits for kids of all ages. The Pritzker Playspace is perfect for babies and toddlers, while older kids can tinker in the Tinkering Lab. Learn about the building structure of the Chicago skyline, drive a CTA bus, get lost in the Treehouse Trails enchanted forest, and get your fill of physical science in the action-packed Zoom Room.

Map 2: Navy Pier, 700 E. Grand Ave., 312/527-1000, www. chicagochildrensmuseum.org; 10am-5pm Mon.-Wed. and Fri.-Sun., 10am-8pm Thurs., $14 adults and children, $13 seniors, children under 1 free

Chicago Children's Museum

Driehaus Museum

For a taste of the Gilded Age, head to the Driehaus Museum. Philanthropist Richard H. Driehaus founded the museum in 2003 to preserve architecture of the past. Today, visitors can stroll through the ornate interiors decorated with marble, carved woods, tiles, and stained glass while viewing original furniture and artwork from designers like George A. Schastey and Louis Comfort Tiffany.

Map 2: 40 E. Erie St., 312/482-8933; www.driehausmuseum.org; Tues.-Sun. 10am-5pm; $20 adults $20, $12.50 seniors, $10 students and children under 12

GALLERIES
RIVER NORTH GALLERY DISTRICT
Catherine Edelman Gallery

This photography gallery is known for showcasing young and emerging artists covering a range of topics—from fashion and street photography to landscape images and socially conscious works. Exhibits include the work of the renowned Sandro Miller, Arno Rafael Minkkinen, Peter Witkin, and Julie Blackmon.

Map 2: 300 W. Superior St., 312/266-2350; www.edelmangallery.com; Tues.-Sat. 10am-5:30pm

ECHT Gallery

For contemporary glass sculpture, head to ECHT Gallery, where the dimly lit, spacious room exhibits beautifully displayed blown glass. Famous glass artists like Dale Chihuly, Scott Chaseling, Chris Ahalt, and Martin Blank have been featured in the rotating collection.

Map 2: 222 W. Superior St., 312/440-0288; www.echtgallery.com; Tues.-Sat. 11am-5pm

PERFORMING ARTS
Chicago Shakespeare Theater

This theater's combination of energetic scenes, incredible actors, and respected directors such as Barbara Gaines make Shakespeare entertaining for everyone. The intimate theater features a thrust stage that extends into the audience with seating on three sides—there's not a bad seat in the house. Tickets are very affordable, and patrons receive discounted parking at Navy Pier.

Map 2: Navy Pier, 800 E. Grand Ave., 312/595-5600, www.chicagoshakes.com; hours and prices vary

Chicago Shakespeare Theater

Lookingglass Theatre

This Tony Award-winning theater at the heart of Michigan Avenue showcases innovative adaptations of original plays like *Moby Dick, The Little Prince,* and *Ethan Frome.* The visually heavy performances are full of elaborate costumes, innovative staging, and a wealth of props. With a small stage and wraparound seats, there's not a bad seat in this intimate venue. Buy tickets online.

Map 2: 821 N. Michigan Ave., 312/337-0665, http://lookingglasstheatre. org; hours vary

MUSEUMS

Polish Museum of America

Opened in 1935, this comprehensive museum details Polish immigration to the United States through artwork and memorabilia. Noble Square, where the Polish Museum of America is located, was once home to the largest Polish population outside of Europe. The Polish Chicago exhibit delves into the history of this community from 1850 to 1939 through photos and artifacts. Other collections include works by notable Polish artists, World War II and postwar posters, and the stunning stained-glass window *Symbol of Poland Reborn* by Mieczysław Jurgielewicz.

Map 3: 984 N Milwaukee Ave., 773/384-3352, www. polishmuseumofamerica.org; 11am-4pm Fri.-Tues., 11am-7pm Wed.; $7 adults, $6 seniors and students

Ukrainian National Museum

Learn the history of Chicago's Ukrainian immigrants through this museum's collection of folk art, instruments, historical documents, and artifacts from the Soviet Union. The small collection is packed with interesting pieces like embroidered clothes, festive dresses, and around 500 paintings and sculptures from Ukrainian artists. A favorite among visitors is the collection of Ukrainian Easter eggs, which are elaborately detailed.

Map 3: 2249 W. Superior Ave., 312/421-8020, www. ukrainiannationalmuseum.org; 11am-4pm Thurs.-Sun., $5 donation

GALLERIES

Mars Gallery

Mars Gallery opened in 1988 as a space for Chicago artists. The three stories of this 19th-century brick loft are packed with contemporary, figurative, pop, and abstract art—some of which hangs from the ceiling. Grab a cocktail from the trendy elevator bar (literally, a bar in an elevator) and head out back to The Vortex, where you can stand in spray-painted "energy vortex circles" for a burst of creativity.

Map 3: 1139 W. Fulton Market, 312/226-7808, www.marsgallery.com; noon-6pm Wed. and Fri., noon-7pm Thurs., 11am-5pm Sat.

Vertical Gallery

This urban art gallery showcases street art, pop culture, graphic design, and graffiti by local and international artists. Though it features big names in current art like Hebru Brantley and Ben Frost, it also hosts exhibits by street artists like Pure Evil and Greg Gossel. The friendly staff can inform you about each piece and the background of the artists.

Map 3: 1016 N. Western Ave., 773/697-3846, www.verticalgallery.com; 11am-6pm Tues.-Sat.

Lincoln Park, Old Town, and Gold Coast

Map 4

MUSEUMS

Chicago History Museum

Visit this museum for a crash course in Chicago history. An ever-changing rotation of modern exhibits examine Chicago's rail history, how the city came to be a transportation hub, and a time when Lincoln called it home. Conveniently located along the #22 Clark bus line and a few blocks from the Sedgwick Brown Line, this small but fascinating place packs in a lot within a quick hour tour.

Map 4: 1601 N. Clark St., 312/642-4600, www.chicagohistory.org; 9:30am-4:30pm Mon.-Sat., noon-5pm Sun.; $16 adults, $14 students and seniors, children under 12 free

Peggy Notebaert Nature Museum

Founded in 1857, this kid-friendly nature museum is one of the oldest scientific institutions in the United States. Interactive exhibits highlight the ecosystems of marshes, frogs, and birds. The Judy Istock Butterfly Haven is a favorite, a 2,700-sqaure-foot greenhouse filled with more than 1,000 butterflies. This affordable museum offers a good alternative to The Field Museum and is an easy stop in Lincoln Park.

Map 4: 2430 N. Cannon Dr., 773/755-5100, www.naturemuseum.org; 9am-5pm Mon.-Fri., 10am-5pm Sat.-Sun.

outside the Peggy Notebaert Nature Museum

PERFORMING ARTS

✪ Steppenwolf Theatre

This famous Chicago theater group started in the basement of a church. Founders Gary Sinise, Terry Kinney, and Jeff Perry began the theater in 1974. The large ensemble cast has since grown to include such well-known names as John Malkovich, Moira Harris, and Laurie Metcalf, among others. The winner of multiple Tony Awards, the artist-focused theater showcases original scripts and innovative interpretations of the classics with exceptional acting in an intimate space. Notable productions include an adaptation of *The Grapes of Wrath*, Sam Shepard's *True West*, and *Coyote Ugly*, which was directed by John Malkovich. Purchase tickets online in advance.

Map 4: 1650 N. Halsted St., 312/335-1650, www.steppenwolf.org; hours vary

Royal George Theatre

Royal George Theatre

At the Royal George Theatre, you can catch a range of pre-Broadway and off-Broadway productions in one of the four medium-sized theaters. While the interior of the Royal George may seem plain compared to other theaters in town, the caliber of the shows make up for it and there isn't a bad seat in the house. Buy tickets online or in person at the box office.

Map 4: 1641 N. Halsted, 312/988-9000; www.theroyalgeorgetheatre.com; box office Mon. 1pm-6pm, Tues.-Sat. 1pm-8pm, Sun. 1pm-7pm

Theatre on the Lake

Set in a historic building with views over Lake Michigan, Theatre on the Lake features the previous season highlights of the best works from other Chicago theaters. Large glass windows showcase a magnificent backdrop for the 330-seat venue.

Map 4: 2401 N. Lake Shore Dr., 312/742-7994, www.chicagoparkdistrict.com; hours vary

Victory Gardens Biograph Theatre

The Biograph Building, with its burnt-orange facade and 1970s signage, is home to the Victory Gardens Theatre. The intimate curved seating of this former movie theater sets the perfect stage for a selection of unique new plays and quality performances by a diversified cast. Playwrights Steve Carter, Claudia Allen, and Douglas Post have all written performances for the theater.

Map 4: 2433 N. Lincoln Ave., 773/871-3000, www.victorygardens.org; hours vary

Lakeview and Wrigleyville Map 5

PERFORMING ARTS
Athenaeum Theatre

This performance complex, the oldest in Chicago outside of the Loop, features five stages and serves as a community theater, food pantry, cultural resource, and gymnasium. Drop in for a cultural heritage event, or take in a cabaret or improv show. While they don't serve food, discounts are available with partner restaurants.

Map 5: 2936 N. Southport Ave., 773/935-6875, www.athenaeumtheater.org; hours vary

CONCERT VENUES
Briar Street Theater

There's only one reason to go to Briar Street Theater: to see the famous Blue Man Group. The theater is home to the long-running show featuring a trio of blue-painted men that includes digital elements and PVC piping as part of the performance—a big change from the original 1901 space originally built to house Marshall Field's horses. Most of the interior hasn't changed, making it a beautiful place to see an otherworldly show.

Map 5: 3133 N. Halsted St., 773/348-4000, www.blueman.com; hours vary

CINEMA
Brew and View

This old-school movie theater plays cult classics and new films just about to exit the theaters. The bar is open throughout each screening, and patrons can bring in their own food. For musicals, singing along is encouraged.

Map 5: 3145 N. Sheffield Ave., 773/929-6713, www.brewview.com; hours vary; $5

Music Box Theatre

The neon marquee and red velvet curtains of the Music Box Theatre are reminiscent of another era, making this the perfect place to watch classic films while munching on popcorn (with real butter). The theater was built in the 1920s and showcases independent, foreign, and cult films. A newer lounge and garden serves specialty cocktails, which can be brought into the theater.

Map 5: 3733 N.. Southport Ave., 773/871-6604, www.musicboxtheatre.com; hours vary

Wicker Park and Bucktown Map 6

GALLERIES
Flat Iron Arts Building

Smack in the center of Wicker Park, the Flat Iron Arts Building houses dozens of art galleries and studios across its three floors. Exhibits represent the work of animators, printmakers, videographers, painters, and sculptors. An open house is held the first Friday of every month, and there are many evening performances and special events. The artist colony is a symbol for the neighborhood, which is a haven for indie art and music.

The L's Blue Line stops at the Damen Station two blocks west.

Map 6: 1579 N. Milwaukee Ave., 312/566-9800, www.flatironartsbuilding.com; 7am-10pm daily; free

PERFORMING ARTS
House Theatre of Chicago

In 2001, a group of friends who wanted to tie community and storytelling together through theater started their own theater group. Today, the House Theatre of Chicago showcases original works with a focus on storytelling and inclusivity. Shows are performed at the Chopin Theatre, a small venue that offers the chance to interact with the cast. The downstairs bar provides refreshments and displays local artwork on the walls.

Map 6: 1543 W. Division St., 773/769-3832, www.thehousetheatre.com; hours vary

CINEMA
Logan Theatre

Logan Theatre first opened in 1915, and a 2012 remodel kept the original design while adding more modern amenities. The result is a beautiful building with a stained-glass arch, refurbished marble walls, and state-of-the-art screens and sound systems. There's also a bar where you can grab a drink before catching mid-run and indie films.

Map 6: 2646 N. Milwaukee Ave., 773/342-5555, www.thelogantheatre.com; hours vary

Hyde Park   Map 7

MUSEUMS
DuSable Museum of African-American History

Founded in 1961, this museum is dedicated to preserving and interpreting the experiences and achievements of people of African descent. Though small, it's packed with moving exhibits that track the history of African Americans in the United States from the slave trade through the election of President Obama. Spend an hour perusing the historic photographs, works by W. E. B. Du Bois, the poems of Langston Hughes, and pieces from the 1960s Black Arts Movement. The museum is free on Tuesday.

Map 7: 740 E. 56th St., 773/947-0600, www.dusablemuseum.org; 10am-5pm Tues.-Sat., noon-5pm Sun.; $10 adults, $7 students, $3 children 6-11, children under 5 free

PRAIRIE AVENUE HISTORIC DISTRICT

After the 1871 Great Chicago Fire, the **Prairie Avenue District** (1800-1900 Prairie Ave., 1800 block of S. Indiana, and 210-217 E. Cullerton St.) was the place of residence for Chicago's elite. Millionaires like Marshall Field and George Pullman bought large, Italianate-style mansions in the neighborhood and moved in. Later, in the 1890s, wealthy homeowners, annoyed by the sound of nearby railroad tracks, abandoned the area and moved north to the Gold Coast and Old Town neighborhoods.

Many of the historic homes in the Prairie Avenue District were torn down to make room for apartments and commercial buildings, a trend that continued after the Great Depression. Fortunately, residents helped preserve some of the mansions, many of which date back to the late 1800s. Today, the Prairie Avenue Historic District is on the National Register of Historic Places.

the Elbridge G. Keith House in the Prairie Avenue Historic District

A guided tour of the **Glessner House Museum** (1800 Prairie Ave., 312/326-1480, www. glessnerhouse.org, 10am-noon Sat. May-Dec., 75 min., $25) offers a fascinating look at nine of the existing homes and the impressive collection of 19th-century artwork within. Walking tours of Prairie Avenue ($15, dates and times vary) are also available.

Greater Chicago Map 8

MUSEUMS

✪ Willie Dixon's Blues Heaven

Willie Dixon's Blues Heaven is a must for any big music lovers visiting Chicago. The former Chess Records Studio, where Chuck Berry, Aretha Franklin, Etta James, Muddy Waters, and many more recorded—including of course Willie Dixon—is now a museum and foundation supporting blues artists and the promotion of music. Berry lived in the basement at one point, The Rolling Stones wrote a song about the studio, and there are many more stories which you'll hear on the tour, often given by Dixon's son.

Map 8: 2120 Michigan Ave., 312/808-1286, www.bluesheaven.com; by appointment only noon-4pm Thurs.-Fri., noon-3pm Sat.; by donation

National Museum of Mexican Art

The National Museum of Mexican Art displays Mexican culture as a bridge between communities, a culture *sin fronteras* (without borders). The Mexican exhibits spanning 3,000 years of history include a fascinating collection from artists on both sides of the Mexican-United States border. The permanent collection explores Mexican history from pre-Cuauhtémoc Mexico to colonial Mexico, independence, revolution, post-revolution, and present day, with a section on the Mexican experience in the United States. The small museum only takes an hour to walk through. There's parking nearby, or access it via the L's Pink Line.

Map 8: 1852 W. 19th St., 312/738-1503, www.nationalmuseumofmexicanart.org; 10am-5pm Tues.-Sun.; free

Swedish American Museum

This small museum in Andersonville, Chicago's traditionally Swedish neighborhood, tells the story of Swedish heritage in the United States. The main exhibit, The Dream of America: Swedish Immigration to Chicago, tells the story of the Swedish immigrant experiment, following fictitious characters on their journey across the Atlantic Ocean and how they chose careers and built lives in Chicago. The show is filled with artifacts like ship tickets and passports, as well as Swedish crafts. One of the highlights for families is the interactive museum playground, which has beautiful murals and Swedish costumes. Kids can dress up while playing in a traditional house, pretending to cook meals, playing with farm animals in the yard, and even packing a suitcase to prepare to make the trip to the United States, where they'll encounter a log cabin and other animals.

Map 8: Andersonville, 5211 N. Clark St., 773/728-8111, www. swedishamericanmuseum.org; 10am-4pm Mon.-Fri., 11am-4pm Sat.-Sun.; $4 adults, $3 seniors, students, and children

PERFORMING ARTS

Neo-Futurists

The Neo-Futurists are known for their fast-paced, experimental theater. Performances like *Too Much Like Makes the Baby Go Blind* and *Infinite Wrench* present a chaotic barrage of short and quick productions in two-minute increments. Fans of unique, unusual, and improvisational sketch comedy will love this. Tickets are sold at the door and shows often sell out.

Map 8: 5153 N. Ashland Ave., 773/275-5255; www.neofuturists.org; shows 11:30pm Fri.-Sat., 7pm Sun.; $9

SPORTS AND ACTIVITIES

ACTIVITIES

Of course, no visit to Chicago is complete without experiencing a Chicago Cubs game. You don't have to be a Cubs fan to feel the magic and camaraderie that

surrounds Wrigley Field. The nine-inning party known as game day attracts thousands of families, visitors, and bleacher bums to drink beer, inhale hot dogs, and cheer on the team. Bars in the Lakeview neighborhood often reach capacity well before the first pitch. No one is as dedicated as a Cubs fan. Prepare to catch a bit of the infectious spirit, whether on a ballpark tour or with coveted tickets in hand.

Chicago's equally devoted outdoor enthusiasts are dedicated to getting the most out of the city's green spaces and sandy shores, rain or shine. Along the 29 miles of spectacular Lake Michigan shoreline are a string of sandy beaches, parks, and bike paths that lure residents and visitors alike in summer. Linking them all is the 18-mile Lakefront Trail, shared by morning joggers and touring cyclists on Divvy bikes. Along the trail, you're sure to see people swimming, kayaking, and getting out their sailboats for a day on Lake Michigan. Beachgoers have many options, from the remote and quiet shore of the Museum Campus's 12th Street Beach to the volleyball games and summer parties that erupt on Lincoln Park's North Avenue Beach.

Cubs spirit at the Garfield Park Conservatory

Chicago's peaceful parks are host to multiple concerts and festivals in summer. Families will love Lincoln Park; the zoo and nature conservatory can fill

142

HIGHLIGHTS

✪ **BEST PLACE TO RELAX:** In the center of downtown, **Grant Park** feels quiet and removed—the perfect getaway from the Loop (page 144).

✪ **BEST RIVERFRONT HISTORY LESSON:** Learn about Chicago's architecture, the Great Chicago Fire, and the Columbian Exposition along the **Chicago Architecture River Cruise** (page 146).

✪ **BEST FOR FOOTBALL FANS:** Those who truly love football, shouldn't miss seeing the **Chicago Bears** at **Soldier Field** (page 146).

✪ **BEST BEACH: North Avenue Beach** is the busiest beach in Chicago with a wealth of options for paddleboarding, swimming, and even yoga (page 148).

✪ **BEST BIKE PATH:** Rent a Divvy bike and ride along the shore of Lake Michigan, taking in the sights and parks along the **Lakefront Trail** (page 149).

✪ **MOST ICONIC:** There's no better place to cheer on the **Chicago Cubs** than at famous Wrigley Field (page 150).

✪ **BEST PLACE TO GET AWAY:** You could spend hours wandering the park pathways and botanic gardens at the **Garfield Park Conservatory** (page 153).

North Avenue Beach

a kid's day, not to mention the skate park, an archery range, and five playgrounds. The younger set will enjoy the whimsical Oz Park filled with statues from *The Wonderful Wizard of Oz* or *The Velveteen Rabbit*-inspired Palmer Square Park. In winter, many of these parks are home to ice-skating rinks that provide a festive feel.

The Loop and Museum Campus

Map 1

PARKS

✪ Grant Park

This 319-acre park sits between the Loop and Lake Michigan, providing a large, green respite from city life. Elms line the park's boulevards, while the rest of it is fairly unadorned, just waiting for picnickers or the hundreds who come in the summer to sprawl out with a book or for a nap, the city skyline in the background. In the center you'll find Buckingham Fountain, the star of the park. There are a few hot dog and ice cream stands throughout that also serve beer and wine. Grant Park was set aside as land not to be built on in 1836, before Chicago was even incorporated, and that has been honored ever since. The walkways were constructed on rubble from the Chicago Fire, and in the 1900s the park was designed in the beaux arts style. Today,

Buckingham Fountain at Grant Park

Millennium Park Ice Skating Rink

Grant Park holds festivals and events, notably Lollapalooza and the 2016 Chicago Cubs World Series rally.
Map 1: 339 W. Randolph St., 312/742-3918; 6am-11pm daily

BEACHES
12th Street Beach
This small beach south of the Adler Planetarium is often quiet, which is odd as it's so close to the busy Museum Campus. It's a great spot to relax, watch the fireworks at Navy Pier, or listen to live bands at Northerly Island. While there's no volleyball, kayaking, or other beach sports, there is a small bathhouse, a snack shop, and a few picnic tables.
Map 1: 1200 S. Linn White Dr., 773/363-2225, www.cpdbeaches.com; 11am-7pm daily

ICE-SKATING
Maggie Daley Ice Skating Ribbon
This unique ice rink winds over a rolling landscape, showing off the Chicago skyline as skaters follow a looped track through Grant Park.

Along the way, stands sell hot chocolate to warm you up while admiring the city views.
Map 1: 337 E. Randolph St., 312/552-3000, http://maggiedaleypark.com; noon-8pm Mon.-Thurs., noon-10pm Fri., 10am-10pm Sat., 10am-8pm Sun. Nov.-Mar.; free admission; $12-14 skate rental

Millennium Park Ice Skating Rink
One of Chicago's favorite winter traditions is ice-skating at Millennium Park. The rink is popular with skaters of all levels—from children trying their first skate to experts performing tricky jumps on the ice. The buzz of Michigan Avenue's Christmas shoppers lends the rink a festive feel, while the city skyline and *Cloud Gate* provide a scenic background. Stands sell hot chocolate and snacks when you need to refuel.
Map 1: 210 E. Randolph St., 312/742-1168, www.cityofchicago.com; noon-8pm Mon.-Thurs., noon-10pm Fri., 10am-9pm Sat.-Sun. mid-Nov.-Mar.; free admission; $12 skate rental

TOURS AND CRUISES
✪ Chicago Architecture River Cruise

On this 90-minute cruise along the Chicago River, you'll learn everything you need to know about Chicago's rapid rise from small town to thriving city—a history deeply tied to its architecture. The Chicago Architecture Foundation's knowledgeable and certified guides know their stuff. They'll guide you past more than 50 buildings, offering historical background and insider knowledge on each as you glide in comfort aboard Chicago's *First Lady* vessel. Upper open-air viewing decks, climate-controlled cabins, and a full-service bar make for luxurious history lessons. Passengers meet at a dock on the southeast corner of the Michigan Avenue Bridge (look for a blue sign). Standard cruises are during the day,

Chicago Architecture River Cruise

but a twilight cruise (7:30pm) adds the twinkling lights of the city.

Map 1: Michigan Ave. and Wacker Dr., www.architecture.org; tours 9am-7:30pm daily; $46-49

SPECTATOR SPORTS
FOOTBALL
✪ Chicago Bears

Home of the Chicago Bears, Soldier Field hosts football games (Sept.-Feb.), international soccer and rugby tournaments, and big-name concerts. With a capacity of 61,500, it's the smallest stadium in the NFL, which makes sight lines for a Bears game pretty good from wherever you're sitting. A one-hour behind-the-scenes tour ($15 adults, $7 seniors, $10 children over age 10, $4 children ages 4-9, children age 3 and under free) of the curved white stadium begins with a historical video then visits the South Courtyard, Doughboy Statue, field, Visitor's Locker Room, Skyline Suite, and Colonnades.

Concessions are heavy on pizza and burgers, although there are a few unique options like the Purple Pig. Tickets for Bears games are available online (www.chicagobears.com). Gates open two hours prior to kickoff in season. Public transportation to Soldier Field is easy. Take the L to Roosevelt on the Orange, Green, or Red Line or hop on the 128 Soldier Field Express bus from Union Station or the Ogilvie Transportation Center.

Map 1: Soldier Field, 1410 Museum Campus Dr., 312/235-7000, www.soldierfield.net; game times vary

Near North and Navy Pier

Map 2

BEACHES

Ohio Street Beach

This small, secluded beach is just a few minutes' walk from Navy Pier and the Lakefront Trail, and is less crowded than the sandy beach at North Avenue. It's especially popular for swimming, with great views of the lake and the small North Avenue Beach lighthouse. Grab a bite at the on-site Caffé Oliva (847/922-3717, 11am-10pm daily) if all that swimming tires you out.

Map 2: 600 N. Lake Shore Dr., 312/742-7529; www.cpdbeaches.com; 11am-7pm daily

BIKING

Divvy Bikes

Chicago's Divvy bike share program is an easy and convenient way to get around. With nearly 600 bike stations across the city, visitors can rent a bike for a day of sightseeing, then return the bike to any station when done. Most major attractions are within steps of a Divvy bike station and payment kiosk. A complete map is online.

Map 2: Navy Pier and various locations, 855/553-4889; www.divvybikes.com; 24-hour pass $9.95

Divvy bike station

SPECTATOR SPORTS
BASKETBALL
Chicago Bulls

The United Center is the largest sports arena in the United States and home to the Chicago Blackhawks and Chicago Bulls. If you're going to a game, stop on the east side of the stadium to see the statues of basketball legend Michael Jordan and hockey stars Bobby Hull and Stan Mikita. Indoors, seating is tiered, and you can see from any seat, though you might need binoculars the higher up you go. The United Center's food and drink options are fantastic for a sports arena. You'll find stands that offer everything from Chicago Beef to authentic tacos to offerings from the Publican, Gibson's, and other top restaurants. The same can be said for the bar, where you'll find beer and cocktails from local breweries and acclaimed cocktail bars. It makes going to a game fun even if you're not into sports. The United Center also hosts big-name concerts, like Jay-Z and Ariana Grande. Parking is available, or you can take the Green or Pink Line L to the Ashland Station and walk a few blocks.

Map 3: 1901 W. Madison St., 312/455-4500, www.unitedcenter.com

HOCKEY
Chicago Blackhawks

The Chicago Blackhawks are one of Chicago's favorite sports teams, partly because they win so often and have taken home the Stanley Cup three times since 2010. Games are raucous and loud, but the fans are friendly and love getting everyone into the spirit. The Blackhawks play in the United Center; on the east side of the stadium, look for the large statues of hockey legends Bobby Hull and Stan Mikita.

Map 3: 1901 W. Madison St., 312/455-4500, www.unitedcenter.com

Lincoln Park, Old Town, and Gold Coast

Map 4

BEACHES
✪ North Avenue Beach

Chicago's busiest beach is packed with activity—sunbathing, stand-up paddleboarding, and volleyball. Stake out a spot in the sand or hang out at Castaways, a beach house serving burgers and tropical drinks. Kayak and Jet Ski rentals are available onsite. Access is along the Lakefront Trail, so bike or walk here to avoid the impossible parking. Alcohol is prohibited.

Map 4: 1600 N. Lake Shore Dr., 773/363-2225, www.cpdbeaches.com

Oak Street Beach

This small beach is walking distance from the Lakefront Trail and features spectacular skyline views and volleyball courts. Since the sand is limited, locals spread out on towels

Fifteen miles of green space and beaches along Lake Michigan make **Lake Shore Drive** (Hwy. 41) one of the prettiest urban parkways in North America. Beaches dot the shoreline every few blocks, while luxurious mansions, towering skyscrapers, and a cluster of parks provide a stunning backdrop. If driving along Lake Shore Drive, plan your travel from south to north for the best views. Even better, get out of the car and onto a bike (or two feet) to explore the shore via the **Lakefront Trail.** Popular stops along the 18-mile path include Grant Park, Navy Pier, Lincoln Park, and **North Avenue Beach.** Divvy bike rentals line much of the path. Pick up a bike at one of the Museum Campus's three docks and ride north.

on the cement walk then dive in for a dip when it gets too hot. Bike rentals, restrooms, and snacks are available seasonally. The Oak Street Beach underpass gets you across Lake Shore Drive.

Map 4: 1000 N. Lake Shore Dr., 773/363-2225, www.cpdbeaches.com

TOP EXPERIENCE

BIKING
✪ Lakefront Trail

The scenic Lakefront Trail stretches 18 miles from north to south along the shores of Lake Michigan. Along the way, the paved trail passes beaches, gardens, and harbors, as well as Lincoln Park, Grant Park, and the Museum Campus. Popular stops include the North Avenue and Oak Street Beaches, Navy Pier, and Jackson Park. Biking a portion of the trail is a great way to see Chicago from a new perspective while enjoying some exercise and skyline views. **Divvy bike rentals** (www.divvybikes.com) line the path, which mirrors Lake Shore Drive.

Map 4: Lake Shore Drive from 5800 N Sheridan Ave. to 7100 S Shore Ave., www. choosechicago.com

PARKS
Lincoln Park

This 1,200-acre park is home to the Lincoln Park Zoo, Lincoln Park Conservatory, and the Peggy Notebaert Nature Museum, making it an easy place to spend the day. Aside from these well-known attractions, there's a nature boardwalk, a rowing canal, a skate park, an archery range, a driving range, and several harbors for boating. Five playgrounds offer amusement for the kids, or you can drop in for a game of basketball, volleyball, or baseball at the connected playfields. The park is named in honor of Abraham Lincoln and its *Abraham Lincoln: The Man* statue is a highlight.

Map 4: 500-5700 N. Lake Shore Dr. between W North Blvd. and W Bryn Mawr Ave., 312/742-7726, www. chicagoparkdistrict.com; 6am-11pm daily

Oz Park

Named in honor of L. Frank Baum, the author of *The Wonderful Wizard of Oz*, this park is great fun for families. Small kids can climb the play

biking along the Lakefront Trail

structures in Dorothy's Playlot, while everyone will enjoy a summertime stroll in the flower-filled Emerald Garden. See if you can spy statues of Tin Man, Scarecrow, Cowardly Lion, and Dorothy and Toto sprinkled throughout the park.

Map 4: 2021 N. Burling St., 312/742-7898, www.chicagoparkdistrict.com/parks/oz-park; 6am-11pm daily

Lakeview and Wrigleyville   Map 5

TOP EXPERIENCE

SPECTATOR SPORTS
BASEBALL
✪ Chicago Cubs

Whether you're a baseball fan or not, there's nothing like watching the Cubs play at **Wrigley Field.** Cubs fans are as loyal as it gets—coming out rain or shine, win or loss, year after year—and their enthusiasm is contagious, even more so after the Cubs' World Series win in 2016. Sit in the bleacher seats for the full fan experience and learn the words "Go Cubs Go" so you don't feel like a total outcast. Cubs fans honor former announcer Harry Caray with boisterous renditions of "Take Me Out to the Ballgame" at each game, often accompanied by a famous guest singer. Wrigley is one of the only fields in the country where you can watch the game from rooftop seats (available with all-you-can-eat-and-drink packages). Reserve these seats as far in advance as possible.

Map 5: Wrigley Field, 1060 Addison St., 773/404-2827, www.wrigleyfield.com; hours and prices vary

Wrigley Field

It's often said that Chicago Cubs fans are the most loyal in the world. Year after year, they turn out for games, cheering on a team with a losing record as if they were the best in the world. It wasn't always this way.

Prior to World War II, the Cubs won four National League pennants over a 10-year period. They won another pennant in 1945. And then they didn't have a winning season for another 20 years. Until 2016, the Cubs had not won a World Series since 1908. Between 1908 and 1945, they didn't even make it to the World Series. From 1945 to 2016, they made it to the postseason seven times. Since 1945, the Cubs finished last or second-to-last more than 40 percent of the time. Fans turned out anyway.

Between 2000 and 2014, the Cubs had the eighth-worst record in baseball—and they drew more fans than all but four other Major League clubs. Why? Some fans cite neighborhood loyalty, while others say it's fun to root for the underdog or worth it for the experience of sitting in a vintage stadium that puts spectators close to the field. Or maybe it's the fact that seeing a game at Wrigley Field is like going to a big block party—the field has been called the "world's largest beer garden." And for years, it was the hope that maybe, just maybe, this time the Cubs would win a game or two.

That hope and loyalty paid off for Cubs fans in 2016, when the team finally won the World Series. The entire city erupted in elation (even White Sox fans had to admit it was a special moment), and the parade and celebration that followed at Grant Park drew more than five million people. That's enough team spirit to last through any number of wins or losses in the years to come. Like any true fan will tell you, sometimes it's heartbreaking to be a Cubs fan, but they wouldn't have it any other way.

Wicker Park and Bucktown

Map 6

PARKS

Humboldt Park

This neighborhood park features a historic field house with two gymnasiums, a fitness center, soccer and baseball fields, a tennis court, and several playgrounds. The inland beach and lagoons are the perfect spot for an afternoon of picnicking, while sports fans should look for the replica of Wrigley Field known as "Little Cubs Field." The former Humboldt Park stables are now home to the **National Museum of Puerto Rican Arts and Culture** (3015 W Division St., 773/486-8345, http://nmprac.org; 10am-5pm Wed.-Fri., 10am-2pm Sat.; free). Check the park's calendar online for events.

Map 6: 1400 N. Sacramento Ave., 312/742-7549, www.chicagoparkdistrict.com/parks/humboldtpark; 6am-11pm daily

Palmer Square Park

This seven-acre park in Logan Square is a favorite among families for its playground inspired by the book *The Velveteen Rabbit*. There's a path linking four scenes from the book around the park. Adults can run on the track that circles the park or relax under the plentiful trees.

Map 6: 2200 N. Kedzie Ave., 312/742-7535; 6am-11pm daily

Wicker Park

Four-acre Wicker Park, with nice gardens and a children's playground, anchors its namesake neighborhood.

Humboldt Park

Adults come for the baseball, basketball, soccer, and football areas, while a pretty fountain with a water spray feature is a hit among kids in the summer. A field house features a gymnasium and meeting rooms that are rented out for large gatherings.

Map 6: 1425 N. Damen Ave., 312/742-7553; 6am-11pm daily

BIKING
606 Trail

A former railroad, the 2.7-mile elevated 606 Trail was converted into a walking and biking trail in 2015. From the northwest side, the trail offers new perspectives of the city, passing historic buildings like the former Churchill Cabinet Co. and the Ludwig Drum Factory. The pleasant path is less crowded than Lakefront and an easier way to get across the northwest side of the city while avoiding busy sidewalks.

Map 6: Walsh Park and N. Marshfield Ave.; 6am-11pm daily

Hyde Park

Map 7

PARKS
Jackson Park

This 543-acre park located behind the Museum of Science and Industry feels a world away from the city. Stroll through winding pathways and across bridges to the Wooded Island, where you'll find the Japanese Garden of the Phoenix. The garden was originally part of the 1893 World's Columbian Exposition and features a Buddhist temple and the lotus-inspired sculpture *Sky Landing,* designed by Yoko Ono. Around Jackson Park are gardens, basketball and tennis courts, a turf field, an 18-hole golf course, boat harbors, and a beach. Soon, it will also hold the Barack Obama Presidential Library.

Map 7: 6401 S. Stony Island Ave., 773/256-0903, www.chicagoparkdistrict. com/parks/jackson-park; 9am-10pm Mon.-Fri., 5pm-10pm Sat.

Washington Park

Landscape architect Frederick Law Olmstead designed this 367-acre park on the south side of Chicago in the 1870s. There are two large swimming pools, basketball, tennis, and racquetball courts; baseball, football, soccer, cricket, and softball fields; a nature area, a garden, and an arboretum. Don't miss the *Fountain of Time,* a sculpture that represents 100 years of peace between the United Kingdom and the U.S. Combine a visit here with a tour of the DuSable Museum, also located within the park.

Map 7: 5531 S.. Martin Luther King Dr., 773/256-1248; www.chicagoparkdistrict. com; Mon.-Fri. 8am-9pm, Sat. 9am-5pm, Sun. 9am-4pm

Greater Chicago   Map 8

PARKS
⭐ Garfield Park Conservatory

Escape the busy pace of the city with a stroll through this giant conservatory, one of the largest in the country. Often referred to as "landscape art under glass," the 184-acre conservatory is home to thousands of plant species in rooms linked by small walkways set within the giant glass structure. The tropical temps offer the perfect respite from chilly Chicago weather. Exhibits include a palm house, fern house, desert house, a kid's garden with interactive activities, as well as outdoor gardens, tennis courts, a fishing pond, and a swimming pool. Parking is available on-site, or take the L's Green Line to the Conservatory stop.

Map 8: 300 N. Central Park Ave., 312/746-5100, www.garfieldconservatory. org; 9am-5pm Thurs.-Tues., 9am-8pm Wed.; free

SPECTATOR SPORTS
BASEBALL
Chicago White Sox

Formerly Cellular Field, Guaranteed Rate Field is the home of the Chicago White Sox. The park features high seating with unobstructed views and some great food options, as well as more than 100 craft beers. Large groups can rent Suite 134, a swanky party room with catered food and drinks. Group tours (312/674-1000) are available with advance reservations and include the press box, field, home dugout, and the Stadium Club.

Map 8: 333 W. 35th St., 866/769-4263, www.mlb.com/whitesox; parking $10-20

SOCCER
Chicago Fire

Toyota Park is about 12 miles south of downtown, but if you're a soccer fan, it's where you'll go to see the Chicago Fire play. Walk through the giant brick archway into the stadium, which fits

the Desert House at the Garfield Park Conservatory

28,000 fans. Concession stands sell hot dogs, pulled pork and other sandwiches, pizza, popcorn, soda, and draft beer, among other food selections. The stadium is also host to big-name concerts and festivals.

Map 8: Toyota Park, 7000 Harlem Ave., 708/594-7200, www.toyotapark.com

SHOPS

Save room in your suitcase because you'll want to do some shopping. Michigan Avenue is a renowned shopper's paradise, while nearby Oak and Rush Streets are where to go for designer stores. The historic Merchandise Mart houses everything you could ever need for the home.

What makes shopping in Chicago stand out, however, are the hundreds of local designers and neighborhood boutiques that sell everything from handmade clothing and curated vintage collections to rare books and unique gifts.

For clothing, accessories, and home items, stroll the Loop and Near North neighborhoods. Stop in South Loop Loft for timeless furniture, or in Ikram for high-end clothing from the woman who dresses Michelle Obama. Or get a completely customized suit at Knot Standard.

In Lincoln Park, Old Town, and the Gold Coast, you'll find charming boutiques and specialty shops. For vintage items, books, and records, Lakeview and Wicker Park have the best options, like the handmade jewelry from local designers at Virtu.

The Merchandise Mart in the Chicago Loop

And for the best souvenirs in the city, stop by the Chicago Architecture Foundation Shop for a unique gift and grab a bag of popcorn from Nuts On Clark.

HIGHLIGHTS

✪ **BEST WINDOW-SHOPPING:** Walk the **Magnificent Mile** for elaborate window displays, especially at Christmas (page 157).

✪ **BEST MEN'S CLOTHING STORE:** At **Knot Standard,** every detail of your new suit is customizable (page 160).

✪ **BEST SURPRISE PURCHASE:** Everything in **Space 519** is so tempting that you'll probably walk out with something, whether you need it or not (page 161).

✪ **BEST INTERNATIONAL FOOD SHOP:** Whisk yourself away to Rome at **Eataly,** where wine, cheese, and pasta are taken seriously and tastings are plentiful (page 161).

✪ **BEST VINTAGE:** At **Randolph Street Market,** you'll find dozens of vintage vendors all in one place (page 163).

✪ **BEST SOUVENIR:** Snack on sweet-and-salty Chicago Mix popcorn from **Nuts on Clark,** but try to save some to take home (page 170).

✪ **BEST ONE-OF-A-KIND GIFT:** Handcrafted jewelry from the artisans at **Virtu** is both beautiful and unique (page 171).

Eataly

SHOPPING DISTRICTS
⭐ Magnificent Mile

The Magnificent Mile is one of the world's famed shopping streets. With the Tribune Tower on one end and the John Hancock Center on the other, it's also a tourist hot spot. On "Mag Mile" you'll find upscale hotels, designer stores, boutiques, department stores, and high-end restaurants and cafés. There are three main department stores: 900 North Michigan Shops, Water Tower Place, and The Shops at North Bridge. These hold national retail chains, a giant Macy's, and the flagship American Girl Place. Along the rest of the mile, you'll find more than 50 flagship retailers like Bloomingdales, Apple, and Gucci. Modern stores blend with historic architecture along Mag Mile, giving it a unique feel. During the winter holidays, store windows showcase festive displays and the city puts up an impressive array of lights and decorations along the strip. The Magnificent Mile isn't known for local or unique shops and it can be quite touristy, but it's still fun to walk down this iconic thoroughfare at least once.

Map 2: N. Michigan Ave. bet. Chicago Ave. and Lake Shore Dr., www.themagnificentmile.com; store hours vary

Rush and Oak Streets

Rush Street in the Gold Coast is home to high-end shops and luxury hotels that spill over onto Oak Street. Rush Street has a history of luxury: It was one of the most desirable places to live in the mid-1800s and is still home to wealthy Chicagoans. Here you'll find designer names like Barney's, Brunello Cucinelli, Emporio Armani, and Saint Laurent alongside more casual shops like Madewell. Grab a coffee from the large Starbucks on the corner and do some window shopping.

Map 2: N. Rush St. at E. Oak St..; store hours vary

The Loop and Museum Campus

Map 1

CLOTHING AND SHOES
Floradora

This boutique vintage store sells women's clothing from a selection of carefully chosen designers. The owner's grandmother worked in the historic Monadnock Building, where Floradora is located, and was the inspiration for its opening. Stop in for special occasion dresses, hats, and jewelry or pop in next door at Floradora Shoes, the sister shop selling women's designers shoes (Coclico, Chie Mihara, and more). It's somewhat pricey, but the quality and selection are exquisite.

Map 1: 330 S. Dearborn St., 312/212-8860, www.floradora.com; 10am-7pm Mon.-Fri., 10am-5pm Sat.

GIFT AND HOME
Chicago Architecture Foundation Shop

This is your one-stop-shop for Chicago souvenirs. The bright store is packed to the brim with Chicago-branded apparel, jewelry, and coasters, as well as a few gifts from local designers and a

BEST SOUVENIRS

It's always fun to take something home with you to remember your trip. While you'll find plenty of magnets, postcards, and other souvenirs along Michigan Avenue, there are a few more unique souvenirs you can pick up.

Grab a few bags of Chicago Mix, the caramel and cheese popcorn mix from **Nuts On Clark** for your foodie friends (or to eat on the plane).

Purchase unique artwork from local artists at the **Andersonville Galleria.**

The **Chicago Architecture Foundation Shop** sells Chicago-themed gifts like coasters with a map of Chicago, state flag candles, and a host of architecture-inspired options.

For unique jewelry, accessories, and other gifts made by local designers head to **Art Effect** or **Virtu.**

book selection full of Chicago history and architecture. Walk away with a set of Frank Lloyd Wright-designed tumbler glasses or a gold cuff bracelet with an engraved CTA map.

Map 1: 224 S. Michigan Ave., 312/922-3432, https://shop.architecture.org; 9am-9pm daily

SHOPPING MALLS
The Shops at Block 37

This five-story mall contains a mix of shopping, restaurants, and entertainment. For shopping, Akira, Sephora, Anthropologie, and The Disney Store are here, as well as a large AMC movie theater. Magnolia Bakery, Farmer's Fridge, Au Bon Pain, and the Latin City Food Hall are quick breakfast and lunch spots in the Loop. The mall is open weekends, when other businesses in the Loop are closed.

Map 1: 108 N. State St., 312/261-4700, www.blockthirtyseven.com; hours vary by store

Near North and Navy Pier

Map 2

CLOTHING AND SHOES
Akira

This Chicago chain of women's clothing is known for European styles, sexy dresses and shoes, and lots of accessories like hats and purses. Stocked with more than 200 designer brands like BCBG and Jeffrey Campbell Shoes and some smaller names as well, it's easy to find an outfit or accessories in a pinch. It's affordable but not cheap, making it popular for trendy items that still look unique.

Map 2: 835 N. Michigan Ave., 312/951-5508, www.shopakira.com; 10am-9pm Mon.-Sat., 11am-6pm Sun.

Azeeza

Local designer Azeeza Khan's label has been worn by many famous names and is a favorite among Chicago women looking for internationally inspired, timeless dresses that can transition easily from day to night. There's a large attention to fabric, craft, and individuality, like silk tops and handwoven sweaters or scarves with exotic prints. Khan brand helps women exude confidence, and that comes through in the shopping experience, where a friendly and honest staff helps you pick the perfect pieces.

Map 2: 900 N. Michigan Ave., 312/649-9373, www.azeeza.us; 10am-7pm Mon.-Sat., 10am-6pm Sun.

Gold Coast Couture

This designer hat store specializes in derby hats, fascinators, bridal headbands, cocktail hats, and other accessories. The owners can help you try on different styles and will tell you about their designs. Some hats are made exclusively for the store, but all of them are exquisitely designed—some are even surprisingly affordable.

Map 2: 980 N. Michigan Ave., Ste. 1473, 312/965-9812, www.goldcoastcouture.com; hours by appointment

Ikram

For high-end women's clothing, there's nowhere better than Ikram. A regular dresser of Michelle Obama, owner Ikram Goldman's high-end clothing boutique carries a curated collection of American, European, and Japanese designers, as well as a few vintage pieces picked by the owner. Cocktail dresses, tops, shoes, pins, gloves, and accessories from Gucci, Alexander McQueen, Sakayori, and Leur Logette fill the bright, modern shop.

Map 2: 15 E. Huron St., 312/587-1000, www.ikram.com; 10am-6pm Mon.-Sat.

Independence

This men's boutique focuses on high-end, ethically sourced clothes made in the United States and Canada; brands include Oak Street Bootmakers, Engineered Garments, Gitman, and Imogene + Willie. The shoes are especially well crafted, with some designs made specifically for the store. The wood floors and large American flag hanging on the wall give the shop a rustic vibe, and it's popular with the hipster crowd.

Knot Standard

THE MERCHANDISE MART

The Merchandise Mart (222 W Merchandise Mart Plaza, 800/677-MART, www.themart. com; 9am-6pm Mon.-Fri., 10am-3pm Sat.) is the world's largest commercial building and design center. The art deco building was erected in 1930 to house Chicago's architecture and design trades all in one place (and was the largest building in the world at that time). Today, it holds a broad range of businesses, shops, and restaurants, and many interior design shops still dominate the ground floor.

Map 2: 47 E. Oak St., 312/675-2105, www. independence-chicago.com; 11am-7pm Mon.-Sat., noon-5pm Sun.

⭐ Knot Standard

This high-end menswear store creates the "ultimate buttoned-up suit in the Windy City." At each one-hour appointment in the modern and open showroom, an expert stylist will take your measurements and help you choose from more than 5,000 fabrics, including silk and cashmere, as well as curated fabrics from Loro Piana and Holland & Sherry. Customize buttons, stitching, lapels, and pant breaks. Knot Standard isn't cheap, but an excellent fit is guaranteed.

Map 2: 220 W. Illinois St., #114, 855/784-8968, www.knotstandard.com/ showrooms/chicago; by appointment

GIFT AND HOME
American Girl Place

Whether your child owns an American Girl doll already or you're hoping to buy one, this store is a delight. Aside from being stocked with every doll and accessory you can imagine, there's also an area to design your own doll clothes, a doll hair salon, and a cute café overlooking Michigan Avenue. The Standard Parking garage (111 E. Chestnut) offers discounted parking with a receipt.

Map 2: 835 N Michigan Ave., 877/247-5223, www.americangirl.com; 10am-8pm Mon.-Thurs., 10am-9pm Fri., 9am-9pm Sat., 9am-6pm Sun.

Classic Remix

If you're looking for the perfect piece to finish your place, but can't quite put your finger on what it is you need, come to Classic Remix. The boutique sells new and vintage furniture and a huge array of home decor, lighting, and art. They also sell jewelry and other accessories and gifts in a beautifully laid-out space. If you find a larger piece you love, they'll ship it to you.

Map 2: 706 N. Wells St., 312/915-0569; 10am-6pm Mon.- Fri., 11am-5pm Sat.

P.O.S.H.

If you're hoping to find unique dishware or other small furnishings for your home, stop at P.O.S.H., a charming shop full of vintage finds from hotel and estate sales, auctions, and European flea markets. Each piece tells a story, as does the building

P.O.S.H.

they're housed in, the Tree Studio, which is the nation's oldest known artist studio and on the National Register of Historic Places. It's worth a visit just to check out the details of the building and flower-filled courtyard, but we're betting you come away with a treasure too.

Map 2: 613 N. State St., 312/280-1602, www.poshchicago.com; 10am-7pm Mon.-Sat., 11am-5pm Sun.

⊕ Space 519

This carefully curated store on Michigan Avenue sources hard-to-find items from designers across a range of categories, from apparel to books to home items. Men's and women's clothing, botanical serums, sunglasses, coffee table books, jewelry, and candles are popular, if eclectic, items that also make a great gift. Space 519 is known for its wide selection, knowledgeable staff, and open layout, which makes shopping easy.

Map 2: 900 N. Michigan Ave., 312/751-1519, www.space519.com; 10am-7pm Mon.-Sat., noon-6pm Sun.

BOOKS
After-Words

Two floors hold more than 70,000 new and used books, from fiction to photography to cookbooks, and everything in between. The store is basic, but always well stocked and with a friendly staff who will help you find titles or authors. There's also a great selection of signed books.

Map 2: 23 E. Illinois St., 312/464-1110, www.after-wordschicago.com; 10:30am-11pm Mon.-Fri., 10am-11pm Sat., noon-7pm Sun.

GOURMET AND SPECIALTY FOODS
⊕ Eataly

At this famed, three-floor Italian marketplace you'll find specialty foods, a huge array of Italian wine labels, and multiple restaurants. Shop for fresh produce and handmade pasta, take cooking classes to perfect your Bolognese sauce, learn about wine from attentive sommeliers, or just stop in for a bite at the pizza, pasta, or fish restaurant. There's also a *birreria* and *osteria*. Finally, browse the sweets section for Italian candies and chocolates you don't often see in the United States, and stop by the Nutella or gelato stand for an authentic dessert. Don't forget to grab an espresso from the coffee bar on your way out!

Map 2: 43 E. Ohio St., 312/521-8700, www.eataly.com; 8am-11pm Mon.-Sat., 8am-10pm Sun.

West Side

Map 3

CLOTHING AND SHOES

Ad Hoc

Ad Hoc stocks a curated selection of women's clothing and handmade jewelry that will survive the trends. What makes Ad Hoc stand out among other local boutiques is the price tag—many pieces ring in at around $50. Choose from a mixed collection of brand-name designers, American-made labels, and local Chicago artists. Take a restful break from browsing on one of the shop's couches or spin some vinyl on the in-store record player.

Map 3: 1948 W. Chicago Ave., 312/343-9991, www.chicagoadhoc.com; noon-7pm Mon.-Fri., 11am-6pm Sat., noon-5pm Sun.

BLVDier

At BLVDier, custom suits and sports coats draw inspiration from the West Loop industrial district, Edwardian lines, Japanese aesthetic, and the meticulous details of Neapolitan fashion to create beautifully fitted pieces made with fabrics from the finest mills in the Biella region of the Italian Alps. You'll find classic yet personalized items here: Jackets can be finished with surgeon's cuffs and customized lapel, buttons, stitches, pockets, and other details. The shop itself is small, but the white walls and minimalist decor feel spacious.

Map 3: 211 N. Green St., 630/200-8583, www.blvdier.com; by appointment

PRSVR

This luxury clothing and luggage label began on Instagram. After became a hit of celebrities like Nicki Minaj and Nelly, the upscale hip-hop fashion brand PRSVR opened this minimalistic storefront specializing in high-end sneakers, track pants, and leather shoes. The store caters to men, but there are options for women and kids as well.

Map 3: 1822 W. Grand Ave., 855/297-7787, www.prsvr.com; 11am-7pm Mon.-Fri., noon-5pm Sat.

Rider for Life

Rider for Life is an upscale women's boutique with a relaxed feel. Vintage clothing, indie styles, and newer trends mix together in the cozy store, where you can buy a small gift from the apothecary or drop lots of money on a lambskin bomber jacket or Maison des Talons shoes. Jewelry, sunglasses, and handbags round out your outfit.

Map 3: 1115 W. Lake St., 312/243-0464, www.shoprider.us; 11am-8pm Mon.-Sat., 11am-6pm Sun.

Tarnish

Tarnish emphasizes the beautiful wear and tear of the motorcycle lifestyle by focusing on the story behind designers like Gracie Roberts, Baghsu, Grifter USA, and Black Arrow Label. The surprisingly affordable collection includes perfectly fitted jackets, men's and women's clothing (i.e., lots of leather), and vinyl items, as well as gifts and jewelry. Owner Nicole can help find the perfect item in this cozy shop.

Map 3: 2024 W. Chicago Ave., 773/227-7290, www.tarnishthestore.com; noon-7pm Mon.-Fri., 11am-6pm Sat., noon-5pm Sun.

BOOKS AND MUSIC

Open Books

Open Books is not your ordinary used bookstore; it's also a nonprofit that provides literacy assistance to thousands of children through book donations and instructional programs. Stroll through the perfectly organized racks of used books from all genres—and all in great condition—and know that your purchase will help the world become a more well-read place.

Map 3: 651 W Lake St., 312/475-1355, www.open-books.org; 9am-7pm Mon.-Sat., noon-6pm Sun.

Permanent Records

The Chicago branch of this Los Angeles shop is known for hard-to-find rock LPs and an incredibly friendly staff that loves the job. The brightly lit store is neatly organized by genre, making it easy to sort through bins holding thousands of records. If you're looking for something specific and can't find it anywhere else, chances are you'll find it here.

Map 3: 1914 W. Chicago Ave., 773/278-1744, www.permanentrecordschicago.com; noon-8pm daily

GIFT AND HOME

The Fig Tree

This small store sells stationery, home decor, kitchen items, party accessories, jewelry, and a large selection of baby gifts such as cute, screen-printed onesies and fairy wings. The sweet and friendly owner is usually on-site and can help you find a unique gift, whether you're looking for a necklace by a local artist, funny coasters, or the perfect handmade card.

Map 3: 1037 W. Madison St., 312/226-6303, www.figtreechicago.com; 11am-7pm Mon.-Fri., 10am-6pm Sat., noon-5pm Sun.

Morlen Sinoway Atelier

Morlen Sinoway's spacious, airy showroom features new and antique pieces from around the world. Browse vintage furniture from Finland or modern Japanese cabinets, as well as lighting, area rugs, and small gifts such as silk scarves and handmade totes. Interior design services are also available.

Map 3: 1052 W. Fulton Market, 312/432-0100, www.morlensinoway.com; 9:30am-5pm Mon.-Fri., 11:30am-5pm Sat.

✪ Randolph Street Market

More than 200 antiques vendors and local designers gather for the Randolph Street Market, a monthly indoor-outdoor festival. Shop for records, jewelry, vintage clothes, local artwork, and vintage furniture, or step into the food market for chocolates, cakes, tacos, and treats from rotating vendors. While many vendors sell vintage goods, there's a healthy mix of local artists and designers too. The indoor market runs all year; it expands outdoors May-September and adds a beer garden.

Map 3: 1340 W. Washington Blvd., 312/666-1200, www.randolphstreetmarket. com; 10am-5pm Sat.-Sun. on the last weekend of each month; $8-10 admission

South Loop Loft

This spacious showroom sells furniture and home decor with one common theme: The collection exudes timeless elegance. The welcoming space invites browsing amid the antique chandeliers, brass bar carts, sofas, and chrome swivel chairs.

Map 3: 308 N. Leavitt, 262/490-4215; www.thesouthlooploft.com; Sat. 11am-5pm or by appointment

Sprout Home Kitchen and Table

This beautiful kitchen and tableware shop opened in 2016 as a companion to Sprout Home (745 N Damen Ave., 312/226-5950; 10am-7pm daily), a garden design store across the street. The small, brightly lit space is full of teak shelves lined with dish towels, serving plates, terra-cotta cookware, unique dishes, and vintage cookbooks. It's a delight to walk through, whether you're window-shopping or stocking your home.

Map 3: 744 N Damen Ave., 312/226-5950, www.sprouthome.com/about/chicago-store; 10am-7pm daily

Lincoln Park, Old Town, and Gold Coast
Map 4

BOOKS AND MUSIC
Dave's Records

Dave's Records is often listed as one of the top record stores in the United States for its devotion to all vinyl, all the time. The well-organized store is stuffed with records of all speeds, formats, and genres, from collector's items to newly released albums.

Map 4: 2604 N Clark St., 773/929-6325, www.davesrecordschicago.com; 11am-8pm Mon.-Sat., noon-7pm Sun.

CLOTHING AND SHOES
Fleet Feet

Fleet Feet is the go-to place for running shoes. Whether you're a serious runner or a beginner, the staff will help you find the perfect pair of shoes for a reasonable price. You'll be asked about your running experience, the type of shoes you wear, and may even run on a treadmill to make sure the shoe fits. The stores host running events too, so check the calendar to see if there's a Fun Run while you're in town.

Map 4: 1620 N. Wells St., 312/587-3338; www.fleetfeetchicago.com; Mon.-Fri. 10am-8pm, Sat. 10am-6pm, Sun. 10am-5pm

Fox's Designer Off Price

Fox's is like a smaller, high-end TJ Maxx. The selection of women's clothing is always changing and you may have to do some digging, but when you find a gorgeous designer jacket for under $100, it's worth it. The dressing rooms leave something to be desired, but the staff's commitment to making every guest feel special makes up for it.

Map 4: 2150 N Halsted St., 773/281-0700, www.foxs.com; 10am-8pm Mon.-Fri., 10am-7pm Sat., 11am-6pm Sun.

Greenheart Shop

This beautiful shop tucked down Wells Street sources fair-trade products from around the world. You'll find scarves from Indonesia, bags from Kenya, wooden bowls from Peru, jewelry from local designers, and ornaments, blankets, and household items from around the world. Learn the stories behind the artists and products, and know your purchase carries an eco or social mission. You never know what you'll find when you walk in, but it's hard to walk out without something special.

Map 4: 1714 N. Wells St., 312/264-1625,
www.greenheartshop.org; 11am-7pm
Mon.-Fri., 10am-6pm Sat., 10am-5pm Sun.

Lori's: The Sole of Chicago

Lori's started as a small designer shoe
store and has since grown to house
4,500 square feet of women's shoes
and accessories (and some apparel).
The owner scours shops in New York,
Los Angeles, Paris, Florence, and
Milan for unique, well-crafted pieces
to bring here. You'll find designers like
Sam Edelman, Pascucci, and Franco
Sarto. Lori's attentive staff knows its
stuff, and the store is a must for any
shoe lover.

Map 4: 824 W. Armitage Ave.,
773/281-5655, www.lorisshoes.com;
11am-7pm Mon.-Thurs., 11am-6pm Fri.,
10am-6pm Sat., noon-5pm Sun.

Mercy Beaucoup

Mercy sells used men's and women's
clothing and accessories to help you
curate an affordable designer ward-
robe. The store organizes its offerings
by size and receives new shipments
each week. Proceeds benefit the Mercy
Home for Boys & Girls.

Map 4: 1545 N. Wells St., 312/202-6794,
www.mercyhome.org/mercybeaucoup;
11am-7pm Tues.-Sat., 11am-5pm Sun.

GIFT AND HOME
Aaron's Apothecary

Entering Aaron's Apothecary is like
stepping back in time. The front of
the store is filled with beautiful per-
fume bottles, natural products, and
boutique makeup—including several
European brands that can be hard to
find in the United States—while an
old-world pharmacy resides in back.

Mercy Beaucoup

Aaron's Apothecary

Map 4: 2338 N. Clark St., 773/360-8595, www.aaronsapothecary.com; 8am-7pm Mon.-Fri., 8am-6pm Sat., 11am-4pm Sun.

Art Effect

This store is a favorite for unique gifts, including women's designer clothes, handmade jewelry, flirty scents and toiletries, and colorful kitchenware. The gift-wrapping is fabulous and always receives compliments. Located right off the Brown Line, this is an easy stop for a quirky souvenir.

Map 4: 934 W. Armitage Ave., 773/929-3600, www.shoparteffect.com; 11am-7pm Mon.-Thurs., 11am-6pm Fri., 10am-6pm Sat., noon-5pm Sun.

Rotofugi

This designer toy shop is beloved for its cool art gallery, pop culture figurines, and toys from established and emerging designers. The husband and wife owners clearly love what they do and are always on hand.

Map 4: 2780 N. Lincoln Ave., 773/868-3308, www.rotofugi.com; 11am-7pm daily

GOURMET AND SPECIALTY FOODS
Old Town Oil

Old Town Oil sells high-quality, small-batch olive oil and vinegars from around the world. Step inside and take your time tasting and asking questions, whether you're looking for a dipping oil, something to cook with, or something to dress a salad. The staff is extremely knowledgeable about pairing flavors and will teach you how to use each oil or vinegar. This shop also sells great gift boxes.

Map 4: 1543 N. Wells St., 312/787-9595, www.oldtownoil.com; 11am-7pm Mon.-Sat., noon-5pm Sun.

Plum Market

This specialty market is great for organic food products, rows of granola and fruit bars, an extensive selection of wine, and samples of local chocolates. Opt for a quick lunch from the hot or cold salad bar or a cup of Intelligentsia coffee to go. The apothecary is stocked with aisles of all-natural face serums, vitamins, and natural makeup.

Map 4: 1233 N. Wells St., 312/229-1400, www.plummarket.com; 8am-10pm daily

The Spice House

It's almost impossible to walk by The Spice House and not go in, so intoxicating are the exotic smells wafting from this shop. Browse extensive collections of imported, high-quality spices, extracts, salts, and rubs or grab a fun in-house spice mix to take home. The knowledgeable staff is happy to answer questions and offer recommendations.

Map 4: 1512 N. Wells St., 312/274-0378, www.thespicehouse.com; 10am-7pm Mon.-Sat., 10am-5pm Sun.

Vosges Haut-Chocolate

Chocolatier Katrina Markoff creates innovative chocolates inspired by her travels around the world. After training at Le Cordon Bleu, Markoff (named one of the 10 Best Chocolatiers in the World by *National Geographic*) opened this small purple-and-white shop to showcase delicious chocolates that incorporate indigenous spices, liqueurs, and herbs. Staff can answer questions, arrange chocolate pairings, or serve drinks like the Mexican hot chocolate. **Map 4:** 951 W. Armitage Ave., 773/296-9866; www.vosgeschocolate.com; 10am-8pm Mon.-Sat., 10am-6pm Sun.

Lakeview and Wrigleyville   Map 5

ANTIQUES

Architectural Artifacts

Explore 80,000 square feet of unique, upscale artifacts and furnishings from around the world. From fine antiques to reproductions, small vintage pieces, and grand furnishings, you could spend hours wandering around this expansive shop. **Map 5:** 4325 N Ravenswood Ave., 773/348-0622, www.architecturalartifacts. com; 10am-5pm daily

BOOKS AND MUSIC

Chicago Comics

Chicago Comics bills itself as the most comprehensive comic shop in the Midwest, and wandering through the massive selection, it's hard to argue. The shop specializes in hard-to-find titles—no matter what you're looking for, you can probably find it here. A subscription service is also available, and you can sell your old comics on Tuesdays (noon-7pm). **Map 5:** 3244 N. Clark St., 773/528-1983, www.chicagocomics.com; noon-8pm Mon.-Fri., 11am-8pm Sat., noon-7pm Sun.

Chicago Music Exchange

Whether you're a musician or a collector, a visit to Chicago Music Exchange is a must. Stroll the aisles of vintage instruments and ask the friendly staff (all musicians themselves) about inventory or any technical questions. You may walk away with a vintage strap or some new picks. **Map 5:** 3316 N. Lincoln Ave., 773/525-7773, www.chicagomusicexchange.com; 11am-7pm Mon.-Sat., 11am-5pm Sun.

Reckless Records

What sets Reckless Records apart from other vinyl shops is their selection—it's huge. Lining the dark walls are shelves packed with an extensive catalog of LPs, 45s, cassettes, CDs, and DVDs. The staff is happy to help or let you linger. The store also hosts live performances and record signings. Two other locations are in the Loop (26 E. Madison, 312/795-0878) and Wicker Park (1379 N. Milwaukee Ave., 773/235-3727). **Map 5:** 3126 N. Broadway, 773/404-5080, www.reckless.com; 10am-10pm Mon.-Sat., 10am-8pm Sun.

Roscoe Books

This isn't the biggest bookstore in Chicago, but it has a nice collection of popular and local titles and great staff recommendations. The kids section is especially welcoming and expansive and has story time on Saturdays and Tuesdays at 11am.

Map 5: 2142 W. Roscoe St., 773/857-2676, www.roscoebooks.com; 10am-7pm Sat.-Wed., 10am-8pm Thurs.-Fri.

Unabridged Bookstore

Stacks of all kinds of books fill this local bookshop, which has outlasted bigger newcomers in the area. Truly a neighborhood gem, the store only sells books and is staffed with knowledgeable folks who are passionate about reading. Check out the handwritten staff recommendations for your next favorite book.

Map 5: 3251 N. Broadway St., 773/883-9119, www.unabridgedbookstore. wordpress.com; 10am-9pm Mon.-Fri., 10am-7pm Sat.-Sun.

CLOTHING AND SHOES

BabyDolls Boutique

BabyDolls Boutique sells girly gifts like charm bracelets and purses for women, children, and, of course, babies. The shop also has a children's clothing line and custom styling sessions which can be booked in advance of a visit.

Map 5: 3737 N. Southport Ave., 773/525-2229, www.babydolls-boutique. com; 11am-7pm Mon.-Fri., 11am-6pm Sat., noon-5pm Sun.

Belmont Army

This massive, five-story thrift shop began as an army surplus store; over the decades it has morphed into a sort-of everything surplus store. You could spend hours browsing the racks here for a unique outfit or accessory—from party dresses to fatigues

Reckless Records

Leahey & Ladue Consignment

and skateboards to jewelry. It's especially popular around Halloween for firefighter uniforms, scandalous lingerie, and everything in-between. If the first floors don't appeal, head to the top floor for higher-end vintage.

Map 5: 855 W. Belmont Ave., 773/549-1038, www.belmontarmy. wordpress.com; 11am-8pm Mon.-Sat., noon-6pm Sun.

Leahey & Ladue Consignment

Leahey & Ladue is a carefully curated and neatly organized consignment shop stocked with designer pieces at reasonable prices. The quality is consistently high—you won't have to dig through racks of clothes to find a stellar piece. Come for pretty dresses, elegant handbags, heavenly jewelry, and a staff that knows their vintage.

Map 5: 3753 N. Southport Ave., 773/929-4865; 11am-7pm Mon.-Thurs., 11am-8pm Fri.-Sat.

GIFT AND HOME
Foursided

This home design and gift store features custom frames and beautiful prints, as well as cute greeting cards and quirky gifts. It's bigger than it looks and hard to step inside without buying at least something small.

Map 5: 2939 N. Broadway St., 773/248-1960, www.foursided.com; 11am-7pm Mon.-Thurs., 10am-7pm Fri.-Sat., 10am-6pm Sun.

Heritage Bicycles

Custom-made bicycles and coffee go hand in hand at this airy shop on Lincoln Avenue. Heritage produces the first completely made-in-Chicago bikes since the 1970s (when Schwinn left the city). Customers can drop in to get a flat tire fixed (or order a new bike built from scratch), chat with friends on the patio, and enjoy a signature Thai iced coffee.

Map 5: 2959 N. Lincoln Ave., 773/245-3005, www.heritagebicycles.com; 7am-7pm daily

GOURMET AND SPECIALTY FOODS

Lush Wine and Spirits

This neighborhood wine shop sells rare beers and offers an eclectic wine selection. The staff is excited to help guests taste their way to something they love; ask them to guide you through the small production wines for a not-at-all intimidating wine education. This is a comfortable, relaxed place to learn about local, unique spirits and brews—and to bring home the perfect bottle.

Map 5: 2232 W. Roscoe St., 773/281-8888, www.lushwineandspirits.com; noon-10pm Sun.-Thurs., noon-11pm Fri.-Sat.

✪ Nuts on Clark

This gourmet popcorn shop is beloved in Chicago, especially for the "Chicago Mix," a blend of caramel and cheese popcorn that is seriously addictive. Nuts on Clark sells what is widely considered the best caramel popcorn. The mom-and-pop label is so popular it's spread to multiple locations around the city and at the airport. Grab a couple bags on your way out of town.

Map 5: 3830 N. Clark St., 773/549-6622, www.nutsonclark.com; 9am-4pm Mon.-Sat.

Windy City Sweets

This candy store is a blast from the past with ring pops, Pez dispensers, licorice, gummy everything, homemade fudge, and even an ice-cream counter. Sample the ice-cream flavors to your heart's content, then order a cone to go or dine in at one of the three small tables.

Map 5: 3308 N. Broadway St., 773/477-6100, www.windycitysweets.com; 11am-11pm daily

Wicker Park and Bucktown

Map 6

CLOTHING AND SHOES

Eskell

This bright and quirky women's boutique sells clothing, jewelry, and gifts geared toward shoppers in their 20s and 30s. Peruse blouses, dresses, and classic denim from many designers, or browse the shop's own label of printed silks in simple silhouettes. While there, stock up on bangles and fragrances, discover local jewelry designers, or pick up some candles for gifts to take home.

Map 6: 1509 N. Milwaukee Ave., 773/486-0830, www.eskell.com; 11am-7pm Mon.-Sat., noon-5pm Sun.

Kokorokoko

If you grew up in the 1980s or 1990s and prefer your vintage only slightly dated, step inside Kokorokoko for a little reminiscing. The owners love the "post-hip-hop, pre-Internet era," and it shows in their exuberance when displaying products. The shop is stocked with a curated selection of graphic tees, dresses, bags, and other clothing and accessories of this generation.

Map 6: 1323 N. Milwaukee Ave., 773/252-6996, www.kokorokokovintage.com; noon-7pm Mon.-Fri., 11am-8pm Sat.

Silver Moon

This small boutique sells vintage bridal wear from the 1890s to late 1900s. They also offer expert tailoring for wedding dresses and have experience working with vintage fabrics and cuts. Aside from wedding wear, you'll find vintage dresses, jewelry, and handbags each with a handwritten tag displaying the designer's name and time period. Filled with plush Victorian chairs and gold mirrors, the shop itself feels vintage.

Map 6: 1721 W. North Ave., 773/235-5797, www.silvermoonvintage.com; 11am-4pm Mon.-Tues., 11am-6pm Wed.-Sat.

Wolfbait & B-Girls

Wolfbait & B-Girls is as local as it gets. This shop sources clothing and accessories from more than 250 local artisans and Chicago-based fair-trade companies, highlighting the city's talent. Sift through soft T-shirts, patterned dresses, soy candles, vegan soaps, printed bags, and unique Chicago memorabilia.

Map 6: 3131 W. Logan Blvd., 312/698-8685, www.wolfbaitchicago.com; 10am-7pm Mon.-Sat., 10am-4pm Sun.

BOOKS AND MUSIC

Dusty Groove Records

Dusty Groove Records offers a massive selection of rare, new, and used LPs and CDs, often landing a spot on "Best Record Store in America" lists from the likes of *Rolling Stone*, *Time*, and the *Wall Street Journal*. The top-shelf collection is neatly organized with plenty of space to browse. There's also a bargain basement with hundreds of new sale items each week. The staff obviously loves music—and really loves Chicago—and can help you discover both.

Map 6: 1120 N. Ashland Ave., 773/342-5800, www.dustygroove.com; 10am-8pm daily

Myopic Books

This neighborhood bookstore may look small from the outside, but inside are aisles of packed bookshelves lined with popular and classic titles, as well as lesser-known authors and limited editions. Grab a few books and head to the top floor to sit at a comfortable chair and table and read. Check online for a schedule of live music (Monday evenings) and author readings.

Map 6: 1564 N. Milwaukee Ave., 773/862-4882, www.myopicbookstore.com; 9am-11pm daily

Volumes BookCafé

In 2016, two Chicago sisters opened this independent bookstore and café, which quickly became a neighborhood hot spot. The long room of spacious tables is full of people working, reading, or chatting while drinking Metropolis coffee, local beer, or wine. Nibble on pastries while browsing the handpicked selection of fiction and nonfiction titles. There are comfy couches and a reading nook in back, where you'll also find a kid's section.

Map 6: 1474 N. Milwaukee Ave., 773/697-8066, www.volumesbooks.com; 9:30am-10pm Mon.-Sat., 10am-8pm Sun.

GIFT AND HOME

✪ Virtu

The amount of care that owner Julie Horowitz puts into this collection of jewelry and gifts is evident in her enthusiasm and attention to detail— from handwritten display notes to the artisans behind each piece. The beautifully crafted jewelry, ceramics, handmade cards, notebooks, and gifts sport a strong emphasis on supporting artists and shopping locally. Choose from cocktail napkins with feminist slogans to necklaces made with precious gems.

Map 6: 2035 N. Damen Ave., 773/235-3790, www.virtuchicago.com; 10am-7pm Tues., 11am-7pm Wed.-Fri., 10am-6pm Sat., 11am-5pm Sun.

GOURMET AND SPECIALTY FOODS
Wixter Market

This Wicker Park shop sells "super-frozen" seafood from around the world. "Super-frozen" means that the mahimahi from Ecuador, salmon from Scotland, and yellowtail from Hawaii is frozen at -76 degrees Fahrenheit the day they are caught and can be kept much longer than fish sold at your typical grocery store. Owner Matt Mixter is often in the shop and happy to talk about his seafood with anyone interested in the process. Wixter Market also sells tinned fish and seafood from gourmet Spanish and Portuguese brands.

Map 6: 2110 W. Division St., 312/248-2800, www.wixtermarket.com; 11am-7pm daily

TOYS
Toy de Jour

The husband and wife team behind Toy de Jour sold vintage toys and knickknacks on eBay before finally opening this small storefront in Logan Square in 2014. A neighborhood favorite, the store is stocked to the brim with nostalgia-inducing toys like G.I. Joe, Ninja Turtles, Cabbage Patch dolls, and Hardy Boys board games. Step inside and ignite your inner kid on a blast to the past.

Map 6: 2064 N. Western Ave., 773/217-9089, www.toydejour.com; 11am-7pm Mon.-Fri., noon-5pm Sat.-Sun.

Hyde Park
Map 7

BOOKS
First Aid Comics

This small store is packed to the brim with well-organized rows of comics of all kinds, from classics to lesser-known titles. The collection is impressive, but what makes this place stand out is the staff, welcoming to everyone from comic newbies to aficionados and kids.

Map 7: 1617 E. 55th St., 312/773-6642, www.firstaidcomics.com; 11am-7pm Mon., Tues., Thurs., and Fri.-Sat., 11am-8pm Wed., noon-5pm Sun.

Powell's Books

This independent bookstore is stocked floor to ceiling with used books and rare titles, especially scholarly tomes of interest to the nearby University of Chicago students. The bright and clean interior is well-organized and constantly restocked, making browsing a breeze.

Map 7: 1501 E. 57th St., 773/955-7780, www.powellschicago.com; 9am-11pm daily

CLOTHING AND ACCESSORIES
The Silver Umbrella

This small consignment boutique features gently used designer and high-end clothing, accessories, shoes, and housewares for men and women. The owners carefully curate their collection to be full of unique, quality pieces.

Powell's Books

Look for barely worn boots, perfectly cut blazers, patterned dresses, bow ties, and hats.
Map 7: 5305 S. Hyde Park Blvd., 773/675-6114, www.thesilverumbrella.com; 11am-7pm Tues.-Fri., 11am-5pm Sat.

GIFT AND HOME
Modern Cooperative

Enter Modern Cooperative and you'll find yourself swept back to the *Mad Men* era. Beautiful 1960s and '70s-style furnishings and accessories are elegantly displayed alongside a more contemporary line of furniture from Toronto designer Gus Modern. The store's clean, open layout invites browsing. Pick up some unique dishware or handmade jewelry crafted by Chicago artists to bring home.
Map 7: 1500 E. 53rd St., 872/244-7477, www.moderncooperative.com; 11am-7pm Tues.-Fri., 11am-6pm Sat.-Sun.

Greater Chicago   Map 8

ANTIQUES
Broadway Antique Market

This sprawling furniture emporium is well organized and priced reasonably for the quality of goods on offer. Styles veer toward midcentury, though modern pieces are found from time to time. Even if you don't have room in your car to drag back a new desk or dresser, it's fun to walk around the shop and check out the relics of days gone by.

Map 8: 6130 N. Broadway St., 773/743-5444, www.bamchicago.com; 11am-7pm Mon.-Sat., 11am-6pm Sun.

BOOKS
Pilsen Community Books

This cozy community bookstore is packed floor to ceiling with books of every genre. Rolling ladders help access titles on the top shelves. Most books are used, and they're all clean and in great shape; there are even rare books, like vintage copies of *The Jungle Book* and several Hemingway titles. All donations help literacy programs around Chicago.

Map 8: Pilsen, 1102 W. 18th St., www.pilsencommunitybooks.org; 11am-7pm Sun.-Mon., 11am-9pm Tues.-Sat.

CLOTHING AND SHOES
The Brown Elephant
This showroom-style thrift store features antique furniture, clothing, and jewelry displayed in an open, bright setting. Visit midday on weekdays for a choice pick of the latest women's and men's apparel, shoes, and household items. All proceeds benefit the Howard Brown Health Center, a facility that specializes in LGBTQ health.

Map 8: 5404 N. Clark St., 773/271-9382, www.howardbrown.org/brown-elephant; 11am-6pm daily

Milk Handmade
This small and charming boutique sells handcrafted women's clothing and accessories, including jewelry, soft T-shirts, and lovely dresses. The store's pale-green walls are lined with racks of clothes organized by color. A few wooden tables display jewelry, scarves, and accessories in the middle of the store. The owner showcases local designers and is usually on hand to tell you about them.

Map 8: 5137 N. Clark St., 773/234-7053, www.milkhandmade.com; 11am-7pm Mon.-Fri., 10am-6pm Sat., 11am-5pm Sun.

GIFT AND HOME
Andersonville Galleria
This spacious gallery housed in an old Swedish deli features more than 90 local vendors selling everything from local artwork from Chicago Artist Inc. to apparel by Sharp Chicago and handmade candles by the Chandler Candle Company. Browse whimsical bags, photo prints, hand-printed cards, unique jewelry, local toffee, and Chicago-centric wall art for the perfect souvenir.

Map 8: Andersonville, 5247 N Clark St., 773/878-8570, www.andersonvillegalleria.com; 11am-7pm Mon.-Thurs. and Sat., 11am-8pm Fri., 11am-6pm Sun.

Transistor
Transistor is a little bit art gallery, a little bit music venue, a lot like a cozy living room that's always worth checking out. Shop for local art, handmade jewelry, vinyl records, books and stationery, and portable electronics curated from more than 100 artists and designers. The venue also screens movies and hosts live music.

Map 8: 5224 N Clark St., 312/631-9408, www.transistorchicago.com; noon-8pm Tues.-Sat., noon-6pm Sun.

WHERE TO STAY

Whether you're visiting for work or play, Chicago has hundreds of accommodation options in a range of tastes and budgets—from extreme luxury at the Four Seasons or Peninsula hotels to affordable stays at the Freehand or Holiday Jones hostels.

For business travel or a quick weekend getaway, plan to stay downtown in the Loop, which has plenty of boutique establishments and chain hotels conveniently located near many of the city's top attractions. However, this is the heart of the business district and the Loop tends to die down on weekends; many shops and restaurants are closed and reaching nightlife venues will require a car or cab ride.

Hotel Lincoln

The Near North neighborhood is much livelier on weekends (particularly the River North district), while still close to many sights. For a more neighborhood feel, head to the Gold Coast, Lincoln Park, Wicker Park, or Lakeview.

While you can usually find a hotel or hostel room year-round, options become more limited in the summer as rates increase. Prices also rise during big sporting events (like when the Cubs play) or festivals such as Lollapalooza and Taste of Chicago. For the best hotel deals, brave the winter weather and travel in January or February.

HIGHLIGHTS

✪ **BEST VIEWS:** The rooftop bar at the **Chicago Athletic Association Hotel** has sweeping views of Lake Michigan and Millennium Park (page 178).

✪ **BEST MINIBAR:** The minibar at the **Virgin Hotel** is set up in a bright-red mini Smeg fridge and everything in it only costs $1 (page 180).

✪ **MOST LUXURIOUS:** For luxury accommodations, unparalleled service, and an on-site spa that can't be beat, stay at the **Four Seasons** (page 182).

✪ **BEST HOTEL BREAKFAST:** The Parisian-style, farm-to-table breakfast at **The Peninsula Chicago** is so good that even locals make it a destination (page 183).

✪ **MOST BUDGET-FRIENDLY:** The **Freehand Chicago** is a hostel that feels more like a hotel (page 185).

✪ **COOLEST DECOR:** The **Robey**'s midcentury furnishings and minimalist palette, lit with pops of burgundy, are straight out of a design book (page 191).

PRICE KEY

$	Less than $150 per night
$ $	$150-300 per night
$ $ $	More than $300 per night

brunch at the Freehand Chicago

CHOOSING WHERE TO STAY

The Loop and Museum Campus

For theater lovers, the Loop is your best bet. For a weekend spent seeing the sights (and your hotel room), staying downtown means you will be well-connected to most attractions, as well as L train stations and CTA bus lines. The Loop tends to be fairly dead on the weekend, as it's primarily a business district. But it's a favorite of business travelers and walking distance to most office buildings and convention centers.

Near North and Navy Pier

The Near North neighborhood has more food and dining options on the weekends, yet is still close to the city's nightlife. If you plan to wine, dine, and dance your weekend away, the River North area is where you'll want to be. The W Chicago offers the closest lodging to the Navy Pier, but more options line Michigan Avenue's Magnificent Mile, a shopper's paradise.

West Side

The West Side has few lodging options, but excellent dining opportunities. Access to the center of the city may become a bit more difficult, but is still navigable. The Ogilvie Transportation Center is located here, as is Union Station.

Lincoln Park, Old Town, and Gold Coast

Lincoln Park, Gold Coast, and Old Town are closer to more attractions, while still maintaining a local vibe. These neighborhoods see less of a late-night crowd, yet still have great boutiques and dining options, so they're great for families. Lincoln Park is well-connected with the Red and Brown CTA lines, as well as many bus lines.

Lakeview and Wrigleyville

If you're here to see a Cubs game, this neighborhood is your best bet. It can get wild on weekend nights when the Cubs win or in June during Pride month.

Wicker Park and Bucktown

Wicker Park and Bucktown have few accommodation options, but these neighborhoods are good for those interested in eating, drinking, and going out to nightclubs. A stay here offers a local feel, though transportation may be more difficult.

Hyde Park

Since it's a bit far south of downtown, Hyde Park may be good for long-term stays. Lodging rates may be better than those more centrally located and with more spacious accommodations.

ALTERNATIVE LODGING OPTIONS

There are several short-term rental options in Chicago; most are in the Loop and Near North neighborhoods. For stays longer than a few weeks, short-term rentals are often more affordable than a hotel. For furnished or unfurnished accommodations for up to a three-month period, visit www.sublet.com, www.csnhousing.com, and ww.chicagorental.com.

Home and apartment rentals from Airbnb (www.airbnb.com) and VRBO (www.vrbo.com) are extremely popular in Chicago and are a great option for longer stays. Apartment rentals are available in every neighborhood and offer a more local feel for living in the city. Plus, some Airbnb "hosts" offer discounts when booking by the week or month.

There are several hotels near

WHERE TO STAY IF...

IF YOU ONLY HAVE A WEEKEND...
...stay in **the Loop,** where the city's biggest attractions are within walking distance.

IF NIGHTLIFE IS YOUR THING...
...head to the **Near North** neighborhood and book a room close to the River North district.

IF YOU'RE HERE FOR THE FOOD...
...you'll have fewer options, but excellent dining choices on the **West Side.**

IF YOU'RE LOOKING FOR A NEIGHBORHOOD VIBE...
...a stay near **Lincoln Park** will make you feel like a Chicago native.

IF YOU'RE HERE TO SEE THE CUBS...
...there's only one place to be: **Wrigleyville.**

IF YOU'RE HERE FOR WORK...
...**the Loop** is the heart of the business district with plenty of hotels.

Chicago O'Hare and a stay here may be less expensive than a hotel room in the city. The Aloft Chicago O'Hare is located one mile from O'Hare, with a free shuttle service to downtown. The Hilton Chicago O'Hare is located *on* the airport grounds, with access to downtown via the CTA Blue Line.

The Loop and Museum Campus   Map 1

The Blackstone $$$
The Blackstone sits in a historic French beaux arts building designed in 1909 by architects Marshall & Fox. The 21-story hotel offers 335 elegant rooms (including historic and modern suites) with pillow-top beds, marble bathrooms, luxury amenities, and views overlooking Grant Park. There's a 24-hour gym, an on-site Starbucks, and free wireless Internet. The hotel is a 10-minute walk to The Art Institute, Michigan Avenue, and Willis Tower.
Map 1: 636 S. Michigan Ave., 312/447-0955, www.theblackstonehotel.com

✪ Chicago Athletic Association Hotel $$$
In 2016, this prestigious Michigan Avenue athletic club from the late 1800s was reborn as the luxurious Chicago Athletic Association Hotel, drawing visitors for its impeccable service and amenities and locals for its dining options and views from the bar. The grand marble staircases and art deco interior design are reminiscent of the neo-Gothic building's past, while the renovated bathrooms, spacious rooms, and upscale amenities are fully modern. Upon arrival, head straight to Cindy's Rooftop Bar for sweeping views across Lake Michigan

and Millennium Park. At night, enjoy bocce or billiards and an esteemed craft cocktail list in the historic game room.

Map 1: 12 S. Michigan Ave., 312/940-3552, www.chicagoathletichotel.com

Fairmont Chicago $$$

This luxury hotel near Millennium Park offers guests magnificent views over the skyline, Lake Michigan, and Grant Park. Spacious rooms feature lots of natural light and are decorated in calm earth tones with artwork from photographer Warwick Orme. Bathrooms include marble furnishings, luxury bath products, and separate soaking tubs and showers. Dine in the on-site Millennium Room, the casual Columbus Tap, or The Bar cocktail bar. Amenities include a 24-hour fitness room, a full-service spa, and free wireless Internet. The Fairmont Chicago is an AAA Four Diamond hotel and has received a Green Seal Silver Certification.

Map 1: 200 N. Columbus Dr., 312/565-8000, www.fairmont.com/chicago

The Alise $$

The Alise (formerly the Hotel Burnham) was designed by Daniel Burnham in the Gothic Revival style. Guests can admire vintage features like the spiral staircases and mosaic floors while enjoying a stay in refreshingly modern rooms. Rooms are on the small side, but are comfortable, with sleek furnishings, flat-screen TVs, and luxury bath amenities. There is an on-site fitness center and a bike rental service. Located walking distance to Michigan Avenue and the Loop, the Alise is also very pet-friendly—dogs are offered a bed and water upon request.

Map 1: 1 W. Washington St., 312/940-7997, www.staypineapple.com

Hampton Inn Majestic Theater District $$

Located inside the PrivateBank Theatre, this hotel is in the center of the Loop and walking distance to Millennium Park, The Art Institute, Willis Tower, and the Magnificent Mile. Rooms are clean and comfortable, with plush bedding, HDTVs, and workstations. Stays include a free breakfast at the on-site restaurant (or to go in a Hampton On the Run Breakfast Bag). Guests can use the gym on-site, and free wireless Internet is available throughout the hotel.

Map 1: 22 W Monroe St., 312/332-5052, www.hamptoninn.com

Hotel Blake $$

This boutique hotel on Printer's Row in the South Loop is housed in a historic 19th-century building, with modern furnishings in inviting golds and reds. Rooms feature large windows, Egyptian cotton sheets, comfortable chairs, rainfall showerheads, and luxury eco-conscious toiletries. Other amenities include free wireless Internet, a 24-hour gym, and a business center. The downstairs Meli Café and Juice Bar is a local favorite for breakfast or lunch; there's also full in-room dining. Printer's Row is full of beautiful historic brick buildings and a quick walk to The Art Institute and Michigan Avenue.

Map 1: 500 S Dearborn St., 312/986-1234, www.hotelblake.com

Hyatt Centric The Loop $$

The Hyatt Centric The Loop stands out for its historic art deco design and knowledgeable service. The hotel works with local bloggers to create neighborhood guides for guests, and the concierge can assist with bookings and restaurant reservations. Spacious rooms fill with natural light by day and feature beds with Egyptian cotton sheets. The rooftop bar, Aire (open seasonally), serves craft cocktails and small plates, or guests can dine at the adjoining Cochon Volant. On-site appeals include a 24-hour fitness center, meeting spaces, a game area, and a communal fireplace. The hotel is a short walk from State Street, Millennium Park, The Art Institute, and Chicago's Theater District.

Map 1: 100 W Monroe St., 312/236-1234, https://theloopchicago.centric.hyatt.com

Kimpton Gray Hotel $$

Located in a landmark building, this beautiful hotel's sophistication is reminiscent of London, decorated in sumptuous grays and browns. Spacious, modern rooms include flat-screen TVs, Atelier Bloem bath products, and plush bathrobes; some rooms have spa baths. Enjoy a cocktail at Vol. 39, a luxury library lounge, or dine on Latin-inspired food at Boleo. There's also a 24-hour fitness center, a complimentary evening wine hour, free wireless Internet, and a full-service salon and spa. The hotel is just blocks from Michigan Avenue and within walking distance to theaters, The Art Institute, and the Washington/Wells CTA stop.

Map 1: 122 W. Monroe St., 877/771-7031, www.grayhotelchicago.com

Kimpton Hotel Allegro $$

The Allegro's glamorous rooms feature beautifully patterned accent walls, silk pillowcases, large bathrooms, and in-room spa program services. There's free Internet and a 43-inch flat-screen LCD TV in each room. An on-site fitness center is fully equipped with cardio machines, weights, and yoga accessories. Complimentary wine is offered at cocktail hour, and the hotel's Italian restaurant is 312 Chicago. You're in the heart of the Theater District and a five-minute walk from Grant Park and State Street.

Map 1: 171 W. Randolph St., 312/236-0123, www.allegrochicago.com

The Palmer House Hilton $$

Built in 1871, The Palmer House Hilton is one of Chicago's great historic hotels. Updated rooms feature modern amenities such as workstations, flat-screen HDTVs, and luxury bath products. There's an indoor pool and hot tub and an on-site spa. Dining options include a rooftop terrace and the lobby bar. The hotel is one block from the Red Line CTA Monroe Station and Millennium Park as well as steps from the Theater District.

Map 1: 17 E. Monroe St., 312/726-7500, www.palmerhousehiltonhotel.com

Radisson Blu Aqua $$

The modern exterior of the Aqua building resembles a wave, with high ceilings and an exposed brick interior. Inside this luxury Radisson, contemporary rooms feature hardwood floors, minimalist furniture, flat-screen TVs, bathrobes, free wireless Internet, and views of Millennium Park, the Chicago skyline, or Lake Michigan. Amenities include a health club with a fitness room, basketball court, and indoor and outdoor pool and an Italian restaurant.

Map 1: 221 N. Columbus Dr., 312/565-5258, www.radissonblu.com/en/aquahotel-chicago

✪ Virgin Hotel $$

The Virgin brand prides itself on breaking tradition, and its hotel is

CHICAGO'S HISTORIC HOTELS

The late 19th and early 20th centuries were a golden age for Chicago architecture. After the Great Chicago Fire of 1871 leveled the city, much of the business district was rebuilt with a new focus on fire codes and design. In 1893, the World's Columbian Exposition made Chicago a hub for architecture, drawing respected architects from across the country who then designed buildings for the city in Gothic and Renaissance Revival styles. Many of the historic buildings constructed during this time are beautiful hotels still in use today.

The **Palmer House**, now a Hilton property in the Loop, was once the largest hotel in the world. Built in 1871 and designed by architect John M. Van Osdel, it has housed Frank Sinatra, Judy Garland, Liberace, and Louis Armstrong. Walk inside to tour the lobby, which is painted with elaborate murals and decorated in gold accents.

The Drake was designed by Benjamin Marshall with Italian Renaissance palaces in mind. Upon opening on New Year's Eve in 1920, the hotel became synonymous with wealth and fame in Chicago. It's a favorite of presidents, from Herbert Hoover to Bill Clinton and Barack Obama, as well as Walt Disney, Princess Diana, and Pope John Paul II. The hotel was also featured in the films *Risky Business* and *My Best Friend's Wedding*.

The **InterContinental** on Michigan Avenue was once the Medinah Athletic Club, built in 1929 at the peak of Chicago's skyscraper glory. The 42-story hotel featured a mix of international styles and included a boxing arena, an archery range, and a large swimming pool, which is still intact. Architect Walter W. Ahlschlager combined a mix of architectural styles, including Egyptian, Greek, medieval, art deco, and Gothic for an impressive tower with various carved sections topped with a golden cupola.

Daniel Burnham designed the **Hotel Burnham** (now The Alise), a steel and glass masterpiece that set the standard for modern skyscrapers while maintaining a classic Gothic Revival exterior. Today guests can take an audio tour of the hotel, which is a National Historic Landmark.

Designed by architect Benjamin Marshall and listed on the National Register of Historic Places, **The Blackstone** features a beautiful beaux arts-style lobby and an ornate Crystal Ballroom. Teddy Roosevelt, Jimmy Carter, and 10 other U.S. presidents, as well as Tennessee Williams and Al Capone, have stayed here.

no different. Rooms feature two large "chambers": A dressing chamber holds the bathroom and soaking tub, with a spacious closet, vanity, and sitting area; the sleeping lounge is separated by a sliding door and features ergonomic beds and a workstation. Each includes a cute minibar in a brightly colored Smeg fridge; all products are $1 (the hotel calls it "street pricing"). A daily social hour is held in the Commons Club. The hotel is in a prime location within walking distance to all Loop sights, as well as Michigan Avenue.

Map 1: 203 N. Wabash Ave., 312/940-4400, www.virginhotels.com

THEWit $$

Located in the Theater District, rooms in this stylish and modern hotel feature pops of color with eclectic art, work spaces, custom furniture, flat-screen TVs, and luxury toiletries. (Spa rooms feature Kohler soaking tubs.) Visit the on-site spa, fitness center, yoga studio, or the private theater. The rooftop lounge (called ROOF) often features DJs and dancing, while the State and Lake Tavern serves gastropub fare. The hotel is next to the State/Lake L stop and a 10-minute walk from Millennium Park.

Map 1: 201 N. State St., 312/467-0200, www.thewithotel.com

Chicago's Essex Inn $

The Essex Inn is in one of the best locations in the city: It's right on Michigan Avenue and close to Museum Campus. A large terrace overlooks the city, as do many of the rooms. Each room is

Chicago's Essex Inn

decorated colorfully, with wood accents and modern amenities like large flat-screen TVs and iPhone docks. All rooms have a refrigerator and desk, making them ideal for a longer stay. There's a nice gym and free wireless Internet throughout the hotel.

Map 1: 800 S. Michigan Ave., 312/939-2800, www.essexinn.com

Club Quarters Hotel $

The Club Quarters Hotel is centrally located for both visitors and business travelers with busy schedules. Rooms are small and basic, yet comfortable with flat-screen TVs, free wireless Internet, toiletries, bottled water, and a coffee machine. Downstairs is Elephant & Castle, an English-style pub, and a Starbucks. A small hotel gym features cardio equipment and weights. The Willis Tower, Grant Park, and multiple subway stations are within a short walk.

Map 1: 111 W. Adams St., 312/214-6400, www.clubquartershotels.com

Congress Plaza Hotel $

Located directly across from Grant Park, rooms at the Congress Plaza Hotel feature sweeping views of the park, Lake Michigan, or the western skyline. Standard rooms feature no-frills amenities—a coffee-maker, TV, and free wireless Internet. The location is the reason to stay here, especially if you're in town for an event at Millennium Park, Grant Park, or along Michigan Avenue. On-site amenities include a 24-hour fitness center, same-day dry cleaning service, and a business center.

Map 1: 520 S. Michigan Ave., 312/427-3800, www.congressplazahotel.com

Near North and Navy Pier

Map 2

✪ Four Seasons $$$

One of Chicago's best hotels, the Four Seasons features skyline views, a luxurious spa, a fabulous on-site restaurant, and rooms with beautiful vintage French furnishings. The skyscraper setting offers panoramic views from guest rooms, and even from marble bathtubs, with LCD flat-screen TVs and high-end Malin + Goetz toiletries. The on-site Allium Restaurant serves fine-dining American cuisine while posh Chicagoans flock to the spa, which features a Roman sauna, pool, hot tub, and a wide array of treatments. There's a fitness center and business center, and a children's club with movies, video games, and other activities. If you can bring yourself to leave the hotel, you're just a few minutes from Millennium Park, Michigan Avenue, Navy Pier, and more. It's no wonder this hotel has received a Forbes 5-Star rating for more than 20 years in a row and the AAA Five Diamond Award for almost 30 years.

Map 2: 120 E. Delaware Pl., 312/280-8800, www.fourseasons.com

InterContinental $$$

Built in 1929 as the Medinah Athletic Club, this hotel combines a mix of Egyptian, Greek, Gothic, and medieval architectural styles that evoke the design of this former men's club. The historic Executive Tower has 315 unique rooms and suites (some with views of the Chicago River or Lake Michigan) featuring plush-top beds, HDTVs, and large baths. The 447 renovated rooms in the Grand Tower are more contemporary, decorated in green earth tones with red accents and with king or double beds. Amenities include an on-site fitness center and spa and a junior Olympic-size pool original to the hotel. There's also a Starbucks and Michael Jordan's Steakhouse. The hotel is within walking distance of Navy Pier and the Museum Campus.

Map 2: 505 N. Michigan Ave., 312/944-4100, www.icchicagohotel.com

The Langham $$$

This Forbes 5-Star Hotel brings British luxury to the heart of Chicago. The skyscraper hotel was designed by architect Mies van der Rohe; the beautiful, light-filled space harbors views of the skyline and Lake Michigan. Neutral-toned rooms are understated and elegant, giving each a welcome feel, and are complemented by floor-to-ceiling windows. Marble bathrooms hold a large soaking tub and rainfall shower. A large pool, fitness center, and restaurant and bar round out the experience.

Map 2: 330 N. Wabash Ave., 312/923-9988, www.langhamhotels.com/chicago

Park Hyatt $$$

The Park Hyatt is the epitome of comfort in downtown Chicago. The large rooms are filled with plush furnishings; bathrooms feature large bathtubs, standing showers, and a spacious double sink. You're assured a good nights' rest thanks to automatic blackout shades and soundproof walls. Room service is available via iPad, or head to the on-site restaurant, NoMi, for fine dining. There's an indoor pool, spa, fitness center, and meeting space. Located on Michigan Avenue, the hotel is in the heart of Chicago shopping, nightlife, and dining, as well as many attractions.

Map 2: 800 N. Michigan Ave., 312/335-1234, www.chicago.park.hyatt.com

☺ The Peninsula Chicago $$$

This five-star hotel takes prides in its service and amenities. Luxurious rooms feature wood and leather details with king-size beds and custom linens, 55-inch televisions, commissioned artwork, and a nutrition bar and espresso machine. Bathrooms include soaking tubs, illuminated mirrors, and a separate shower. The indoor pool is a highlight, with floor-to-ceiling windows and views of the city. The gym offers classes, plus guests have access to an outdoor terrace with views, an on-site restaurant, and an afternoon tea service. The location is close to Michigan Avenue and Navy Pier.

Map 2: 108 E. Superior St., 312/337-2888, www.chicago.peninsula.com

drinks at the Conrad hotel bar

The Waldorf Astoria $$$

This luxurious hotel is situated in a quiet part of the Gold Coast within walking distance to Michigan Avenue, the Museum of Contemporary Art, and other attractions. Rooms are classic and elegant with flat-screen TVs, minifridges, microwaves, and large bathtubs. The on-site spa and sauna are a destination for Chicagoans, as is the European bistro and cocktail bar. There's a fitness center and pool and a fully equipped business center.

Map 2: 11 E. Walton St., 312/646-1300, www.waldorfastoria3.hilton.com

Conrad $$

The Conrad hotel is geared toward the busy traveler who wants to see a local side of the city. The hotel opened in late 2016, with spacious and modern rooms, mirrored bathrooms, and city views. The rooftop sushi restaurant has become a favorite among Chicagoans. The on-site Baptise & Bottle serves farm-to-table American fare and cocktails, and there is a small Italian café downstairs. The hotel lobby features a gorgeous winding staircase and floor-to-ceiling windows that look down onto the city—a relaxing space after a long day.

Map 2: 101 E. Erie St., 312/667-6700, www. conradchicagohotel.com

The Drake $$

This historic hotel opened in 1920 and has been a favorite of politicians and celebrities. Barack Obama and Princess Diana have both stayed here, among others, and it's been the setting for iconic films like *Risky Business*. The hotel was designed in the Italian Renaissance Revival style with arched walkways, sweeping staircases, and ornate ceilings. Rooms feature luxury beds and marble bathrooms with flat-screen HDTVs, iPod docking stations, luxury bath products, a minibar and coffee-maker, and unique artwork. The hotel is steps from Oak Street Beach, and many rooms have views over Michigan Avenue. There's an on-site convenience store, coffee shop, and souvenir shop. The hotel is right off Michigan Avenue, within walking distance of the John Hancock Center, Millennium Park, and The Art Institute.

Map 2: 140 E. Walton Pl., 312/787-2200, www.thedrakehotel.com

The Godfrey $$

This stylish hotel features unique textiles and colored furniture in the large guest rooms. If you're here to work, you'll appreciate the ergonomic desk chairs, while if you're here for leisure, you'll love the L'Occitane toiletries, plush bathrobes, and in-room entertainment options. The hotel is steps from Michigan Avenue and a short trip from the heart of downtown, but set apart from the noise of the city. Head up to the IO Rooftop Lounge, which is one of the hottest spots in the city come summer.

Map 2: 127 W. Huron St., 312/649-2000, www.godfreyhotelchicago.com

Acme Hotel

Palomar Hotel $$

This boutique, luxury hotel is for those who like things a little different. Rooms are decorated with art inspired by the Chicago World's Fair and dotted with colored rugs and accents. There's an indoor pool, a 24-hour fitness center, a spa, and the on-site restaurant, Sable Kitchen & Bar. Guests are within walking distance to many of the city's famous attractions.

Map 2: 505 N. State St., 312/755-9703, www.hotelpalomar-chicago.com

W Chicago $$

The glamorous W Chicago sparkles—from its gleaming lobby to its shimmering rooms featuring wide windows with skyline views, glass desks, comfortable beds, and minimalist furnishings. Bliss bath products line the shower and are available in the connected spa. Head up to the Wet Deck for panoramic views of Navy Pier, cocktail in hand. The handy SPG app allows guests to automatically check in and unlock the room door.

Map 2: 644 N. Lake Shore Dr., 312/943-9200, www.wchicago-lakeshore.com

Acme Hotel $

The Acme Hotel is pretty much the definition of hip. It's a boutique hotel for those who love design, music, and tech. It's trendy and fun, with cool amenities like a free hotspot to go, a great bonus for international travelers. Rooms are decorated with quirky art and cater to the tech-savvy. PC compatible hookups, wireless Bowers and Wilkins Zeppelin audio systems, and possibly the fastest Internet in Chicago make each room feel like home.

Map 2: 15 E. Ohio St., 312/894-0800, www.acmehotelcompany.com

✪ Freehand Chicago $

This downtown Chicago hostel is in a historic building and has one of the coolest cafés in the city. The former Tokyo Hotel, built in 1927, was renovated in 2015 to feature spacious dorm rooms and funky decor.

BEST HOTEL BARS

BROKEN SHAKER AT FREEHAND CHICAGO
Hostel guests and trendy Chicagoans come to **Freehand Chicago** (page 185) for unique cocktails in a low-key, dimly lit setting.

CINDY'S ROOFTOP BAR AT THE CHICAGO ATHLETIC ASSOCIATION HOTEL
The **Chicago Athletic Association Hotel**'s (page 178) rooftop bar is the place for expertly mixed cocktails with some of the best views in the city.

THE J. PARKER ROOFTOP BAR AT THE HOTEL LINCOLN
The **Hotel Lincoln**'s (page 188) rooftop bar has a spacious patio with skyline views and late-night dancing.

SABLE KITCHEN & BAR AT PALOMAR HOTEL
The hotel bar at the **Palomar Hotel** (page 185) is a destination on its own, with 1940s glamour and old-school cocktails with a twist.

VOL. 39 AT THE KIMPTON GRAY HOTEL
This library-themed bar at the **Kimpton Gray Hotel** (page 180) uses gilded cocktail carts to serve caviar and champagne.

Female-only and male-only rooms, plus mixed dorms are available, as are private rooms. The 20-something clientele often takes over the Broken Shaker mixology bar before heading to bed. In the morning, Cafe Integral's long tables fill with visitors and Chicagoans. The young, fun staff is always up on the city's events calendar and often host its own events in the hotel.

Map 2: 19 E. Ohio St., 312/940-3699, www.freehandhotels.com/chicago

Holiday Inn Chicago Mart Plaza $
Like most Holiday Inns, this one is basic but reliable. Less than a five-minute walk from the Merchandise Mart, it's a great base for your Chicago vacation, especially if you plan to spend time along the river and downtown. There's a restaurant and bar, and a large room service menu, as well as an attached coffee shop. Rooms each have refrigerators, coffee-makers, LCD TVs, and wireless Internet. On-site you'll find a business center, fitness center, pool, and sauna. Parking is $39/night, which is cheaper than at many hotels in the area.

Map 2: 350 W. Mart Center, 312/836-5000, www.holidayinn.com

Hotel Felix $
This boutique hotel prides itself on being ecofriendly and was Chicago's first hotel to become Silver LEED certified by the U.S. Green Building Council. The four-star hotel combines sustainability with luxury rooms and modern furnishings. While rooms are on the small side, they feature luxury amenities and sleek bathrooms. There's a full-service spa, fitness center, and 24-hour business center on-site, and you'll be within walking distance of Michigan Avenue, Millennium Park, and other top sights.

Map 2: 111 W. Huron St., 312/447-3440, www.hotelfelixchicago.com

Inn of Chicago $
Like many Chicago hotels, the Inn of Chicago is housed in a historic building, renovated for modern expectations. Just half a block from the

Warwick Allerton

Magnificent Mile you'll be within walking distance of hundreds of shops, restaurants, and sights. Back at the hotel, you can choose between a traditional or modern room, which applies to the decor. All amenities are modern, and rooms feature wireless Internet, luxurious toiletries, and all other basic amenities you would expect from a hotel. There's a fitness center in the building, and a bar with skyline views upstairs.

Map 2: 162 E. Ohio St., 312/787-3100, www.theinnofchicago.com

Warwick Allerton $

This historic 1920s hotel offers a timeless look with modern amenities. Standard rooms are on the small side, but include comfortable beds, a desk, and marble bathrooms. Each room lets in a lot of light, and many offer great views of the city. If you are traveling with small children, they can spend time at the Children's Club while you dine at the in-house restaurant. When arriving, you might notice a skyscraper sign reading "Tip-Top Tap." The hotel's historic bar is now a meeting room, but you can still go up and look for a flashback to a time when Sinatra and Bing Crosby hung out here.

Map 2: 701 N. Michigan Ave., 312/440-1500, www.warwickhotels.com/allerton-hotel-chicago

The Westin $

Rooms at The Westin are simple and polished, with wood furnishings and crisp white accents. Many rooms offer incredible views of the skyline or Chicago River. The concierge can set up an architecture tour, research theater tickets, or recommend one of the many nearby restaurants. Or dine in at the on-site sushi restaurant and bar or at a second bar overlooking the river. The gym is open 24 hours a day; guests can rent New Balance gear. A cozy group work space can be booked for last-minute meetings.

Map 2: 320 N. Dearborn St., 312/744-1900, www.westinchicago.com

The Whitehall Hotel $

The Whitehall Hotel is in a historic high-rise residence from the 1920s. The renovated boutique hotel sits just a block from Michigan Avenue near multiple bus lines. Due to the building's age, rooms are small and somewhat basic, but feature romantic decor and modern bathrooms. There are two restaurants and a fitness center on-site. The hotel is known as one of the best values downtown; while not luxurious, it is nice and close to everything.

Map 2: 105 E. Delaware Pl., 312/944-6300, www.thewhitehallhotel.com

West Side   Map 3

Soho House $$$

This hotel and members-only club in the heart of the West Loop is the place to be for posh Chicagoans. With a comfortable lounge, a large circular bar, a music room stocked with instruments, multiple restaurants, a huge gym with a boxing ring, a movie screening room, an impressive art collection, and a rooftop pool with skyline views (and great parties come summer), a stay at Soho House can make it hard to want to leave. Rooms come in a variety of sizes and feature king-size beds with Egyptian cotton sheets, plush armchairs, luxury toiletries, and rain showerheads in the bathroom. Lots of jewel tones and rich wooden accents throughout make it feel like you're in a luxurious living room. Nonmembers can book hotel rooms online or by phone.

Map 3: 113-123 N. Green St., 312/521-8000, www.sohohousechicago.com

Lincoln Park, Old Town, and Gold Coast   Map 4

Belden-Stratford Hotel $$$

This beautiful hotel sits across from the Lincoln Park Zoo and offers large rooms with sweeping views of the skyline and Lake Michigan. The Belden-Stratford provides fully furnished apartments for one-night stays as well as short-term housing. Classically decorated units include fully equipped kitchens, comfortable beds, a seating area, spacious closets, and dry cleaning service. A free continental breakfast is served each morning, or dine at the attached French bistro, Mon Ami Gabi. Other amenities include a fitness center and spa.

Map 4: 2300 N. Lincoln Park W., 773/823-0919, www.beldenstratford.com

Hotel Lincoln $$

This quirky hotel dates to the 1920s and is filled with vintage details and original artwork by local artists. Rooms are decorated in royal blues and deep yellows with bright mirrors and artistic throw pillows. Located close to Lincoln Park, Second City, and within walking distance of shops and restaurants, the hotel features a 24-hour gym, free wireless Internet, a fine-dining restaurant, bike rentals, and rooftop yoga. The on-site Elaine's Coffee Call and J. Parker rooftop bar are favorites of Chicagoans.

Map 4: 1816 N. Clark St., 312/254-4700, www.jdvhotels.com

Hotel Lincoln lobby

Public Chicago Hotel $$

This Gold Coast hotel is just a five-minute walk to the beach and blocks from Michigan Avenue. Large rooms are decorated in calm, neutral hues and postcards of Chicago jazz legends adorn the walls. The connected Pump Room restaurant is a favorite for brunch, and a bar and café are on-site. The 24-hour fitness center and projection center with couches and a 110-inch screen make for another reason to book here.

Map 4: 1301 N. State St., 312/787-3700, www.publicchicago.com

Chicago Getaway Hostel $

This chic hostel feels like a hip hotel with fun extras like a social events,

bike and guitar rentals, and a game room and a communal kitchen stocked with high-quality cookware. Basic yet spacious rooms feature bunk beds in a range of configurations (two, four, or eight beds); some rooms are private with shared baths, but there are two dorm-style rooms. Sheets, towels, and blankets are included, and breakfast and wireless Internet are free.

Map 4: 616 W Arlington Pl., 773/929-5380, www.getawayhostel.com

Hotel Indigo Gold Coast $

This small, pastel-colored hotel in the Gold Coast is great for those who want to spend their time on the beach or Michigan Avenue, both just a short walk away. Also within walking distance of Lincoln Park, the hotel is housed in a renovated, older building. Rooms are on the small side, but are very clean with bright accents, beachy furniture, and modern amenities like a fitness center, a restaurant and bar with breakfast, a lounge, and a business center.

Map 4: 1244 N. Dearborn Pkwy., 312/787-4980, www.hotelindigo.com

Inn at Lincoln Park $

This budget hotel on the north edge of Lincoln Park is filled with architectural details from the early 1900s, giving it character and charm. The hotel's age does show when it comes to the small, somewhat dated rooms and bathrooms, but if you're looking for an inexpensive option within walking distance to Lincoln Park and don't plan on spending much time in your room, this can be a good option. A continental breakfast is included.

Map 4: 601 W. Diversey Pkwy., 866/774-7275, www.innlp.com

Lakeview and Wrigleyville   Map 5

Best Western Plus Hawthorne Terrace $

This small branch of the Best Western chain is one of the few hotels in the area, 0.5 mile from Lake Michigan and 0.6 mile from Wrigley Field and the closest L station. In the heart of Boystown, you're steps away from dozens of bars and restaurants. While amenities are basic, the large suites include full kitchens—nice for longer stays. Sip free coffee in the courtyard and enjoy people-watching on Broadway.

Map 5: 3434 N. Broadway St., 773/244-3434, www.hawthorneterrace.com

Best Western Plus Hawthorne Terrace

City Suites Chicago $

This affordable hotel sits just off the Belmont L line (brown), making it convenient for travelers. Rooms are basic but clean and comfortable. The art deco lobby is stocked with 24-hour coffee, and cookies in the afternoon. Perks include a free pass to a nearby gym, a complimentary breakfast, and free wireless Internet.

Map 5: 933 W. Belmont Ave., 773/404-3400, www.chicagocitysuites.com

Days Inn $

The Lakeview Days Inn is the most basic of the area hotels, but it's also the most budget-friendly. The historic redbrick building sits minutes from Wrigley Field and is just a short walk from the Diversey L station, a line that runs throughout the city. A complimentary breakfast buffet, wireless Internet, and an exercise room are on-site.

Map 5: 644 Diversey Pkwy., 773/525-7010, www.daysinnchicago.net

Old Chicago Inn $

At this older, but charming bed-and-breakfast, each room is uniquely decorated with antique furniture and includes a continental breakfast and a complimentary dinner at Trader Todd's nearby. Relax near the lobby fireplace and peruse books about Chicago's past. Guests receive access to Room 13, the 1920s speakeasy that's notoriously hard for Chicago residents to get into.

Map 5: 3222 N. Sheffield Ave., 773/472-2278, www.oldchicagoinn.com

Wicker Park and Bucktown

Map 6

✪ The Robey $$

One of Chicago's most iconic buildings, the 12-story art deco Northwest Tower was one of the first skyscrapers built outside of downtown. In 2016, this building designed by Perkins, Chatten & Hammond in the early 1920s was turned into the boutique Robey hotel. The lobby of this Chicago landmark gives a nod to the last century with its dark-paneled walls, leather furniture, and emerald accents. The tower's triangular shape helps every room receive a lot of light. Amenities from Le Labo, 400-thread-count sheets, soft denim robes, free wireless Internet, and plush beds add a touch of luxury.

Map 6: 1600 N. Milwaukee Ave., 872/315-3050, www.therobey.com

Holiday Jones Hostel $

Holiday Jones Hostel sits right off the CTA Blue Line, conveniently located in Wicker Park. The hostel is clean and spacious, with dorms and shared rooms at affordable rates (linens and towels provided). Bunk beds line the walls of the rooms, which include big windows and a shared bathroom. Play foosball, watch movies, rent bicycles, or hang out with the other guests in the common areas. A complimentary breakfast is included.

Map 6: 1659 W. Division St., 312/804-3335, www.holidayjones.com

Hyde Park

Map 7

Chicago Lakeshore Hotel $$

This small, independently owned hotel boasts rooms with a personalized feel and views over Lake Michigan. Rooms are basic, with a comfortable bed and desk area, complimentary toiletries, free wireless Internet, and a flat-screen TV. On-site amenities include Friday night jazz in the restaurant and a seasonal outdoor pool. There's free parking for guests and shuttle service to local areas, and you're just a short walk from the beach and Hyde Park attractions.

Map 7: 4900 S. Lake Shore Dr., 773/288-5800, www.chicagolakeshorehotel.com

Hyatt Place Chicago South/University District $$

Located next to the University of Chicago and the University Medical Center, the Hyatt Place Chicago is a great choice if you're visiting the university. Rooms feature plush beds, comfortable work centers, a 42-inch HDTV, free wireless Internet, and spacious bathrooms with granite countertops and complimentary toiletries. Other amenities include an indoor pool, fitness center, a guest kitchen with 24-hour snacks, and a bakery with a bar, desserts, and Starbucks coffee. The hotel is four miles from the McCormick Place Convention

Center and receives overflow from conference-goers who want something more in a neighborhood. A daily shuttle service travels between the hotel, the Loop, and the airport.

Map 7: 5225 S. Harper Ave., 773/752-5300, www.chicagosouthuniversity.place.hyatt.com

Greater Chicago   Map 8

The Guesthouse Hotel $$$

This luxury Andersonville guesthouse is ideal for extended stays, located within walking distance of neighborhood coffee shops and restaurants. Each guesthouse suite enjoys natural light from large windows with plush beds, a gourmet kitchen, flat-screen TV, spa-style bathroom, and a private outdoor area with barbecue. Mingle with other guests in the common lounge, work out in the fitness center, do laundry on-site, relax on the rooftop deck, or enjoy afternoon tea in the lounge.

Map 8: Andersonville, 4872 N. Clark St., 773/564-9568, www.theguesthousehotel.com

Aloft Chicago O'Hare $$

This branch of the Aloft chain is about a mile outside Chicago O'Hare and has a free airport shuttle and CTA shuttle to downtown. The stylish blue-and-white-themed rooms are minimalistic with high ceilings, large windows, and platform beds. Amenities include minifridges, tea and coffee, and 42-inch flat-screen cable TVs. Bathrooms feature spacious showers and toiletries from Bliss. There's an indoor pool and fitness center, a business center, free wireless Internet, an on-site restaurant, a bar, and a cappuccino bar. Across the street is one of Chicago's largest fashion outlet malls.

Map 8: 9700 Balmoral Ave., 847/671-4444, www.aloftchicagoohare.com

Four Points by Sheraton Chicago O'Hare Airport $$

Less than two miles from Chicago O'Hare and with a 24-hour free airport shuttle, this Four Points by Sheraton is great for business travelers. Rooms feature a work desk and armchair in addition to plush beds, spacious bathrooms, flat-screen TVs, and coffee and tea. The hotel is decorated in warm hues, making the rooms inviting after a day of work. Facilities include a business center and a well-equipped gym with a sauna. Dine at Mirage, the hotel restaurant, or grab a drink at the on-site Oasis Lounge. The hotel is in a convenient location for those visiting the Allstate Arena, Casino Rivers, or the Fashion Outlets of Chicago, about a 10-minute drive away.

Map 8: 10249 W. Irving Park Rd., 847/671-6000, www.fourpointschicagoohare.com

Hilton Chicago O'Hare Airport $$

The Hilton Chicago O'Hare is the only hotel on the airport grounds, so you're within steps of a shower and a comfy bed after your plane lands. Spacious beige-toned rooms feature quilt-top beds, blackout curtains and sound-resistant windows, 42-inch HDTVs, work desks, bathrooms with large sinks and a shower, and a well-stocked minibar. There are a gym and swimming pool on-site, a steakhouse, a sports bar, and access to the CTA Blue Line downtown. The hotel is located in a no-fly zone; follow the indoor walkway between the hotel and domestic Terminal 2, or opt for the free shuttle from the International Terminal.

Map 8: 10000 W. O'Hare Ave., 773/686-8000, hwww3.hilton.com

South Loop Hotel $$

This boutique hotel just a few minutes from McCormick Place is great for business travelers. The spacious rooms include plush beds, 32-inch TVs, ergonomic workstations, and soaking bathtubs. It offers a 24-hour business center, a fitness center, a salon, a gift shop, free wireless Internet, and free guest parking. It's close to the United Center, which is convenient if you're planning to see a game or a concert.

Map 8: 11 W. 16th St., 312/225-7000, www.chicagosouthloophotel.com

DAY TRIPS

DAY TRIPS

There's much to see and do in Chicago, but sometimes it's nice to take a break from the city. On a day trip, you can truly enjoy the nature of the Midwest.

The village of Oak Park is only an L train ride from downtown Chicago, yet it feels a world away. The pedestrian-friendly town is a walking museum of Frank

Wisconsin Dells

Lloyd Wright architecture as well as the childhood home of author Ernest Hemingway.

With a 1.5-hour drive southwest, you can explore the natural beauty of Starved Rock State Park where you can hike and camp amid canyons, waterfalls, and sandstone bluffs.

West of Chicago, the town of Galena is home to hundreds of historic buildings and dedicated to preserving its Civil War history. Its notable claim to fame is Ulysses S. Grant. Today, tours of Grant's home, as well as an accompanying museum, offer insight into the former general and president.

Across the state line in Wisconsin are the stunning mansions surrounding beautiful Lake Geneva. Their history is displayed along the Geneva Lake Shore Path. An array of luxury accommodations provide a relaxing overnight option for a weekend getaway.

Quirky side trips in Wisconsin include the House on the Rock, a unique structure built on a chimney of rock and filled with eclectic and whimsical displays, and the Wisconsin Dells, the world's largest water park with dozens of slides, a lazy river, a giant wave pool, and a water-coaster.

PLANNING YOUR TIME

If you only have one day, visit **Oak Park.** You can easily see the sights in a few hours or spend a full day wandering the downtown. Oak Park is also your best bet if you don't have a car as it's easily accessible on the L.

HIGHLIGHTS

⊛ **BEST ARCHITECTURE:** The **Frank Lloyd Wright Home and Studio** explores the famous architect's life and work in the residence he designed and lived in until 1909 (page 197).

⊛ **BEST SUMMER GETAWAY:** Just an hour's drive from Chicago, you'll find hiking trails, nature, and tranquility at **Starved Rock State Park** (page 197).

⊛ **BEST FOR HISTORY BUFFS:** History lovers won't want to miss wandering through the **Ulysses S. Grant Home,** where they can learn about the former general and president (page 201).

⊛ **BEST PLACE TO RELAX:** Walk around beautiful Lake Geneva and admire the historic mansions along the **Geneva Lake Shore Path** (page 203).

⊛ **MOST UNIQUE:** There's nothing in the world quite like the **House on the Rock,** a museum with an eclectic collection and a house that hangs off a cliff (page 204).

⊛ **BEST FOR KIDS:** The water coasters, waterslides, and wave pools at the **Wisconsin Dells** are a summer paradise for kids (page 208).

Frank Lloyd Wright Home and Studio

If you do have a car and don't mind driving, head to **Galena.** You can explore the downtown in a day, but history buffs might want to spend the night so that there's more time to dive into the town's Civil War history.

If you have a night or two, **Lake Geneva** is a nice retreat away from the city. Make sure to walk the Lake Shore Path, as it's the most beautiful and interesting part of town. While farther away, **House on the Rock** and the **Wisconsin Dells** could be worth the drive. (For architecture lovers, House on the Rock is a must.) You might get there early in the morning, spend a few hours, then make the trip back to the city or spend the night in the Wisconsin Dells, leaving a full day for Noah's Ark.

Oak Park

Ten miles west of downtown Chicago, the suburban village of Oak Park has a character all its own. Home of the Frank Lloyd Wright-Prairie School of Architecture District, Oak Park has the largest concentration Frank Lloyd Wright Prairie School homes—27 in all. The sights are walkable, and the quaint downtown harbors boutique shops, cafés, and restaurants. Even better is the L access from Chicago via the CTA Green Line.

Ernest Hemingway Birthplace and Museum

SIGHTS
ERNEST HEMINGWAY BIRTHPLACE AND MUSEUM

Author Ernest Hemingway was born in Oak Park, Illinois. Today, visitors can tour both his childhood home and the museum that bears his name. At the **Ernest Hemingway Birthplace and Museum** (200 N. Oak Park Ave., 708/524-5383, www.ehfop.org; 1pm-5pm Wed.-Fri. and Sun., 10am-5pm Sat.; adults $10, youth and seniors $8, children 5 and under free), the Victorian edifice holds childhood photos, early writings, and a variety of memorabilia from Hemingway's early life.

Located down the same street, the museum offers a detailed portrait of the author's life. Spend an hour here learning about Hemingway's time as a war reporter in Spain, his writing years in Paris, and his coverage of World War II. Hemingway at the Movies exhibits posters, photographs, and clips of Hemingway novels turned into films. There's also an extensive section on his childhood years in Oak Park, which is best taken in as part of a highly informative one-hour guided tour (offered when purchasing tickets).

❂ STARVED ROCK STATE PARK

Starved Rock State Park

To get out of the city and into nature, head to **Starved Rock State Park** (2688 E. 875th Rd., Oglesby, 815/667-4906, www.starvedrockstatepark.org; visitor center open 9am-4pm daily). Located on the Illinois River, the park is home to waterfalls, hiking trails, and 18 canyons with moss-covered walls and sandstone bluffs that provide a striking contrast to the relatively flat Illinois landscape.

Visitors can hike to the scenic Eagle Cliff or Lover's Leap overlooks, look for bald eagles and other birds, and go canoeing or rafting in the river. The park provides overnight accommodations with 133 campsites (www.reserveamerica.com; June-Dec., $25) plus cabins and hotel rooms at the on-site **Starved Rock Lodge** (815/667-4211, www.starvedrocklodge.com; $90-155).

Starved Rock State Park is 93 miles southwest of Chicago, about a 1.5- to 2-hour drive. From Chicago, take I-90 East to I-55 South. Follow I-55 South for 42 miles to I-80 West near Shorewood. Merge onto I-80 West and drive 44 miles to Highway 178. Take Exit 81 and turn left to follow Highway 178 South for three miles to Deer Park Township. Turn left onto Highway 71 South/East 8th Road for 3.3 miles. The park entrance will be on the left.

FRANK LLOYD WRIGHT HOME AND STUDIO

Frank Lloyd Wright designed this small home, where he lived with his wife and children from 1889 to 1909. Today, the **Frank Lloyd Wright Home and Studio** (951 Chicago Ave., 312/994-4000, www.flwright.org; 11am-4pm daily; adults $15, children and seniors $12) is a National Historic Landmark and listed on the National Register of Historic Places.

The modest home served as an experimental place for the architect. While it includes some Victorian features—a front porch and a large, main stairwell—the house also provides unusual spaces, such as a small entryway leading into a wide living space with a hearth in the center. These features formed the beginning of what would become Wright's famous Prairie School style.

The one-hour tour offers a glimpse into Wright's working style and personal life, as well as architectural details of the home, such as the murals on the floors and walls and the original furniture. The vaulted second-floor space built for Wright's children was a unique feature at the time. After the tour, take

Day Trips

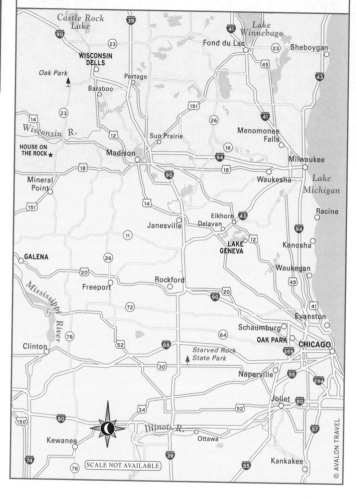

a few minutes to walk the surrounding blocks, where you'll find other Prairie Style homes. Grab a brochure from the museum for a self-guided tour and learn what makes each significant.

If visiting on a weekend, book a tour in advance—they fill quickly.

RESTAURANTS

In historic Scoville Square, **Winberie's** (151 N. Park Ave., 708/386-2600, www. oakpark.winberies.com; 11:30am-9:30pm Mon.-Thurs., 11:30am-10:30pm Fri.-Sat., 10am-9pm Sun.; $7-17) is an Oak Park staple. It serves the basics—burgers, steaks, soups, and salads—and does them well. The restaurant is conveniently located next to the Ernest Hemingway Birthplace and Museum and the Frank Lloyd Wright Home and Studio.

Novo (734 Lake St., 708/628-3454, www.novooakpark.com; 5pm-10pm Tues.-Thurs., 5pm-11pm Fri., noon-11pm Sat., noon-9pm Sun.; $12-32) is also in the Hemingway District and serves chef-driven, seasonally inspired dishes like cornmeal gnocchi and diver scallops with bok choi slaw. The elegant, brick-walled restaurant with copper accents also has a sustainable wine list.

The Little Gem Café (189 N. Marion St., 708/613-5491, www.the-littlegemcafe.com; 5pm-10pm Mon., 11am-10pm Sun. and Tues.-Thurs., 11am-11pm Fri.-Sat.; $18-32) is a European-style eatery with live music on Tuesday night. Try the brie crostini with fig to start, then choose from an array of pasta and meat dishes for your main course.

On the go? Stop in at **Felony Franks** (6427 W. North Ave., 708/948-7483, www.felonyfranks.com; 11am-8pm daily; $3-7), a gourmet, Chicago-style hot dog spot dedicated to providing meaningful employment to formerly incarcerated individuals.

SHOPS

In downtown Oak Park a strip of boutique shops line Lake Street between Harlem and Oak Park Avenues. **The Book Table** (1045 Lake St., 708/386-9800, www.booktable.net; 9am-9pm Mon.-Sat., 11am-6pm Sun.) is a "fiercely independent" bookstore stocked floor to ceiling with shelves of new and used books of every genre. The helpful staff can recommend picks or answer questions. Take time browsing or settle in to read. There are a few autographed books from local authors, which make great gifts.

At **Divine Consign** (809 S. Oak Park Ave., 708/386-3366, www.divine-consign.com; 11am-6pm Mon.-Tues., 11am-7pm Wed.-Fri., 11am-6pm Sat., noon-5pm Sun.), consignment furniture is pulled from six Merchandise Mart showrooms, as well as from homes in the neighborhood. The spacious showroom makes it easy to browse new furniture and home accessories, and the passionate owner is usually on hand to answer questions.

Stop in at the **Careful Peach Boutique** (1024 North Blvd., 708/383-3066, www.carefulpeach.com; 10am-7pm Mon.-Fri., 10am-6pm Sat., noon-5pm Sun.), which is meant to model an old-fashioned European department store. You'll find a curated selection of high-quality home accessories, linens, fragrances, candles, bath items, glassware, and watches. The charming shop features elaborate displays that are even more beautiful around Christmas. You'll find a little bit of everything here, with a focus on luxury.

Upscale boutique **Gem Jewelry + Lifestyle** (135 N. Oak Park Ave., 708/386-8400, www.shopgemjewelry.com; 11am-6pm Tues.-Sat., noon-5pm Sun.) opened as a place for owner Laura Kitsos to sell her jewelry designs. Today, it stocks her pieces as well as those from other small, independent jewelers. The beautiful space features custom cases, shelving, lighting, and a sophisticated air.

HOTELS

Oak Park has a couple of charming spots to stay overnight. **The Write Inn** (211 N. Oak Park Ave., 203/564-5228, www.writeinn.com; $150) is a boutique hotel just across from the Ernest Hemingway Museum. Each room in the historic 1920s building is unique and features comfortable beds and antique-style furnishings with armchairs, ornate mirrors, patterned carpets and bedspreads, 1970s-style footstools, and TVs. Updated bathrooms are stocked with toiletries and towels.

In the Historic District, **Bishop's Hall Bed & Breakfast** (605 Iowa St., 708/383-7774, www.bishopshallusa. com; $200) is a beautiful home with multiple room types ranging from a luxurious suite to simple, cozy rooms. The Georgian Revival home is decorated with plush furniture, beautiful rugs, and four-poster beds. Each room is stocked with luxury toiletries, robes, hair dryers, flowers, and chocolates. A full breakfast is served in the common area or on the terrace, and the adjoining garden is a great place to relax. The hosts are knowledgeable about all Oak Park has to offer.

INFORMATION AND SERVICES

Stop by the **Oak Park Visitor Center** (1010 Lake St., 708/848-1500 or 888/625-7275, www.visitoakpark. com; 10am-5pm Sat.-Wed., 10am-6pm Thurs.-Fri.) for information about walking tours, other sights, and to learn more about the town's history.

GETTING THERE AND AROUND

Oak Park is quick and easy to reach from downtown Chicago. The 10-mile drive usually takes about 15 minutes, but can take up to an hour in rush-hour traffic. From downtown Chicago, take West Congress Parkway to I-290 West. Drive approximately 8.5 miles on I-290 West to either Exit 23A (Austin Blvd.) or 21B (Harlem Ave.). From the Harlem Avenue exit, turn right onto Highway 43 and continue 0.3 mile to Chicago Avenue. The Frank Lloyd Wright Home is on Chicago Avenue; the Hemmingway Museum is around the block on North Oak Park Avenue.

From the Loop, it's easy to reach Oak Park by public transportation. Take the CTA Green Line or the Metra Union Pacific West line from the Ogilvie Transportation Center to the Oak Park Station (the Green Line runs more regularly). From the station, the Frank Lloyd Wright Home is a 0.8-mile walk north.

From Chicago O'Hare or Midway (Oak Park is close to both), a taxi to Oak Park should cost around $30. Once in Oak Park, you can easily walk around most areas.

Galena, Wisconsin

Galena, Illinois, sits about 160 miles west of Chicago. Once a major port city on the Mississippi River, Galena (a term for the mineral form of lead) formerly exported iron. Today, it's a tourist town that boasts hundreds of buildings on the National Register of Historic Places, including the home of Ulysses S. Grant. In winter, it also hosts

some of Illinois's only ski slopes. In recent years, small wineries have become popular stops for summer visitors.

SIGHTS

Galena's historic Main Street is full of shops, hotels, and buildings on the National Register of Historic Places. Spend an hour or two walking the street and stop for photos or pop inside one of the many shops and restaurants.

❂ ULYSSES S. GRANT HOME

This mansion, built in 1859 and designed in the Italianate style by William Dennison, was given to General Ulysses S. Grant by the residents of Galena as a thank-you present upon his return from the Civil War. The **Ulysses S. Grant Home** (500 Bouthillier St., 815/777-3310, www.granthome.com; 9am-4pm Wed.-Sun., $5 adults, $3 children) has been maintained as a memorial since 1904. The square redbrick home features covered porches, green shutters, and a balustrade balcony. Visitors can tour the home, which is still furnished with the Grant family's original belongings. Knowledgeable guides dress in period costumes for the optional 30-minute **tour,** which covers Grant's time during the Civil War through his presidency.

GALENA AND U.S. GRANT MUSEUM

Housed in the 1858 Barrows Mansion, the **Galena and U.S. Grant Museum** (211 S. Bench St., 815/777-9129, www.galenahistory.org; 9am-4:30pm daily, $10 adults, $9 seniors, $8 youth ages 10-18) educates visitors about the history of Galena, the Upper Mississippi River Lead Mine District, and Ulysses S. Grant through permanent and rotating exhibitions featuring Civil War memorabilia, photos, old Galena artifacts, and historic testimonials.

A tour of the museum includes the adjoining blacksmith shop, filled with old equipment still in use by blacksmiths who make items for the gift shop. The museum also offers the one-hour **Walking Tour with General Grant,** which follows Galena's historic

Main Street and is led by a General Grant reenactor. You'll learn about the miners, steamboat captains, and Civil War heroes who put Galena on the map.

Tours begin at 10am every Saturday (May-Oct.). A second tour begins at noon daily departing from the DeSoto House Hotel (230 S. Main St.). Tickets can be purchased at either the museum or the hotel.

RESTAURANTS

There are about two dozen restaurants in Galena and most are along Main Street. A popular local choice is **Fried Green Tomatoes** (213 N. Main St., 815/777-3938, www.friedgreen.com; 4:30pm-8:30pm Mon.-Thurs., 4:30pm-9pm Fri., noon-9:30pm Sat., 4:30pm-9pm Sun.; $14-33), an Italian American spot serving USDA choice steaks, seafood, and a *Wine Spectator* award-winning wine list. The restaurant is housed in a historic building with tall ceilings, brick pillars, and a polished wooden bar. The welcoming staff will make you feel like family. Steak and seafood are popular entrées, though there are also chicken dishes, pastas, and salads. Order the fried green tomatoes as an appetizer.

Fritz and Frites (317 N. Main St., 815/777-2004, www.fritzandfrites.com; 4pm-8pm Tues.-Thurs., 4pm-9pm Fri.-Sat., 9am-8pm Sun.; $10-20) is a cute European bistro blending French and German cuisine. You'll find mussels, *pomme frites,* and quiche served alongside schnitzel and smoked sausages. There's a large selection of bottled European beers, as well as a comprehensive European wine list.

The downtown **Galena Cellars Vineyard and Winery** (515 S. Main

Chestnut Mountain Resort

St., 815/777-3330, www.galenacellars.com; 9am-5pm Mon.-Thurs., 9am-8pm Fri.-Sat., 9am-6pm Sun. Jan.-Apr.; 9am-8pm Mon.-Sat., 9am-6pm Sun. May-Dec.; $10-20), housed in a historic 1840s granary building, serves local wine made just a few miles away. While Illinois isn't the ideal location for growing grapes, the sweeter wines and some of the fruitier options like those made with cherry or peach or the honey mead wine are decent.

The **Galena Brewing Company** (227 N. Main St., 815/776-9917, www.galenabrewery.com; 4pm-9pm Mon.-Thurs., 11am-11pm Fri.-Sat., 11am-9pm Sun.; $9-15) offers a rotating selection of brews made on-site ranging from farmer's blonde ale to oatmeal stout. They also serve some great wings and bar food.

HOTELS

Galena hotels are housed in historic buildings, and the **Main Street Inn** (404 S. Main St., 815/777-3454, www.mainstinn.com; $270) is no exception. This adorable inn was built around 1850 and features six luxurious rooms in a perfect location on Main Street. Each room is uniquely decorated with wallpaper, paintings, pretty bedspreads, and antique furniture. Bathrooms have a shower, bathtub, and pedestal sinks. There's free wireless Internet throughout the hotel.

The **DeSoto House Hotel** (230 S. Main St., 815/777-0090, www.desotohouse.com; $140) features large rooms beautifully decorated in Victorian furnishings that include wireless Internet, TVs, and coffee/tea; suites have fireplaces. There are three restaurants on-site: a charming breakfast spot, a pub, and a fine-dining option, as well as a business center.

If you are visiting in winter, consider staying outside of downtown at the **Chestnut Mountain Resort** (8700 W. Chestnut Mountain Rd., 800/397-1320, www.chestnutmtn.com; $120), Galena's ski resort overlooking the Mississippi River. Rooms are comparable to a standard chain hotel, with basic amenities, toiletries, TVs, and wireless Internet. Ski hills are appropriate for all levels and range from novice to black diamond. The restaurant and bar on-site serve pizza, burgers, and other American food options.

INFORMATION AND SERVICES

The **Galena-Jo Daviess County Visitors Convention Bureau** (720 Park Ave., 815/777-3557) serves as a resource for overnight guests. Stop in for information about Galena's history,

sights, tours, hotels, and more, or to pick up a map or brochures.

GETTING THERE AND AROUND

To visit Galena from Chicago, you will need a car. From Chicago, take I-90 west for 79 miles to Rockford. Follow US-20 west for 85 miles until you reach Galena. Once in Galena, park your car (most spots are free). The town is only about two miles long and easily walkable. The **Galena Trolley Tour** (314 W Main St., 815/777-1248; departs hourly year-round; $20 pp) lasts one or 2.5 hours and offers a narrated trip through the historic district.

Lake Geneva, Wisconsin

About 80 miles north of downtown Chicago, across the state line into Wisconsin, is the resort town of Lake Geneva, a favorite getaway for Chicagoans. The town is filled with giant, Gilded Age mansions, beautiful state parks, beaches, spas, and high-end boutiques. Summer is a peak season for visitors.

SIGHTS
✪ GENEVA LAKE SHORE PATH

After the Civil War, wealthy Chicagoans started coming to Lake Geneva in the summer and built mansions that still surround its waters. The 21-mile **Geneva Lake Shore Path** (www.visitlakegeneva.com) offers an up close look at these lakeside mansions. The trail was originally used by the Potawatomi tribe and later became a path for laborers working on the estates. The shoreline is open

to the public, and the footpath travels through the gardens of some of the historic estates; some homeowners decorate their portions of the path with artwork or benches for visitors. The path eventually leads into the surrounding woods and up to the water of Geneva Lake, where antique wooden boats line the docks. While you probably can't walk all 21 miles on one visit, any stretch is historic and beautiful. Popular starting points include the **Lake Geneva Public Library** (918 W. Main St.) and **Big Foot Beach State Park** (1550 S. Lake Shore Dr.), which are a 2.2-mile walk apart.

BIG FOOT BEACH STATE PARK

Big Foot Beach State Park (550 S. Lake Shore Dr., 262/248-2528, www.dnr.wi.gov; 6am-11pm daily; $8 per vehicle) is right off the Geneva Lake Shore Path, about two miles from

✪ HOUSE ON THE ROCK

House on the Rock (5754 State Rd. 23, Spring Green, WI, 608/935-3639, www.houseon-therock.com; regular season: 9am-5pm daily Mar.-Nov., winter: 11am-3pm Fri.-Sun. Jan.-Mar.; $14.95-29.95 adults, $8.95-15.95 children age 4-17) is both exactly what it sounds like and something indescribable. Located in Spring Green, Wisconsin, about three hours from downtown Chicago, atop Dear Shelter Rock, the "house" is a complex of disjointed rooms that contain the vast and varied personal collection of Alex Jordan Jr.

From the exterior, the House on the Rock resembles a haphazard home by architect Frank Lloyd Wright. Slanted, angular walls and windows jut out into space, while flat roofs and wooden slats appear layered one upon another. Inside, an overwhelming collection of random rooms include a maritime museum, *Titanic* memorabilia, Venetian masks, the world's largest collection of dollhouses, a room based on Dante's *Divine Comedy,* a reproduction of a Victorian street, hundreds of mannequin angels, a 200-foot whale model, a collection of automatic music machines, and the world's largest carousel featuring 182 chandeliers. The highlight feature is the Infinity Room, a long and narrow glass room that projects a nerve-wracking 250 feet into the air from the rock.

If it sounds strange, that's because it is … but it's also why it's so fascinating to walk through. Both beautiful and bizarre, House on the Rock is a worthy detour in Wisconsin.

House on the Rock is about 200 miles northwest of Chicago. From Chicago, take I-90 West for 109 miles to Janesville, Wisconsin. From Janesville, turn left onto U.S. 14 West and follow it for 39 miles to U.S. 18. Continue west on U.S. 18 for 45 miles to Dodgeville. In Dodgeville, take Exit 47 to head north on Highway 23 and drive 14 miles. Turn left onto House on the Rock Road. Plan about four hours for the drive.

downtown Lake Geneva. In the summer, wildflowers are abundant along the trails and the crystal clear water is warm enough to hop in for a quick dip. (The swimming area is small, so it's better for a cool-down swim than a day at the beach.) For those who want to camp during their stay, Big Foot Beach State Park has 100 wooded **campsites** (Apr.-Oct., $18-28 per site, $9.65 reservation fee) for tents and RVs with picnic areas and showers.

BLACK POINT MANSION

Perched on a bluff overlooking the lake, **Black Point Mansion** (812 Wrigley Dr., 262/248-6206, www.cruiselakegeneva.com; adults $39, seniors $37, youth $27) is one of the oldest mansions in Lake Geneva. Built in 1888 as a summer home for Conrad Seipp, the estate was designed in the Queen Anne style with 13 bedrooms and a four-story tower. The home opened to visitors in 2007. On a tour, you'll see many of the original furnishings, learn about the architecture style and the Seipp family, walk through the ornate gardens, and hear about this era in Chicago and Wisconsin history. Visitors reach the estate via a 45-minute boat ride, just as guests would have done when the home was in regular use. Tours from Lake Geneva Cruise Line depart from the Riviera Docks in Lake Geneva.

YERKES OBSERVATORY

Operated by the University of Chicago Department of Astronomy and Astrophysics, the **Yerkes Observatory** (373 W. Geneva St., 262/245-5555, www.astro.uchicago.edu/yerkes; tour schedule varies; $10 donation suggested) is the birthplace of modern astrophysics. It was founded in 1897 with the idea to turn observatories into a space for laboratories in addition to pure observation. A highlight for visitors is the 90-foot domed telescope, which is best visited at night. (Check the night-viewing schedule online to see when the observatory will be open.) For Chicagoans

Geneva Lake Shore Path

usually surrounded by city lights, star-gazing from the Yerkes Observatory is magical.

SHOPS

The Main Street shopping district offers plenty of small-town charm and dozens of local shops selling everything from antique furniture to handmade jewelry, apparel, and specialty food. A favorite among visitors is **Estate Art & Collectibles** (529 Main St., 312/833-6058; 9am-5pm daily), where you'll find paintings, pottery, glass dishes, antiques, Native American artifacts, old maps, and memorabilia from the town's estates. All proceeds benefit Sower's House, a nonprofit that helps orphans, widows, and the homeless in the community.

At **AEppelTreow Winery and Distillery** (1072 288th Ave., 262/878-5345, www.aeppeltreow.com; 11am-4pm Sat., noon-4pm Sun.) you can sip small-batch hard cider made with local apples, as well as whiskey and brandies made from local crops.

Geneva Gifts (150 Broad St., 262/248-6756, www.genevagifts.com; 9am-5pm daily) is the perfect place to stock up on souvenirs. The shop sells everything from locally branded T-shirts to homemade fudge, as well as sandals and Minnetonka moccasins.

RESTAURANTS

Lake Geneva has a range of restaurants, from family-friendly to fine dining. **Popeye's** (811 Wrigley Dr., 262/248-4381, www.popeyeslkg. com; 11:20am-8:30pm Sun.-Thurs., 11:30am-9:30pm Fri.-Sat.; $12-25) opened in 1972 and quickly became a local favorite for its slow-roasted rotisserie chicken and famous Wisconsin fish fry (beer-battered fish-and-chips, with fish caught from the nearest lake). Nautical-themed Popeye's is just the right amount of kitsch, balanced by tranquil lake views.

Baker House (327 Wrigley Dr., 262/248-4700, www.historichot-elsoflakegeneva.com; 5pm-10pm Thurs.-Sat. Sept.-May, 4pm-10pm

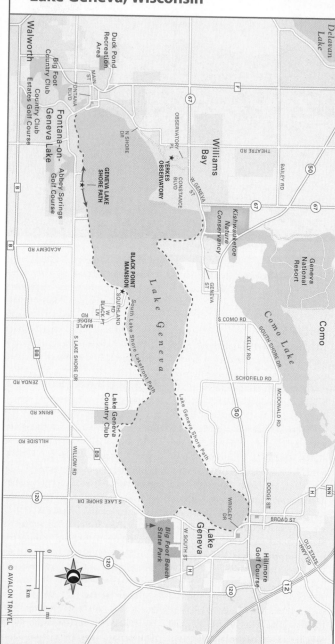

Lake Geneva, Wisconsin

© AVALON TRAVEL

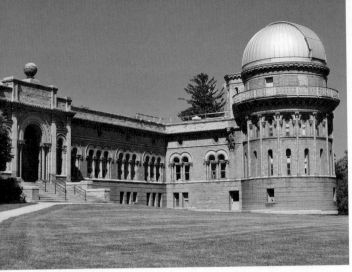

Yerkes Observatory

daily Memorial Day-Labor Day; $24-28) is located in a historic mansion decorated with detailed tiles, hand-carved accents, and a large fireplace. Crab cakes are the signature dish with an elaborate Sunday champagne brunch (9:30am-2pm, $32) popular on weekends.

For a local feel, stop in at **Simple Café** (525 Broad St., 262/248-3556, www.simplelakegeneva.com; 6am-3pm Mon.-Fri., 7am-3pm Sat., 8am-3pm Sun.; $7-12) where farm-fresh food is what's on the menu. You won't go wrong with egg dishes and local veggies; if it's on the menu, get the apple crumble French toast with cinnamon baked apples. For lunch, the grilled cheese and tomato soup or the veggie burger are favorites. The cozy, sunlit restaurant features polished wooden floors and bright yellow walls.

HOTELS

Lake Geneva draws couples who like to stay at the adults-only **Seven Oaks** (682 S. Wells St., 262/248-4006, www.

sevenoakslakegeneva.com; $200). The bed-and-breakfast features spacious, sunny rooms that have their own entrance and offer fireplaces, soaking tubs, and a picturesque porch. Large bathrooms come with toiletries and a plush robe, as well as heated floors. Wireless Internet, breakfast, and a welcome package are included in your stay.

The AAA Four Diamond **Grand Geneva Resort & Spa** (7036 Grand Geneva Way, 800/558-3417, www.grandgeneva.com; $230) is ideal for those looking for a luxurious getaway. Rooms feature Innerloft feather blankets, lake country-style estate home furniture, minifridges, LCD flat-screen TVs (plus a TV embedded in the bathroom mirror), granite-top sinks, luxury toiletries, and panoramic balconies. Guests can take advantage of luxury spa services, head to the on-site stable for horseback riding, use the fitness center and 35-foot climbing wall, play tennis or basketball, or spend a few hours at the on-site water

☼ WISCONSIN DELLS

Wisconsin Dells

Three hours from Chicago, **Wisconsin Dells** (www.wisdells.com) bills itself as the "Water-park Capital of the World." The Wisconsin city is part of the Dells of the Wisconsin River, a glacially formed gorge, which makes for a beautiful landscape, the original reason for tourism here. Today, it holds the largest water park in the country, Noah's Ark, as well as tourist attractions such as mock German villages, kitschy souvenir shops, golf courses, old-time photo booths, go-karts, zip lines, amusement parks, and **Ripley's Believe It Or Not** (115 Broadway, 608/254-2184, www.ripleysdells.com; 9am-11pm daily late May-early Sept.; $14.99 adults, $9.99 children). Wisconsin Dells riverboats drew tourists in the early 1900s and are still a popular activity.

The entire city is built for tourists, most of whom come for **Noah's Ark** (1410 Wisconsin Dells Pkwy., 608/254-6351, www.noahsarkwaterpark.com; 10am-5pm or later daily June-Sept.; $41.99 adults, $29.99 children, $15 parking cash only), a giant water park featuring thrilling waterslides, a water roller coaster, and a wave pool. In the winter, visitors enjoy the indoor water parks that are adjoined with hotels; the most popular are the **Kalahari Resort** (1305 Kalahari Dr., 877/525-2427, www.kalahariresorts.com), the **Chula Vista Resort** (2501 River Rd., 855/388-4782, www.chulavistaresort.com), and the **Great Wolf Lodge** (1400 Great Wolf Dr., 866/976-9653, www.greatwolf.com). Down on Broadway, you'll find restaurants, bars, shops, and plenty of tourist information offices.

park. It has two championship golf courses.

For families, the **Abbey Resort** (269 Fontana Blvd., 262/275-6811, www.theabbeyresort.com; $200) offers indoor and outdoor pools, 90 acres of space for lawn games, bonfires, and movies, plus boat rides and babysitting services. Spacious lake-house-style rooms feature balconies or patios, free wireless Internet, a coffee-maker and refrigerator, and flat-screen TVs. There's also a fitness center and spa on-site.

INFORMATION AND SERVICES

The **Lake Geneva Visitors Center** (201 Wrigley Dr., www.visitlakegeneva.com) has maps and tour guides, as well as a wealth of information on local events, shops, and restaurants.

GETTING THERE AND AROUND

Lake Geneva, Wisconsin, is located about 80 miles northwest of downtown Chicago, about a two-hour drive. From Chicago, take I-90 West to I-94

West (multiple tolls, $0.70-1.50). Once on I-94 West, drive 56 miles north to Kenosha, Wisconsin. From I-94, take Exit 344 to Highway 50 and drive 25 miles west to Lake Geneva.

It is possible to reach Lake Geneva by train from Chicago, though it is a bit of a hassle. From the Ogilvie Transportation Center in downtown Chicago, take the Metra UP-N to Kenosha. From Kenosha, the #2 bus travels from 56th and 13th Avenues to Southport Plaza. From Southport Plaza, take the Kenosha bus to Aurora Medical-Twinlakes, and switch to the Geneva bus toward the Lake Geneva Square bus stop. The trip takes 4-5 hours, depending on the time of day.

BACKGROUND

The Landscape

Chicago, the Windy City

GEOGRAPHY

Chicago sits on the south end of Lake Michigan, which curves along the east side of the city. The basin of Lake Michigan was formed during the Wisconsin Glacial Episode and overtook Lake Chicago, a prehistoric lake formed by a glacier about 13,000 years ago. The bottom of what was Lake Chicago is now the Chicago plain, home to the city of Chicago.

Because Chicago lies at such a low (and flat) elevation, the glacial clay below the grass made the surrounding area something of a wetland. In the 19th century, settlers found ways to benefit from this by building the Chicago portage and canal. The portage is a strategic water gap that connects the drainage basins and waterways of the Great Lakes and the Mississippi River. The central point of this gap lies in the city of Chicago; it's one of the reasons Chicago was able to thrive as a city. (The portage is even pictured on the Chicago flag, which has two blue stripes that symbolize waters meeting.) The geographical highlight of the city though, is Lake Michigan, which Chicagoans flock to the second the weather warms.

CLIMATE

Chicago has four distinct seasons, and each brings extreme variations in temperature. Winter (Nov.-Feb.) is very cold, very windy, and often snowy. The average high temperatures in January and February are in the upper 20s with snowfall around 10 inches. Temperatures can fall well below freezing as locals bundle up in warm boots, jackets, hats, and gloves.

The size of Lake Michigan exerts a thermal effect on the city. Northeast winds off the lake result in larger snowfalls than in other Midwest cities. This "windchill effect" can feel especially strong near the lake in the winter—with such an icy breeze it's hard to believe that the lake actually helps warm temperatures. When walking outside in winter, try to stay close to the sides of nearby buildings in order to reduce windchill.

Summer (late June-Sept.) is often hot and humid. The average daytime temperature is around 75°F, with highs in the 90s. Chicagoans flock to the beaches and outdoor patios to escape the heat; however, most indoor spaces are icy with air-conditioning.

Spring (Mar.-June) and fall (late Sept.-Oct.) are less predictable. These seasons are usually mild, with warm, clear days and crisp evenings; however, there may also be random patches of hot or cold weather. During April and May average highs reach 69°F; by the end of October, highs have dropped to the low 30s to high 40s.

The average yearly precipitation for Chicago is 34 inches, comprised of snow in winter and thunderstorms in summer.

ENVIRONMENTAL ISSUES

Water resources are integral to Chicago. Lake Michigan and the Chicago River are at the heart of the city, and Chicago has invested heavily in water conservation and stormwater infrastructure. Chicago water is safe to drink, and travelers are encouraged to bring their own water bottles and refill as needed rather than purchasing drinking water in plastic bottles.

The popular Chicago Riverfront was revitalized to provide economic opportunities for businesses on the water while at the same time reducing flood risk from the lake and river. In 2015, the city of Chicago passed laws enforcing the cleanup of the Chicago River, resulting in a more enjoyable experience for kayakers and boaters.

The city's grid plan supplies reliable electricity and encourages citizens to reduce energy use. When staying in hotels, be sure to turn off all lights and televisions before departing the room. Recycling is also highly encouraged throughout the city. Every home and apartment building has both a trash and recycling bin, something travelers can also make use of during vacation rentals or Airbnb stays. Chicago imposes $0.07 tax on plastic checkout bags, so bring a reusable shopping bag with you when planning your trip.

Public transportation is plentiful, affordable, and highly encouraged. The City of Chicago has worked to reduce emissions for CTA services by replacing older buses and parts with more efficient vehicles, adding bus routes for commuters, and examining more efficient traffic patterns.

In 2015, Illinois was first in the nation for LEED certification, a designation given to buildings that follow a standard for Leadership in Energy and Environmental Design. There are more than 400 LEED-certified works in the city, including the Radisson Blu Aqua, Hyatt Regency, and Aloft hotels.

Many Chicagoans bike to work, and there are dozens of Divvy bike-share rental stands throughout the city for both locals and visitors. Credit cards are accepted at the Divvy bike stands;

after paying for a day pass, grab a rental bike to scoot around the city and simply drop it off at the stand closest to your final destination. The Divvy bike website includes a helpful map of all stations within the city.

History

EARLY HISTORY

Chicago was originally inhabited by Native Americans, specifically the Mascouten and Miami tribes. For several decades, there had been fighting for land between the Miami, Algonquin, Iroquois, Ojibwe, and Potawatomi peoples.

In the 1670s, French explorers—drawn to the area's connection of river systems—began exploring the region. They named it the "Checagou," after the Native American word "shikaakwa" (both words meant "wild garlic," which was popular in the area). By 1696, the French settlers had built the Mission of the Guardian Angel and were attempting to Christianize the Miami people, who had initially reached out to the French for protection. The Algonquin tribes, now allied with the French, began a takeover of the territory in the early 1700s. However, by the 1720s, the Potawatomi were in control.

It would be decades before the first permanent settler arrived in Chicago. Jean Baptiste Point Du Sable, considered the founder of the city of Chicago, came to the area in the 1780s and built a farm on the Chicago River. His former site is now home to Pioneer Court Plaza, near Chicago's Magnificent Mile.

The decades from 1795 to 1833 saw battles and land disputes between the United States and Native Americans, which resulted in treaties ceding land to the United States and the forced removal of Native American tribes. In 1816, the Potawatomi yielded land covering the Chicago area, river, and Lake Michigan to the United States in the Treaty of St. Louis. By 1833, the Potawatomi had been forcibly removed and the town of Chicago was established.

AGRICULTURE AND TRANSPORTATION

In 1829, the area was plotted by James Thompson, who quickly recognized its potential as a transportation hub. The lake and abundant farmland were beneficial for trade between New York and Chicago, and settlers from the northeast quickly began building roads and docks. As agriculture boomed, the new roads allowed large amounts of produce to be shipped from the surrounding farms to the Erie Canal, where it could continue to New York City via the Hudson River. In 1837, the city of Chicago was incorporated.

The Illinois and Michigan Canal opened in 1848, allowing the delivery of more products via the Mississippi River to the Gulf of Mexico. The Galena & Chicago Union Railroad was also completed in 1848 and with that, Chicago became the heart of the Midwest. Transportation throughout the country was now accessible thanks to Chicago's multiple rail and water connections. Department stores such as Sears & Roebuck Co.

made Chicago their base for shipping across the country. Soon there were 30 railroad lines into Chicago, making it the center for transcontinental shipments. Factories sprang up in Chicago, producing goods that could be easily delivered elsewhere.

IMMIGRATION AND EARLY POLITICS

By the 1830s, Chicago's newest residents were immigrants. Irish Catholics were the first and largest group to arrive, soon followed by Germans, Swedes, Norwegians, Dutch, and English. The city's population grew quickly; by 1870, Chicago was the second-largest city in the country. Between 1870 and 1900, the population grew from 299,000 people to 1.7 million—it was the fastest-growing city at the time largely thanks to this influx of European immigrants.

However, this population boom wasn't just the result of European immigration. Folks from the East Coast saw an opportunity in moving to a city that was quickly becoming a transportation hub. Chicago's canals led to the Great Lakes and the Mississippi River, making it a prime location for shipping. Warehouses sprang up everywhere, drawing investment opportunities. As the city grew and expanded, the Chicago Consolation Act of 1851 split the city into nine wards, forming Chicago's neighborhoods.

In 1855, Mayor Levi Boone passed a law stating that any member of the Chicago police must be born in the United States. Sunday closing laws were enacted, forcing the shuttering of saloons and drinking establishments—primarily German beer gardens and Irish pubs. As a result, the Lager Beer Riot broke out and martial law was imposed.

In 1857, John Wentworth was elected as the new mayor. Known as the reformist mayor, Wentworth led an effort to clean up "The Sands," a district of prostitution houses. He also supported U.S. Senator William H. Seward for presidential election. In 1860, Chicago hosted the Republican National Convention where Abraham Lincoln was nominated instead.

Lincoln's nomination for president was a surprise. Seward, an experienced politician from New York, had been favored to win against the rural and less experienced Lincoln. The convention organizers had printed extra tickets for Chicagoans and told them to show up at the Wigwam Hall early. When Lincoln won after three tense rounds of voting, Chicagoans went crazy.

GREAT CHICAGO FIRE

In 1871, Chicago suffered an enormous fire that devastated the city. On the evening of October 8, a small barn on DeKoven Street caught fire. (The exact cause is unknown, though rumors attribute it to Mrs. O'Leary's cow knocking over a lantern.) At the time, most buildings and sidewalks in Chicago were made of wood, and the flames caught and spread quickly. After the fire jumped the Chicago River and headed north, it struck the city's water source, depriving the small force of firefighters of their only tool to battle the blaze. The Great Chicago Fire continued to rage for two days, finally petering out on October 10 as rain began to fall.

The fire burned almost four square miles of the city to the ground, with huge amounts of damage in the Loop and areas north of the Chicago River. It is estimated that 300 people died and 18,000 buildings were destroyed. As the city rebuilt, it incorporated strict fire codes and building guidelines including more brick, steel, and other materials. Today, the origin point of the Great Chicago Fire is now home to the Chicago Fire Academy.

WORLD'S COLUMBIAN EXPOSITION

In 1893, Chicago hosted the World's Columbian Exposition on what is now Jackson Park near the Hyde Park neighborhood. Landscape architect Frederick Law Olmsted along with architect Daniel Burnham imagined the exposition as a glowing "White City," with gleaming neoclassical-style pavilions, electric lights, and verdant lagoons filling in the former wetlands.

The exposition drew 27.5 million visitors to Chicago, and its architecture and design influenced building styles throughout the country. Today, visitors can step back in time with a trip to the exposition's two surviving structures: the Museum of Science and Industry (the former Palace of Fine Arts) and The Art Institute (the former World's Congress Building).

INDUSTRY

Manufacturing, shipping, and railroads kept Chicago at the heart of the U.S. economy. The city quickly became the world's largest rail hub and was home to one of the busiest shipping ports in the world. The Chicago Union Stock Yards were the premier packing yards in the country. The city became a hub for processing lumber, iron, and coal.

CHICAGO RACE RIOT

As migration to Chicago boomed in the early 1900s, immigrants from eastern and southern Europe settled into specific neighborhood communities. African Americans from the southern

United States also moved north to Chicago and settled on the South Side of the city. While this segregation was not enforced by the city, it happened anyway as many of the European immigrants refused to tolerate those of other races or ethnicities in their neighborhoods. Tensions worsened after World War I, as thousands more African Americans moved north for better jobs and demanded respect from their working peers.

In 1919, the Chicago Race Riot started when Eugene Williams, an African American teenager, accidentally swam too far past a line of segregated beach between 25th and 29th Streets. As a result, Williams was stoned and then drowned. When police refused to arrest his assailant, crowds gathered and the violence that erupted lasted for 13 days. The U.S. government called in 6,000 National Guard troops to end the riot. More than 500 people were injured and 38 were killed.

The riots occurred mostly in neighborhoods where both Irish and African American families resided. Bridgeport and South Side neighborhoods saw the worst of it. The impact of the Chicago Race Riot forced the country to recognize its poor race relations.

PROHIBITION

In 1920, the 18th Amendment was added to the U.S. Constitution and the Prohibition era began. From 1920 to 1933, the distribution of alcohol was illegal—but, of course, this didn't stop Chicagoans. Alcohol was still legal in Canada, and Chicago's proximity made it easy to smuggle it in. Prohibition offered lucrative opportunities for those able to do so, primarily gangsters. Two of the most famous and well-known Chicago gangsters and bootleggers were Al Capone and George "Bugs" Moran. Capone's territory covered southern Chicago, while Moran controlled the north. The influx of illegal alcohol helped speakeasies flourish around the city. A strip along the 2200 block of South Wabash was particularly notorious for its speakeasies and casinos. The two gangsters battled for control, resulting in numerous violent run-ins throughout the city. On February 14, 1929, Capone's gang gunned down seven members of Moran's North Side Gang in what was called the St. Valentine's Day Massacre.

CENTURY OF PROGRESS

To celebrate the Chicago centennial, the city hosted a second World's Fair in 1933-1934. Called the Century of Progress, its centennial theme of technological innovation gave people hope during the Great Depression. The fair featured rainbow-colored buildings and "dream cars" like the limousine, as well as the Home of Tomorrow, the first Major League Baseball All-Star Game, and the first streamlined train.

POST-WORLD WAR II

Chicago experienced a postwar economic boom after World War II. As new housing, commuter railways, and highways were being built, Chicagoans with higher incomes began moving to the suburbs. The city tried to counter this urban flight by building suburb-like communities along the lakefront to entice residents to stay. In 1955, then-mayor Richard J. Daley emphasized city improvements by building major expressways around the downtown Loop and

ordering the construction of Chicago O'Hare International Airport. Daley received credit for creating a "suburb in the city" effect in neighborhoods outside of the downtown area.

1968 DEMOCRATIC NATIONAL CONVENTION

In 1968, as the country erupted in violence both domestic (following the assassinations of Martin Luther King Jr. and John F. Kennedy) and abroad in Vietnam, President Lyndon B. Johnson announced that he would end his bid for reelection. The remaining Democratic candidates were Vice President Hubert Humphrey and senators Robert F. Kennedy, Eugene McCarthy, and George McGovern. On June 5, Robert F. Kennedy was assassinated, and the Democratic Party, already divided by the war in Vietnam, fractured further.

In August 26-29, the Democratic National Convention was held at Chicago's International Amphitheatre (no longer standing). On August 28, approximately 10,000 protesters convened in Grant Park. In response, Mayor Richard J. Daley called in 23,000 Chicago police and National Guard troops. The uniformed presence responded with force, and the riots and confrontations that followed between protestors and police were broadcast widely on national television. Mayor Daley's actions were both criticized and praised, a response that mirrored the country's division.

The Democratic Party eventually nominated Hubert Humphrey as the Democratic candidate. Humphrey lost to Republican candidate Richard Nixon.

CHICAGO MAYORS
HAROLD WASHINGTON

In February 1983, Congressman Harold Washington became the first African American elected as mayor of Chicago. Washington ran against incumbent Jane Byrne (Chicago's first female mayor) and Richard M. Daley, son of former mayor Richard J. Daley, winning with 37 percent of the vote. Washington's accomplishments include the first environmental affairs department for the city and the establishment of the Political Education Project, which promoted his political interests outside of office. Washington was reelected in April 1987 and served as mayor of Chicago until his death while in office on November 25, 1987.

RICHARD M. DALEY

Son of former Chicago mayor Richard J. Daley, Richard M. Daley was mayor of Chicago from 1989 to 2011. He served six terms and was the city's longest-serving mayor. Notable issues during his tenure include revamping the Chicago Public School system, the building of downtown's Millennium Park, support for sustainable housing projects, and benefits for same-sex partners of city employees. Daley was a successful, if sometimes controversial mayor. During his term, the city budget was plunged into deficit, and he was criticized for not controlling police violence.

RAHM EMANUEL

Mayor Rahm Emanuel was first elected in 2011 and reelected in 2015. Chicago's first Jewish mayor, Emanuel has a long history in politics as a congressman and working for presidents Bill Clinton and Barack Obama. While Emanuel has done much to promote Chicago and is popular with business owners, his decision to shut down 50 public schools in primarily African American and Latino neighborhoods as well as his handling of the controversial Laquan McDonald shooting have been widely criticized.

BARACK OBAMA

President Barack Obama got his political start in Chicago in 1983 while working as a community organizer. From 1992 to 2004, Obama taught constitutional law at the University of Chicago near his home in Hyde Park. It's in Chicago that he met his wife, Michelle, and launched his presidential campaign. Obama's presidential win was also seen as a win for Chicago, especially on the South Side where he lived and worked.

The Obamas home in the Hyde Park neighborhood has drawn tourism to the area. The Obama Presidential Center is scheduled to open in Hyde Park's Jackson Park in 2020. The Obamas continue to give back to Chicago through volunteering and multiple donations.

CONTEMPORARY TIMES

Today, Chicago's population of almost three million thrives on the city's architecture, music, food, and performing arts. It is home to world-renowned theaters, prestigious universities, and is a business hub for national and international companies. The city's diversity is represented in its festivals, food, and museums.

Chicago is also at the center of national issues surrounding race, immigration, and politics. Citizens grapple with education issues, loving (or hating) the mayor, trying to stem urban violence, and rallying around young or lesser-known politicians, such as Barack Obama before his run for presidency.

Local Culture

DIVERSITY

Chicago's population is 45.3 percent European descent, 32 percent African American, 5 percent Asian, and 3 percent other races. Chicago has the fifth-highest foreign-born population in the country. Approximately 21 percent of the population was born outside the United States: 56 percent are from Latin America, 23 percent are from Europe, 18 percent are from Asia, and 2.6 percent are from elsewhere around the world. Ethnic groups represented in the city include Irish, German, Italian, Mexican, Assyrian (Chicago has one of the largest Assyrian diaspora populations), Arab, Bangladeshi, English, Bulgarian, Czech, Greek, Chinese, Indian, Puerto Rican, and Iranian.

SUBCULTURES

In the 1830s, Irish immigration to the United States was on the rise, and this period coincided with Chicago's founding and growth as a city. Chicago's Irish population is very influential in the city, especially in the police and fire departments, churches, hospitals, and schools. The St. Patrick's Day parade and the tradition of dying the Chicago River green make up one of the city's most popular and beloved events.

Chicago is also one of the most important Polish diaspora centers in the country. When Polish immigrants first came to Chicago in the late 1800s, their communities spanned five neighborhoods, with most concentrated along the near northwest side and Bridgeport. Polish culture remains in evidence today, most notably at the Polish Museum of America on the city's West Side.

Germans and Swedes comprise a large part of Chicago's population. Andersonville is still home to a sizable Swedish population, and many of the storefronts and businesses in this greater Chicago neighborhood reflect this heritage. Chicago is also home to the third-largest Italian American population in the United States.

Chinese immigrants to Chicago lived in the Chinatown neighborhood on the South Side. Today, Chicago's Chinatown continues to grow. Exploring this area, you'll hear dialects of Chinese widely spoken and see many Chinese businesses and restaurants.

While Chicago is a melting pot of ethnicity and culture, for some groups the city is extremely segregated. Neighborhoods on the South and West Sides are overwhelmingly African American, while Pilsen is home to a large Hispanic population.

In the Lakeview neighborhood, Boystown is home to a thriving lesbian, gay, bisexual, and transgender community, one of the largest LGBTQ populations in the country.

RELIGION

Chicago represents most religions, including Christianity, Judaism, Islam, Buddhism, Hinduism, Jainism, Sikhism, and Bahá'í. Residents attend churches, mosques, and synagogues, and the city is home to one of only seven Bahá'í temples in the world. However, Christianity is the most common religion, with about 70 percent of Chicago's religious population identifying as Christian.

ESSENTIALS

Getting There

AIR

Chicago has two major airports, **Chicago O'Hare International Airport** (ORD, 10000 W O'Hare Ave., 800/832-6352, www.flychicago.com/ohare) and **Chicago Midway International Airport** (MDW, 5700 S Cicero Ave., 800/832-6352, www.flychicago.com/midway). Most visitors fly into Chicago O'Hare, about 17 miles northwest of downtown Chicago.

O'Hare serves a wide variety of domestic and international carriers, including United and American Airlines. If you are departing from O'Hare, plan additional time to go through airport security as lines are notoriously long and last-minute gate changes are not uncommon.

Chicago Midway is about 10 miles southwest of downtown Chicago. Midway serves small and low-cost carriers such as Southwest Airlines and some Delta flights. This airport is generally less crowded

Chicago's transit system covers the city.

than O'Hare and a shorter drive from downtown, but with fewer flight options.

AIRPORT TRANSPORTATION
Bus

The **CTA bus's Blue Line** (312/836-7000, www.transitchicago.com) runs 24/7 from the airport to Forest Park, with stops in Logan Square, Wicker Park, and the Loop. It takes about 30 minutes to travel from the airport to the Loop ($5 one-way). The CTA Orange Line runs daily (4am-1am) from Chicago Midway to downtown Chicago in about 20 minutes ($2.25 one-way).

Taxi

Taxis depart from the lower level of each terminal in Chicago O'Hare. Take a taxi from the designated taxi stands, as other drivers offering rides inside the airport are usually not licensed. The fare is meter-based and depends on traffic; expect to spend around $40 to reach downtown Chicago. The drive takes 25-30 minutes with normal traffic, but can be up to an hour or more during rush hour or due to other traffic delays.

Taxis are available outside the main terminal at Midway. From Midway to downtown Chicago, the trip will take about 20-25 minutes and cost $30.

Ride Shares

Ride sharing applications such as **Uber** (www.uber.com) and **Lyft** (www.lyft.com) pick up from designated areas at Chicago O'Hare and Midway. Each terminal at O'Hare has a designated area on the departure level; at Midway, all pickups occur at the main terminal. At O'Hare, you can choose your terminal from the mobile app when booking your ride.

Car Rental

Both O'Hare and Midway airports have a wide range of rental car options. Each company offers free, 24-hour shuttle service from the arrivals curb to the car rental offices, which are usually just past the parking garages. Ace, Alamo, Avis, Budget, Dollar, Enterprise, Hertz, National, Thrifty, Corporate Rent A Car, and Payless Car Rental are all available from each airport. Many national brands have rental offices throughout the city as well, especially in the Loop.

CAR

Several expressways lead into Chicago. They are referred to by their names, rather than by their highway numbers.

The **Dan Ryan** (I-90/I-94) enters Chicago from the southeast via the Chicago Skyway (I-90) and the Bishop Ford Freeway (I-94). From central Illinois, the Dan Ryan (I-90/I-94) enters Chicago via I-57.

The **Edens Expressway** is the stretch of I-94 specifically from the northern suburbs to downtown Chicago. It's often crowded and experiences delays. The Edens Expressway runs into the Tri-State (I-294), which is a tollway.

Arriving in downtown Chicago from the south or north gives you great views of the skyline. Even better views can be seen along Lake Shore Drive (U.S. 41).

If arriving or departing Chicago around rush hour (7am-10am and 4pm-7pm), be prepared for heavy traffic. Sometimes getting into or out of downtown can take up to an hour. Weekends, early mornings, late evenings, and midday are generally the least congested times to drive.

TOLLWAYS

Illinois tollways are comprised of the **Kennedy** (I-90), which enters Chicago from the northwest and south, and I-88, which heads to the west suburbs, as well as the **Veterans Memorial Tollway** (I-355) and the **Tri-State** (I-294), which runs from the South Side to the northwest past O'Hare. Tolls run $1.50 each, and pay stations are located on the right side of the road. An **I-Pass** (a prepaid toll collection tool) is used to pay tolls. Visitors without an I-Pass should keep cash and coins on hand.

TRAIN

Chicago is a hub for **Amtrak** (800/872-7245, www.amtrak.com), which operates its Midwestern and cross-country routes out of **Union Station** (225 S Canal St.). Amtrak train lines out of Chicago include:

Empire Builder: Seattle to Chicago via Portland, Spokane, and St. Paul/Minneapolis

California Zephyr: San Francisco to Chicago via Denver

Capitol Limited: Washington, DC to Chicago via Pittsburgh and Cleveland

Cardinal: New York to Chicago via Washington, DC, Cincinnati, and Indianapolis

Metra (312/322-6777, www.metrarail.com) trains make daily runs to the suburbs from Union Station and **Ogilvie/Northwestern Station** (500 W Madison St.). Trains reach the suburbs and carry on to Joliet, Aurora, South Bend, Indiana, and Kenosha, Wisconsin.

BUS

Greyhound (312/408-5821, www.greyhound.com) operates frequent buses throughout the Midwest. The main Greyhound terminal is just southwest of the Loop (630 W. Harrison St.) and is open 24 hours. Other terminals are at the Blue Line Cumberland CTA Station (5800 N Cumberland Ave.) and the Red Line 95th/Dan Ryan CTA Station (14 95th St.).

Burlington Trailways (800/992-4618, www.burlingtontrailways.com) and **Indian Trails** (800/292-3831, www.indiantrails.com) also depart from the Greyhound's Loop station.

Burlington Trailways buses leave daily for Davenport, Iowa City, Des Moines, and Omaha. Indian Trails buses have daily service to Grand Rapids, East Lansing, and the Upper Peninsula of Michigan.

Megabus (877/462-6342, www.us.megabus.com) offers some of the most affordable bus options from Chicago. The bus picks up outside of Union Station (225 S Canal St.) and provides express services to many Midwest cities with connections to the rest of the country. Seats start at $1 when booking online, depending upon how far in advance you reserve and your travel dates.

Coach USA (773/648-5000, www.coachusa.com) buses offer daily transit throughout the country, with service to Arkansas, Georgia, Iowa, Indiana, Kentucky, Michigan, Minnesota, Missouri, Nebraska, Ohio, Tennessee, Texas, and Wisconsin. Buses pick up from Union Station (225 S Canal St.) and the O'Hare (10000 W O'Hare Ave.) and Midway (5700 S Cicero Ave.) airports.

Wisconsin Coach (262/542-8861, www.web.coachusa.wisconsincoach) travels from O'Hare to southeastern Wisconsin, Milwaukee, and the Milwaukee General Mitchell Airport. There are 14 buses daily; prices are $20-30 depending upon the destination.

Peoria Charter Coach Company (309/662-6951, www.peoriacharter.com) is great for those visiting university campuses around Chicago. The bus departs from O'Hare with service to Peoria, Normal, Champaign, and downtown Chicago.

Getting Around

DRIVING

For those unused to driving in a large, metropolitan city, driving a car in Chicago may feel hectic. Downtown in the Loop, there are many one-way streets that can be especially chaotic during morning and afternoon **rush hours** (7am-10am and 4pm-7pm weekdays).

Chicago also has some "bi-level" streets downtown. These streets include both a lower, ground-level stretch (i.e., Lower) and an elevated street directly above (i.e., Upper). For example, bi-level Wacker Drive is split into an Upper Wacker and a Lower Wacker. The lower level allows drivers to turn into the Loop; the upper level is for through traffic.

If you don't have the time to negotiate traffic, or if you're staying in an area where parking is limited (most of downtown), consider using public transit instead.

Parking in the city is expensive and often hard to find. For an easier (and cheaper) way to find parking, try **SpotHero** (www.spothero.com), a mobile phone app that shows where to find discounted parking spots in lots or garages around the city.

If you do need a car, consider signing up for a car-sharing service like **Zipcar** (312/589-6300, www.zipcar.com). After paying a membership fee, drivers can then pick up and drop off cars at any time of day from various Zipcar locations in the city.

PUBLIC TRANSPORTATION

The **Chicago Transit Authority** (CTA, 312/836-7000, www.transitchicago.com) refers to Chicago's integrated train, metro, and bus system. However, when Chicagoans refer to a CTA stop they're usually referring to the **L**, shorthand for the elevated tracks of the train system.

Disposable single-ride passes, daily Ventra tickets, and reusable Ventra cards ($5 for card) are available for purchase from kiosks at all CTA L stations. Kiosks accept cash and credit. Ticket are accepted on both L trains and on buses. The L train fare costs $2.25 (must prepurchase fare from kiosk); bus fares are $2 (exact cash accepted). Transfers are $0.25 for two rides within two hours.

Chicago's public transit is safe, but keep an eye on your belongings and be careful when taking public transit alone late at night. L cars have an emergency button, which when pressed requires the driver to stop the train.

THE L

The L is divided into colored lines; all lines lead into the Loop with the exception of the Yellow Line, which runs between the suburbs of Skokie and north Chicago. The Red, Green, Brown, Blue, Purple, Orange, and Pink Lines offer an expansive network throughout the city. The Red and Blue Lines run 24/7; the remaining lines run 4:30am-1am daily. Each station and L car includes a full route map, which is also available online. Train stations are staffed with an attendant who can help you plan your route.

- The Red Line runs north-south through the Loop with stops in

Lakeview, Lincoln Park, and the Gold Coast.

- The Green Line runs west-east from Forest Park to the South Side, with stops in Oak Park and the Loop.
- The Brown Line runs north-south from Albany Park to the Loop, with stops in Lakeview, Lincoln Park, Old Town, and River North.
- The Blue Line makes a U-turn from Chicago O'Hare to Forest Park, with stops in Wicker Park and the Loop.
- The Purple Line is a small line serving the north suburb of Evanston.
- The Orange Line runs south-north from the Chicago Midway Airport to the Loop.
- The Pink Line runs west-east from the 54th St./Cicero Station to the Loop.

BUS

CTA bus stops are frequent throughout the city and found on almost every major street. Stops downtown run about a block apart; stops elsewhere are located about three blocks apart. Major routes run every 7-15 minutes daily and more frequently during rush hour. OWL routes run 24/7; look for a picture of an owl on the bus stop sign to locate an OWL route.

Each bus stop sign displays the bus route. All buses have a lit display with the name of the streets and stops, so that you can track your trip.

Bus rides with a Ventra card cost $2; when paying cash, rides are $2.25. (Bring exact change, as change is not available on board and transit cards cannot be purchased.) A Ventra card may be purchased at kiosks at the CTA train station or L station. The **CTA Bus Tracker website** (www. ctabustracker.com) and mobile app provide real-time information for all bus routes.

METRA

Metra (312/322-6777, www.metrarail. com) is Chicago's commuter rail service, which travels to the suburbs and as far as Kenosha, Wisconsin, and South Bend, Indiana. If you are staying in the suburbs, Metra is a cheap and quick way to get to the city; however, cars can become very crowded during rush hour (7am-10am and 4pm-7pm). Purchase tickets at the automated machines in each train station ($2, depending on destination) or on the train for $3. Unlimited weekend passes are $7.

TAXIS AND RIDE-SHARES

Taxis are readily available on most major streets, especially downtown. Rates are set by the city and calculated by meter. Each ride starts at $2.25, with $0.20 added for each 1/9 mile (or 35 seconds). There's a $1 fuel charge for each ride, a $1 charge for a second passenger, and a $0.50 charge for third or fourth passengers. Payment is via cash or credit card.

When outside of downtown Chicago or on the Near North Side, you may have to call a taxi. The main companies are: **Yellow Cab** (312/829-4222, www.yellowcabchicago.com), **Flash Cab** (773/561-4444, www.flash-cab.com), and **Checker Cab** (312/243-2537, www.checkertaxichicago.com).

Uber (www.uber.com) and **Lyft** (www.lyft.com) are the most popular ride sharing apps in Chicago. Rides typically cost about half the price of a taxi, though they can be significantly cheaper during non-busy periods. (They can also be more expensive during surge pricing hours.) Both Uber and Lyft routinely run deals during the week, so check the apps for current specials. Uber Pool and Lyft Line, where you share your ride with someone going in the same direction for an even lower price, are also popular.

THE PEDWAY

More than 40 blocks of downtown Chicago are linked by the pedestrian Pedway. The Pedway started in 1951 with a few one-block tunnels connecting the Red and Blue line subways, but soon expanded to connect more than 50 buildings and multiple subway stops. While used mostly by commuters bustling from the train to work, visitors may enjoy seeing the underground network, which contains a few shops and food stalls. It's especially nice for traveling through the city in the winter months, when freezing temperatures and cold winds can make walking above ground for sustained periods of time unbearable.

Travel Tips

ACCESS FOR TRAVELERS WITH DISABILITIES

All CTA buses (and some train stations) are wheelchair accessible. The international wheelchair symbol on L stations advises whether the station is accessible. If it is, it will have an elevator at ground level. If the station is not accessible, an alternate bus route will be offered.

Chicago is a crowded city with congested sidewalks, especially downtown. In winter, sidewalks are shoveled and salted quickly; however, wheelchair users could have trouble navigating snow and ice.

TRAVELING WITH CHILDREN

Chicago is a great family destination. Many sights and museums have sections tailored toward children and include educational components. Popular sights include the zoo and the Shedd Aquarium, as well as Navy Pier, which is home to the Chicago Children's Museum. Admission rates for children are often a fraction of the price for adults.

GAY AND LESBIAN TRAVELERS

Chicago is friendly to gay and lesbian travelers. The annual pride parade is held in June and runs through Lakeview, specifically Boystown, Chicago's predominantly gay neighborhood. Same-sex marriage has been legal in Illinois since 2013.

INTERNATIONAL TRAVELERS
PASSPORTS AND VISAS

Foreign travelers will need a valid passport and, in some cases, a visa. For a list of visa requirements by country, visit www.travel.state.gov/visa. Visa requirements can change and additional restrictions may apply. At the time of publication, citizens from Syria, Iran, Yemen, Libya, Somalia, and Sudan must undergo special screening. If traveling from one of these countries, plan additional time for your visa application and process, and factor in extra time upon arrival for airport security. Canadian citizens do not need a visa, but do need a passport or passport card.

CUSTOMS

When entering the United States via an airport, foreign travelers must fill out a customs form. The form requires your destination name, address, and phone number. There are limits on the amount of money and gifts you can bring into the country, as well as limits on tobacco and some alcohol. Fruits and vegetables are generally not allowed either. If carrying prescription medication, bring your prescription with you. Additional customs information can be found online at www.cbp.gov.

Health and Safety

HOSPITALS AND EMERGENCY SERVICES

For nonemergency care, visit one of the more than 70 urgent care clinics in Chicago. Concentra (1030 W Chicago Ave., 312/243-1574, www.concentra.com), Immediate Care (180 Michigan Ave., 312/201-1234, www.michiganavenueimmediatecare.com), and Medspring (219 W Chicago Ave., 312/878-1945, www.medspring.com) are three larger providers with locations around the city.

For emergency hospital services, some recommended options include Advocate Illinois Masonic Medical Center (836 W Wellington Ave., 773/975-1600, www.advocatehealth.com) in Lakeview, Rush University Medical Center (1653 W Congress Pkwy., 888/352-7874, www.rush.edu) on the West Side, Lurie Children's Hospital downtown (225 E Chicago Ave., 312/227-4000, www.luriechildrens.org), Northwestern Memorial Hospital (251 E Huron St., 312/926-2000, www.nmh.org) downtown, or University of Chicago Medicine (5841 S Maryland Ave., 773/702-1000, www.uchospitals.edu) in Hyde Park.

CRIME

While relatively safe, Chicago is a big city and with that comes some crime. When you are downtown or in the North and Near West Sides, petty crime can be a concern. Keep your luggage within reach and keep your wallet hidden when taking public transit. In the Loop, be careful at night (again, watch your purse or wallet).

Chicago does have a high rate of violent crime, but this is concentrated in a few very small areas on the far South and West Sides. It's best to avoid the far South Side, especially the blocks between King Drive, 43rd Street, 79th Street, and Western Avenue. On the far West Side, avoid the blocks between Western Avenue, Central Avenue, Harrison Street, and Chicago Avenue. Lawndale, Chatham, Roseland, and Auburn Gresham should also be avoided when possible. These blocks are residential; most tourists will not visit this area.

Homelessness is a problem in Chicago, and you may encounter people asking for money, especially downtown.

Information and Services

VISITORS CENTERS

Chicago has two visitors centers where you can learn more information about the city's history, culture, and attractions and pick up maps and brochures. At the **Chicago Cultural Center Visitor Information Center** (Chicago Cultural Center, 77 E Randolph St., 312/742-1168, www. choosechicago.com, 9am-6pm daily), there are plenty of free materials and it's a good excuse to stop and marvel at the beautiful interior. The other visitor information center is located inside **Macy's** (111 State St., 800/887-9103, www.visitmacysusa. com, 10am-9pm daily).

POST OFFICE

Post offices throughout Chicago are open 8am-6pm weekdays, with limited weekend hours (closed Sun. and national holidays). One of the most accessible post offices is on the first floor of the Merchandise Mart (222 W Merchandise Mart Plaza). There are several post offices throughout the Loop, as well as in each major neighborhood. Blue post boxes can be found every few blocks, especially downtown.

Internet Resources

NEWSPAPERS

Chicago Reader
www.chicagoreader.com
The *Chicago Reader* is a literary newspaper covering all things Chicago, from politics to nightlife.

Chicago Sun-Times
www.chicago.suntimes.com
The *Chicago Sun-Times* is a daily newspaper covering Chicago sports, politics, events, entertainment, and weather.

Chicago Tribune
www.chicagotribune.com
The *Chicago Tribune* is Chicago's largest daily newspaper covering everything from breaking news, city news, sports, features, and global politics.

The Daily Herald
www.dailyherald.com
The Daily Herald is the largest newspaper for Chicago's suburbs, covering breaking local and national news.

Newcity
www.newcity.com
Newcity is a free, cultural weekly magazine focusing on Chicago artists, musicians, chefs, and more.

RedEye Chicago
www.chicagotribune.com/redeye
RedEye Chicago offers tips on the best places to eat, drink, and go out in the city.

GENERAL INFORMATION

The City of Chicago
www.cityofchicago.org

Chicago History
www.chicagohistory.org

Chicago Park District
www.chicagoparkdistrict.com

Chicago Transit Authority
www.transitchicago.com

Visit Chicago
www.choosechicago.com

Index

Restaurants Index

Nightlife Index

Shops Index

Hotels Index

Photo Credits

All photos © Rebecca Holland except page 2 (bottom left) © Americanspirit | Dreamstime.com, (bottom right) © Benkrut | Dreamstime.com, (bottom) © Joshua Wanyama | Dreamstime.com; page 4 (top) © Danny Raustadt | Dreamstime.com, (middle) © Eugene Feygin | Dreamstime.com, (bottom) © Alexandre Fagundes De Fagundes | Dreamstime.com; page 5 © F11photo | Dreamstime.com; page 6 © James Kirkikis | Dreamstime.com; page 8 (top) © Amadeustx | Dreamstime.com, (bottom) © Miroslav Gritsenko | Dreamstime.com; page 9 (top) © Benkrut | Dreamstime.com, (middle) © Lightpainter | Dreamstime.com, (bottom) © Nyker1 | Dreamstime.com; page 10 (top) © Adeliepenguin | Dreamstime.com, (bottom) © Haveseen | Dreamstime.com; page 11 (top) © Courtesy of The Second City/Todd Rosenberg, (bottom) © Sabrina Young; page 12 © Amadeustx | Dreamstime.com; page 13 © Afagundes | Dreamstime.com; page 14 © Cafebeanzphoto | Dreamstime.com; page 17 © Americanspirit | Dreamstime.com; page 21 © Marynag | Dreamstime.com; page 27 (top) © Marynag | Dreamstime.com, (middle) © Adeliepenguin | Dreamstime.com, (bottom) © Del7891 | Dreamstime.com; page 29 © Cafebeanzphoto | Dreamstime.com; page 31 © Nyker1 | Dreamstime.com; page 33 (top) © Suzanne Tucker | Dreamstime.com, (bottom) © Carroteater | Dreamstime.com, (top) © Dibrova | Dreamstime.com, (bottom) © Jessica Kirsh | Dreamstime.com; page 39 (top) © Adeliepenguin | Dreamstime.com, (middle) © Benkrut | Dreamstime.com, (bottom) © Haveseen | Dreamstime.com; page 41 © Boscophotos1 | Dreamstime.com; page 43 (top) © Wickedgood | Dreamstime.com, (bottom) © Nathan Resnick | Dreamstime.com, (top) © Cafebeanz Company | Dreamstime.com, (bottom) © Ernitz | Dreamstime.com; page 49 (top) © Cafebeanzphoto | Dreamstime.com, (bottom) © Jim Roberts | Dreamstime.com, (top) © Jannis Werner | Dreamstime.com, (bottom) © Jannis Werner | Dreamstime.com; page 51 © Marek Lipka Kadaj | Dreamstime.com; page 52 © Benkrut | Dreamstime.com; page 55 © Luca Petruzzi | Dreamstime.com; page 58 © Shedd Aquarium/Brenna Hernandez; page 61 © Sgoodwin4813 | Dreamstime.com; page 63 © Tupungato | Dreamstime.com; page 67 © Filedimage | Dreamstime.com; page 69 © Cmlndm | Dreamstime.com; page 70 © Jbatt | Dreamstime.com; page 71 © Jim Roberts | Dreamstime.com; page 72 © Tehnik83 | Dreamstime.com; page 73 © Ellesi | Dreamstime.com; page 110 © Anthony Moser; page 125 © Anthony Moser; page 127 © Kobby Dagan | Dreamstime.com; page 128 © Andrey Bayda | Dreamstime.com; page 129 © Rudi1976 | Dreamstime.com; page 131 © Pkorchagina | Dreamstime.com; page 132 © Flamingo, 1974 Alexander Calder, PhotoSmontgom65 | Dreamstime.com; page 133 © Amadeustx | Dreamstime.com; page 134 © Tinamou | Dreamstime.com; page 136 © Wendy Goeckner | Dreamstime.com; page 137 © Helgidinson | Dreamstime.com; page 140 © Jim Roberts | Dreamstime.com; page 143 © Ellesi | Dreamstime.com; page 144 © Dibrova | Dreamstime.com; page 146 © Vlad Ghiea | Dreamstime.com; page 147 © Smontgom65 | Dreamstime.com; page 149 © Stefano Armaroli | Dreamstime.com; page 152 © Benkrut | Dreamstime.com; page 154 © Glenn Nagel | Dreamstime.com; page 194 © Kwiktor | Dreamstime.com; page 195 © Thomas Barrat | Dreamstime.com; page 196 © Manuel Hurtado Ferrández | Dreamstime.com; page 197 © Jason P Ross | Dreamstime.com; page 205 © Rhbabiak13 | Dreamstime.com; page 207 © Rhbabiak13 | Dreamstime.com; page 209 © Kwiktor | Dreamstime.com; page 219 © Lightpainter | Dreamstime.com

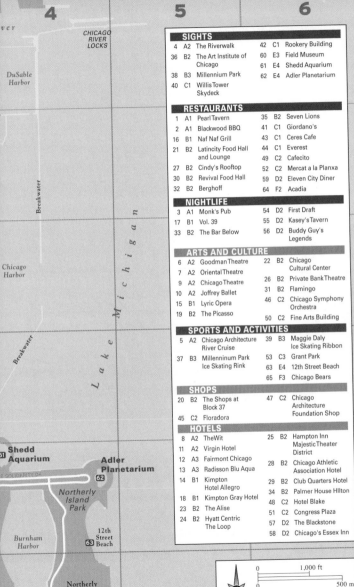

4   **5**   **6**

CHICAGO RIVER LOCKS

DuSable Harbor

Breakwater

Chicago Harbor

Lake Michigan

Breakwater

SIGHTS

4	A2	The Riverwalk
36	B2	The Art Institute of Chicago
38	B3	Millennium Park
40	C1	Willis Tower Skydeck
42	C1	Rookery Building
60	E3	Field Museum
61	E4	Shedd Aquarium
62	E4	Adler Planetarium

RESTAURANTS

1	A1	Pearl Tavern
2	A1	Blackwood BBQ
16	B1	Naf Naf Grill
21	B2	Latincity Food Hall and Lounge
27	B2	Cindy's Rooftop
30	B2	Revival Food Hall
32	B2	Berghoff
35	B2	Seven Lions
41	C1	Giordano's
43	C1	Ceres Cafe
44	C1	Everest
49	C2	Cafecito
52	C2	Mercat a la Planxa
59	D2	Eleven City Diner
64	F2	Acadia

NIGHTLIFE

3	A1	Monk's Pub
17	B1	Vol. 39
33	B2	The Bar Below
54	D2	First Draft
55	D2	Kasey's Tavern
56	D2	Buddy Guy's Legends

ARTS AND CULTURE

6	A2	Goodman Theatre
7	A2	Oriental Theatre
9	A2	Chicago Theatre
10	A2	Joffrey Ballet
15	B1	Lyric Opera
19	B2	The Picasso
22	B2	Chicago Cultural Center
26	B2	Private Bank Theatre
31	B2	Flamingo
46	C2	Chicago Symphony Orchestra
50	C2	Fine Arts Building

SPORTS AND ACTIVITIES

5	A2	Chicago Architecture River Cruise
37	B3	Millenninum Park Ice Skating Rink
39	B3	Maggie Daly Ice Skating Ribbon
53	C3	Grant Park
63	E4	12th Street Beach
65	F3	Chicago Bears

SHOPS

20	B2	The Shops at Block 37
45	C2	Floradora
47	C2	Chicago Architecture Foundation Shop

HOTELS

8	A2	The Wit
11	A2	Virgin Hotel
12	A3	Fairmont Chicago
13	A3	Radisson Blu Aqua
14	B1	Kimpton Hotel Allegro
18	B1	Kimpton Gray Hotel
23	B2	The Alise
24	B2	Hyatt Centric The Loop
25	B2	Hampton Inn Majestic Theater District
28	B2	Chicago Athletic Association Hotel
29	B2	Club Quarters Hotel
34	B2	Palmer House HIlton
48	C2	Hotel Blake
51	C2	Congress Plaza
57	D2	The Blackstone
58	D2	Chicago's Essex Inn

61 Shedd Aquarium

62 Adler Planetarium

E. SOLIDRITY DR.

Northerly Island Park

Burnham Harbor

12th Street **53** Beach

Northerly Island (Old Meigs Field)

| 0 | | 1,000 ft |
| 0 | | 500 m |

DISTANCE ACROSS MAP
Approximate: 2.8 mi or 4.7 km

© AVALON TRAVEL

SEE MAP 4

SEE MAP 3

SEE MAP 1

Newberry Library

Washington Square

NEAR NORTH

Chicago/ State

Chicago/ Franklin

Magnificent Mile

MAGNIFICENT MILE

Grand/ State

Tribune Tower

RIVER NORTH

Wrigley Building

Merchandise Mart

Lincoln Park

Connors Park

360 Chicago

SIGHTS		56 C6 Navy Pier	63 D1 Bavette's
1 A2 Newberry Library		57 C6 Centennial Wheel	Bar & Boeuf
11 A3 360 Chicago		82 D3 Tribune Tower	65 D2 Beatrix
41 C3 Driehaus Museum		84 D3 Wrigley Building	66 D2 Sunda
43 C3 Magnificent Mile			67 D2 Naha
			69 D2 Bohemian House
RESTAURANTS		35 C2 Portillo's	71 D2 Xoco
4 A3 Cafe Spiaggia		36 C2 Brindille	
12 B1 Big & Little's		44 C3 Tru	**NIGHTLIFE**
22 B3 Gino's East		46 C3 Uno's	13 B1 Headquarters
26 C1 Mr. Beef		48 C3 Shake Shack	Beercade
27 C1 Bernie's		49 C3 Bandera	25 C1 Green Door Tavern
Lunch and Supper		58 C6 DMK Burger Bar	29 C1 Spy Bar
28 C1 Nacional 27		61 D1 Lou Malnati's	30 C1 Sound Bar
31 C1 Al's Chicago Beef		62 D1 Doughnut Vault	39 C2 Pops for Champagne
32 C1 GT Fish & Oyster			51 C4 Green River

72 D2 Frontera Grill	
74 D2 Ramen-san	
76 D2 RPM Steakhouse	
78 D2 Siena Tavern	
80 D3 The Purple Pig	
86 E1 Chicago Cut	
87 E2 River Roast	
68 D2 Underground	
73 D2 Three Dots and	
a Dash	
75 D2 Studio Paris	
Nightclub	
77 D2 Untitled	
83 D3 Andy's Jazz Club	

GOLD COAST

N DEWITT PL

Lincoln Park

N LAKE SHORE DR

E PEARSON ST

Lake Shore Park

24

E SUPERIOR ST

E HURON ST

41

E ERIE ST

51

N FAIRBANKS CT

N MCCLURG CT

52

E ONTARIO ST

E OHIO ST

STREETERVILLE

E ILLINOIS ST

N LAKE SHORE DR

Ogden Plaza

Chicago River

N WACKER DR

41

Outter Harbor

0   500 ft

0   250 m

DISTANCE ACROSS MAP
Approximate: 1.7mi or 2.75 km

FILTRATION PLANT PIER

Milton Lee Olive Park

Ohio Street Beach
53

Olive Park Woodland

54

Navy Pier
56

NAVY PIER

55   57 58 59

Centennial Wheel

Gateway Park

CHICAGO RIVER LOCKS

DuSable Harbor

SEE MAP 1

Breakwater

ARTS AND CULTURE

14	B1	Catherine Edelman Gallery
15	B1	ECHT Gallery
20	B3	Lookingglass Theatre
24	B4	Museum of Contemporary Art
55	C6	Chicago Children's Museum
59	C6	Chicago Shakespeare Theater

SPORTS AND ACTIVITIES

| 53 | C5 | Ohio Street Beach |
| 54 | C5 | Divy Bikes |

SHOPS

3	A3	Independence
5	A3	Gold Coast Couture
9	A3	Space 519
10	A3	Azeeza
16	B1	Classic Remix
17	B3	American Girl Place
18	B3	Akira
37	C2	Ikram
38	C2	P.O.S.H.
47	C3	Eataly
60	D1	Knot Standard
79	D3	After-Words Books

HOTELS

2	A2	The Waldorf Astoria
6	A3	The Drake
7	A3	The Whitehall Hotel
8	A3	Four Seasons
19	B3	Park Hyatt
21	B3	The Peninsula Chicago
23	B3	Warwick Allerton
33	C2	The Godfrey
34	C2	Hotel Felix
40	C2	Acme Hotel
42	C3	Conrad
45	C3	Freehand Chicago
50	C3	Inn of Chicago
52	C5	W Chicago
64	D1	Holiday Inn Chicago Mart Plaza
70	D2	Palomar Hotel
81	D3	Intercontinental
85	D3	The Langham
88	E2	The Westin

© AVALON TRAVEL

SIGHTS

45	D6	Haymarket Memorial	55	E6	Union Station
53	E6	Old St. Patrick's Church			

RESTAURANTS

2	A2	Black Dog Gelato	38	D5	J. P. Graziano Grocery and Sub Shop
5	A2	Atomix			
6	A2	Roots	39	D5	Girl & the Goat
7	A2	Homestead	43	D5	Monteverde Restaurant & Pastificio
9	A3	El Taco Veloz			
16	B4	Two	46	D6	Blackbird
17	B5	The Dawson	47	D6	Avec
25	C5	Publican	49	D6	Sepia
27	C5	Momotaro	50	E5	Artopolis Bakery, Cafe and Agora
31	D4	BellyQ			
34	D5	Leña Brava	50	D6	French Market
35	D5	Maude's Liquor Bar	51	E5	Athena Greek Restaurant
37	D5	Au Cheval	54	E6	Lou Mitchell's

NIGHTLIFE

10	A3	Five Star Bar	33	D4	City Winery
15	B4	G&O	36	D5	Lone Wolf Tavern
18	B5	Richard's Bar	40	D5	Haymarket Brewery
20	C4	The Aberdeen Tap	41	D5	RM Champagne Salon
24	C5	The Aviary	48	D6	CH Distillery

ARTS AND CULTURE

1	A1	Vertical Gallery	12	B1	Ukrainian National Museum
11	A4	Polish Museum of America	21	C4	Mars Gallery

SPORTS AND ACTIVITIES

29	D2	Chicago Blackhawks	30	D2	Chicago Bulls

DISTANCE ACROSS MAP
Approximate: 2.6 mi or 4.4 km

0 — 1,000 ft
0 — 500 m

© AVALON TRAVEL

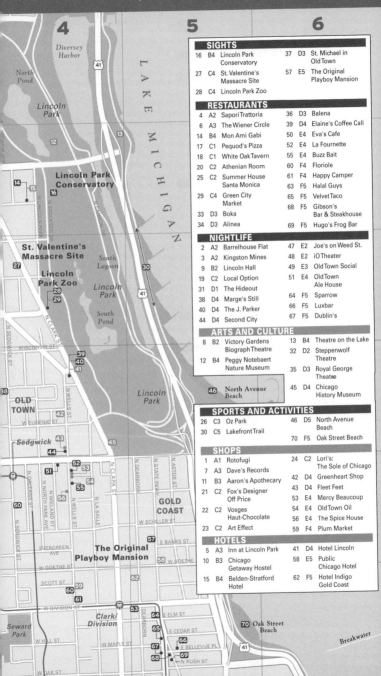

SIGHTS

16	B4	Lincoln Park Conservatory	37	D3	St. Michael in Old Town
27	C4	St. Valentine's Massacre Site	57	E5	The Original Playboy Mansion
28	C4	Lincoln Park Zoo			

RESTAURANTS

4	A2	Sapori Trattoria	36	D3	Balena
6	A3	The Wiener Circle	39	D4	Elaine's Coffee Call
14	B4	Mon Ami Gabi	50	E4	Eva's Cafe
17	C1	Pequod's Pizza	52	E4	La Fournette
18	C1	White Oak Tavern	55	E4	Buzz Bait
20	C2	Athenian Room	60	F4	Floriole
25	C2	Summer House Santa Monica	61	F4	Happy Camper
29	C4	Green City Market	63	F5	Halal Guys
33	D3	Boka	65	F5	Velvet Taco
34	D3	Alinea	68	F5	Gibson's Bar & Steakhouse
			69	F5	Hugo's Frog Bar

NIGHTLIFE

2	A2	Barrelhouse Flat	47	E2	Joe's on Weed St.
3	A2	Kingston Mines	48	E2	iO Theater
9	B2	Lincoln Hall	49	E3	Old Town Social
19	C2	Local Option	51	E4	Old Town Ale House
31	D1	The Hideout	64	F5	Sparrow
38	D4	Marge's Still	66	F5	Luxbar
40	D4	The J. Parker	67	F5	Dublin's
44	D4	Second City			

ARTS AND CULTURE

8	B2	Victory Gardens Biograph Theatre	13	B4	Theatre on the Lake
12	B4	Peggy Notebaert Nature Museum	32	D2	Steppenwolf Theatre
			35	D3	Royal George Theatre
46		North Avenue Beach	45	D4	Chicago History Museum

SPORTS AND ACTIVITIES

| 26 | C3 | Oz Park | 46 | D5 | North Avenue Beach |
| 30 | C5 | Lakefront Trail | 70 | F5 | Oak Street Beach |

SHOPS

1	A1	Rotofugi	24	C2	Lori's: The Sole of Chicago
7	A3	Dave's Records	42	D4	Greenheart Shop
11	B3	Aaron's Apothecary	43	D4	Fleet Feet
21	C2	Fox's Designer Off Price	53	E4	Mercy Beaucoup
22	C2	Vosges Haut-Chocolate	54	E4	Old Town Oil
23	C2	Art Effect	56	E4	The Spice House
			59	F4	Plum Market

HOTELS

5	A3	Inn at Lincoln Park	41	D4	Hotel Lincoln
10	B3	Chicago Getaway Hostel	58	E5	Public Chicago Hotel
15	B4	Belden-Stratford Hotel	62	F5	Hotel Indigo Gold Coast

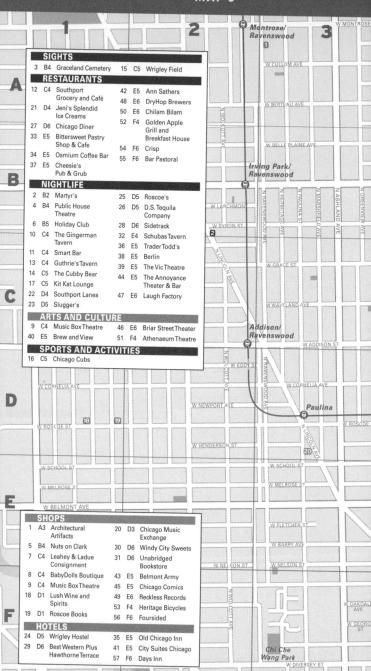

SIGHTS

| 3 | B4 | Graceland Cemetery | 15 | C5 | Wrigley Field |

RESTAURANTS

12	C4	Southport Grocery and Café	42	E5	Ann Sathers
21	D4	Jeni's Splendid Ice Creams	48	E6	DryHop Brewers
27	D6	Chicago Diner	50	E6	Chilam Bilam
33	E5	Bittersweet Pastry Shop & Cafe	52	F4	Golden Apple Grill and Breakfast House
34	E5	Osmium Coffee Bar	54	F6	Crisp
37	E5	Cheesie's Pub & Grub	55	F6	Bar Pastoral

NIGHTLIFE

2	B2	Martyr's	25	D5	Roscoe's
4	B4	Public House Theatre	26	D5	D.S. Tequila Company
6	B5	Holiday Club	28	D6	Sidetrack
10	C4	The Gingerman Tavern	32	E4	Schubas Tavern
11	C4	Smart Bar	36	E5	Trader Todd's
13	C4	Guthrie's Tavern	38	E5	Berlin
14	C5	The Cubby Bear	39	E5	The Vic Theatre
17	C5	Kit Kat Lounge	44	E5	The Annoyance Theater & Bar
22	D4	Southport Lanes	47	E6	Laugh Factory
23	D5	Slugger's			

ARTS AND CULTURE

| 9 | C4 | Music Box Theatre | 46 | E6 | Briar Street Theater |
| 40 | E5 | Brew and View | 51 | F4 | Athenaeum Theatre |

SPORTS AND ACTIVITIES

| 16 | C5 | Chicago Cubs |

SHOPS

1	A3	Architectural Artifacts	20	D3	Chicago Music Exchange
5	B4	Nuts on Clark	30	D6	Windy City Sweets
7	C4	Leahey & Ladue Consignment	31	D6	Unabridged Bookstore
8	C4	BabyDolls Boutique	43	E5	Belmont Army
9	C4	Music Box Theatre	45	E5	Chicago Comics
18	D1	Lush Wine and Spirits	49	E6	Reckless Records
19	D1	Roscoe Books	53	F4	Heritage Bicycles
			56	F6	Foursided

HOTELS

24	D5	Wrigley Hostel	35	E5	Old Chicago Inn
29	D6	Best Western Plus Hawthorne Terrace	41	E5	City Suites Chicago
			57	F6	Days Inn

4 **5** **6**

0   1,000 ft
0   500 m

DISTANCE ACROSS MAP
Approximate: 2.7 mi or 4.5 km

W CUYLER AVE

W BITTERSWEET PL

Lincoln
Park

N CLARENDON AVE

N CLARK ST

N KENMORE AVE

N SHERIDAN RD

N BROADWAY

41

Graceland
Cemetery

3

W IRVING PARK RD

6

Sheridan

N SOUTHPORT AVE

4

W BYRON ST

N SEMINARY AVE

N SHERIDAN RD

N WILTON AVE

N FREMONT ST

N CLARENDON AVE

W SHERIDAN RD

W GRACE ST

5

W GRACE ST

Gill
Park

PINE GROVE AVE

WRIGLEYVILLE

7
8
9

10
11

N CLARK ST

Wrigley
Field

15
16

N RACINE AVE

W WAVELAND AVE

17

W WAVELAND AVE

41

13

Addison/
North Main

N HALSTED ST

N SHEFFIELD AVE

W ADDISON ST

BROMPTON

12

14
23

W ADDISON ST

24

W EDDY ST

W CORNELIA AVE

W CORNELIA AVE

W STRATFORD PL

W HAWTHORNE PL

Southport

W NEWPORT AVE

27

29

N BROADWAY

21

W ROSCOE ST

25
26

28

W ROSCOE ST

22

W HENDERSON ST

LAKE VIEW

N CLARK ST

BOYSTOWN

W BUCKINGHAM PL

30

W ALDINE AVE

N SOUTHPORT AVE

N RACINE AVE

W SCHOOL ST

W MELROSE ST

W ALDINE AVE

31

33

38
37
35

45

Belmont/
North Main

W MELROSE ST

47
48

32

34

36

39 40

42
44
43

46

W BRIAR PL

W BRIAR PL

49

N CLIFTON AVE

N KENMORE AVE

41

W FLETCHER
ST

W BELMONT AVE

50

W FLETCHER ST

W BABRY AVE

W WELLINGTON AVE

Wellington

N CLARENDON AVE

54

55

56

51

52
53

W OAKDALE AVE

W GEORGE ST

W WOLFRAM ST

W WOLFRAM ST

W DIVERSEY ST

57

Diversey

SEE MAP 4

© AVALON TRAVEL

RESTAURANTS

1	A2	Yusho
4	A2	Longman & Eagle
5	A2	Cellar Door Provisions
6	A3	Fat Rice
15	C4	Ipsento Coffee
18	D3	Osteria Langhe
20	D5	Mindy's HotChocolate
23	E5	Buzz Killer Espresso
24	E5	Sultan's Market
26	E5	Stan's Donuts
28	E5	Piece Brewery and Pizza
30	E5	Taxim
31	E5	Dove's Luncheonette
32	E5	Big Star

NIGHTLIFE

2	A2	Lost Lake
7	B2	Lula Cafe
8	B2	Mezcaleria Las Flores
9	B2	Billy Sunday
11	B3	Heavy Feather
12	B3	Revolution Brewing
17	D2	Scofflaw
19	D5	Map Room
33	E5	The Violet Hour
42	F6	Evil Olive

ARTS AND CULTURE

3	A2	Logan Theatre
43	F6	House Theatre of Chicago

SPORTS AND ACTIVITIES

13	C2	Palmer Square Park
21	D6	606 Trail
22	E3	Humboldt Park
34	E5	Wicker Park

SHOPS

10	B2	Wolfbait & B-Girls
14	C4	Toy de Jour
16	C5	Virtu
27	E5	Flat Iron Arts Building
29	E5	Myopic Books
35	E5	Volumes Book Cafe
36	E5	Eskell
37	E6	Silver Moon
38	F5	Wixter Market
39	F6	Kokorokoko
41	F6	Dusty Groove Records

HOTELS

25	E5	The Robey
40	F6	Holiday Jones Hostel

MAP 7

SIGHTS

11	C6	Promontory Point	19	E2	*Fountain of Time*
12	C6	Museum of Science and Industry	20	E4	Oriental Institute Museum
15	D3	Smart Museum of Art	22	E4	Robie House
			23	E6	Osaka Garden

RESTAURANTS

2	B5	A10	16	D4	Medici on 57th
4	B5	Valois	21	E4	Plein Air Cafe
9	C6	Cafe 53			

NIGHTLIFE

| 5 | C4 | Woodlawn Tap | 10 | C6 | The Cove Lounge |
| 7 | C5 | The Promontory | | | |

ARTS AND CULTURE

| 14 | D2 | Dusable Museum of African-American History |

SPORTS AND ACTIVITIES

| 13 | D2 | Washington Park | 24 | F6 | Jackson Park |

SHOPS

| 3 | B5 | Modern Cooperative | 17 | D5 | First Aid Comics |
| 8 | C5 | The Silver Umbrella | 18 | D5 | Powell's Books |

HOTELS

| 1 | A5 | Chicago Lakeshore Hotel | 6 | C5 | Hyatt Place Chicago South/ University District |

DISTANCE ACROSS MAP
Approximate: 2.3 mi or 3.75 km

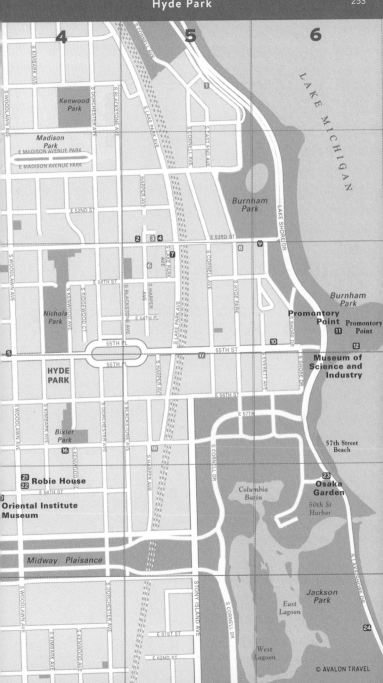

© AVALON TRAVEL

DISTANCE ACROSS MAP
Approximate: 30mi or 48km

0   2.5 km

0   2.5 mi

INSET (INS)

Chase Park

Dover Street District

St. Boniface Catholic Cemetery

ANDERSONVILLE

UPTOWN

W AINSLIE ST
W WINNEMAC AVE
W AINSLIE ST
W LAWRENCE AVE
W WINNEMAC AVE
W CARMEN AVE
W FOSTER AVE
W WINONA ST
W ASHLAND AVE
W BALMORAL AVE
W SUMMERDALE AVE
W FARRAGUT AVE
W BERWYN AVE
N CLARK ST
N ARGYLE ST
N GLENWOOD AVE
N MAGNOLIA AVE
N RACINE AVE
N BROADWAY
W BROADWAY
W WINTHROP AVE
N WINONA ST
N KENMORE AVE

Chicago Midway International Airport

LAKE MICHIGAN

S CICERO AVE
S PULASKI RD
S JERSEY AVE
S WESTERN AVE
S HALSTED ST
W GARFIELD BLVD
63RD ST
W PERSHING RD
ROOSEVELT RD
S DAMEN AVE
W 87TH ST
W 83RD ST
HARLEM AVE
S CICERO AVE
W GRAND AVE
W NORTH AVE
W JERSEY AVE
W 35TH ST
W 87TH ST
S JEFFERY BLVD
S COTTAGE GROVE AVE
S MARTIN LUTHER KING DR
S HALSTED ST
CLARK ST

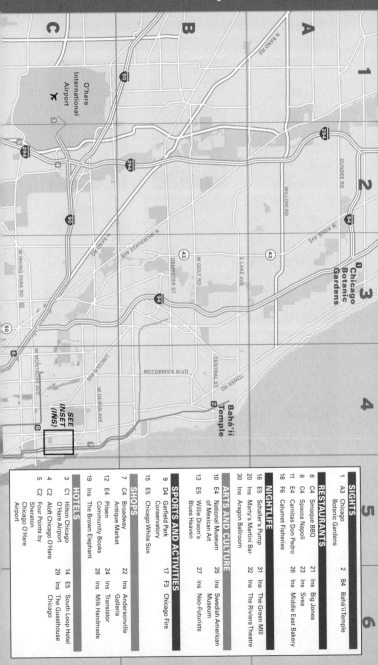

1
2
3
4
5
6
A
B
C
Chicago Botanic Gardens
Bahá'ií Temple
DUNDEE RD
WILLOW RD
N RAND RD
N RIDGE AVE
E LAKE AVE
W GOLF RD
DEMPSTER ST
N MILWAUKEE AVE
TOWER RD
CENTRAL ST
MCCORMICK BLVD
LINCOLN AVE
W DEVON AVE
W MONTROSE AVE
W IRVING PARK RD
O'hare International Airport
SEE INSET (INS)
294
94
90
43
50

SIGHTS

1	A3	Chicago Botanic Gardens	2	B4	Bahá'ii Temple

RESTAURANTS

6	C4	Smoque BBQ	21	Ins	Big Jones
8	C4	Spacca Napoli	23	Ins	Svea
11	E4	Carnitas Don Pedro	26	Ins	Middle East Bakery
18	F6	Calumet Fisheries			

NIGHTLIFE

16	E5	Schaller's Pump	31	Ins	The Green Mill
20	Ins	Marty's Martini Bar	32	Ins	The Riviera Theatre
30	Ins	Aragon Ballroom			

ARTS AND CULTURE

10	E4	National Museum of Mexican Art	25	Ins	Swedish American Museum
13	E5	Willie Dixon's Blues Heaven	27	Ins	Neo-Futurists

SPORTS AND ACTIVITIES

9	D4	Garfield Park Conservatory	17	F3	Chicago Fire
15	E5	Chicago White Sox			

SHOPS

7	C4	Broadway Antique Market	22	Ins	Andersonville Galleria
12	E4	Pilsen Community Books	24	Ins	Transistor
19	Ins	The Brown Elephant	28	Ins	Milk Handmade

HOTELS

3	C1	Hilton Chicago O'Hare Airport	14	E5	South Loop Hotel
4	C2	Aloft Chicago O'Hare	29	Ins	The Guesthouse Chicago
5	C2	Four Points by Sheraton Chicago O'Hare Airport			

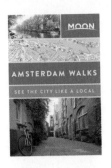

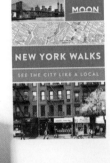

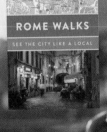

MOON NATIONAL PARKS

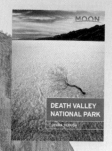

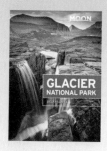

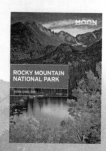

In these books:
- Full coverage of gateway cities and towns
- Itineraries from one day to multiple weeks
- Advice on where to stay (or camp) in and around the parks

PREPARE FOR ADVENTURE

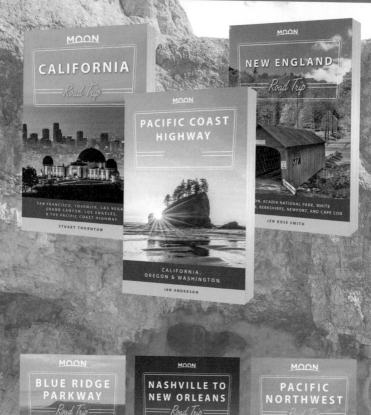

MOON ROAD TRIP GUIDES

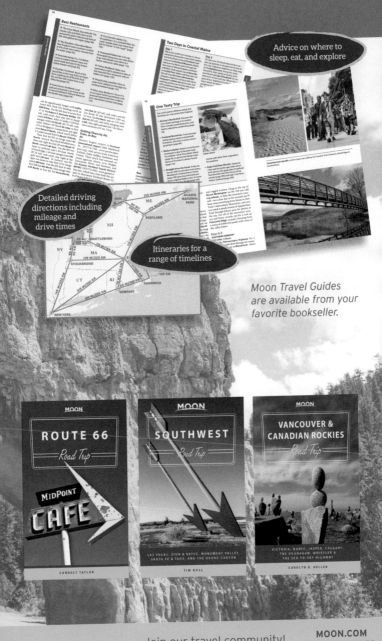

Advice on where to sleep, eat, and explore

Detailed driving directions including mileage and drive times

Itineraries for a range of timelines

Moon Travel Guides are available from your favorite bookseller.

MOON
ROUTE 66
Road Trip
MIDPOINT CAFE
LAS VEGAS, ZION & BRYCE, MONUMENT VALLEY, SANTA FE & TAOS, AND THE GRAND CANYON
CANDACY TAYLOR

MOON
SOUTHWEST
Road Trip
LAS VEGAS, ZION & BRYCE, MONUMENT VALLEY, SANTA FE & TAOS, AND THE GRAND CANYON
TIM HULL

MOON
VANCOUVER & CANADIAN ROCKIES
Road Trip
VICTORIA, BANFF, JASPER, CALGARY, THE OKANAGAN, WHISTLER & THE SEA-TO-SKY HIGHWAY
CAROLYN B. HELLER

Join our travel community!
Share your adventures using **#travelwithmoon**

MOON.COM
@MOONGUIDES

MAP SYMBOLS

≡≡≡ Expressway	○ City/Town	✈ Airport	⚓ Golf Course		
≡≡≡ Primary Road	◉ State Capital	✗ Airfield	🅿 Parking Area		
≡≡≡ Secondary Road	◉ National Capital	▲ Mountain	⛩ Archaeological Site		
⋯⋯ Unpaved Road	★ Point of Interest	✦ Unique Natural Feature	⛪ Church		
------ Trail	• Accommodation	⚐ Waterfall	⛽ Gas Station		
⋯⋯⋯ Ferry	▾ Restaurant/Bar	♠ Park	♾ Glacier		
⊶⊶ Railroad	• Other Location	▣ Trailhead	▩ Mangrove		
≡≡ Pedestrian Walkway	∧ Campground	⛷ Skiing Area	▱ Reef		
⚎⚎ Stairs			▭ Swamp		

CONVERSION TABLES

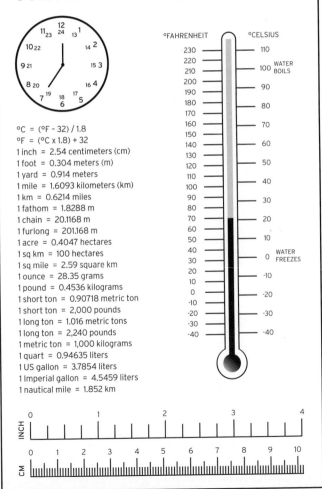

°C = (°F − 32) / 1.8
°F = (°C x 1.8) + 32
1 inch = 2.54 centimeters (cm)
1 foot = 0.304 meters (m)
1 yard = 0.914 meters
1 mile = 1.6093 kilometers (km)
1 km = 0.6214 miles
1 fathom = 1.8288 m
1 chain = 20.1168 m
1 furlong = 201.168 m
1 acre = 0.4047 hectares
1 sq km = 100 hectares
1 sq mile = 2.59 square km
1 ounce = 28.35 grams
1 pound = 0.4536 kilograms
1 short ton = 0.90718 metric ton
1 short ton = 2,000 pounds
1 long ton = 1.016 metric tons
1 long ton = 2,240 pounds
1 metric ton = 1,000 kilograms
1 quart = 0.94635 liters
1 US gallon = 3.7854 liters
1 Imperial gallon = 4.5459 liters
1 nautical mile = 1.852 km

MOON CHICAGO
Avalon Travel
Hachette Book Group
1700 Fourth Street
Berkeley, CA 94710, USA
www.moon.com

Editor: Sabrina Young
Series Manager: Leah Gordon
Copy Editor: Ashley Benning
Production and Graphics Coordinator: Darren Alessi
Cover Design: Faceout Studios, Charles Brock
Interior Design: Megan Jones Design
Moon Logo: Tim McGrath
Map Editor: Albert Angulo
Cartographers: Moon Street Cartography (Durango, CO), Albert Angulo, and Brian Shotwell
Proofreader: Caroline Trefler
Indexer: Rachel Kuhn

ISBN-13: 978-1-63121-7081

Printing History
1st Edition — April 2018
5 4 3 2 1